BESIDES PASTA

My Early Years

A MEMOIR

by

PETER RIZZOLO

To Betsy

Pete Rizzolo

Acknowledgements

I want to thank to my writing group leader, Charlotte Hoffman for her encouragement and insightful analysis of my memoir. Other group members include, Hal Glickman. Chuck Hauser, Beverly Lemons, Tom Shetley, Frank Stellone, and Fabianne Worth. Each contributed their unique perspectives and insights to my early drafts.

Lee Smith read a first draft and offered me sage advice and encouragement. My wife Alyce read the memoir chapter by chapter as I churned it out. As my first reader, her commentary has been useful and much appreciated.

My siblings, Tony, Phyllis and Frances, helped bring some of my fuzzy memories into focus. At times they disagreed on historical events, which in itself was invaluable, since it gave me the option of relating events as I recalled or imagined them to be.

The writing of this memoir was started in a class at North Carolina State University. My instructor was the inimitable charmer of people, as well as snakes, Tim McLaurin. Unfortunately, because of health problems, he was not able to give me feedback on the completed manuscript. Tim's and my fellow students took issue with presenting the memoir in the point of view of a child, since it limited the degree of nuance and literary devices that could be utilized to add greater depth and richness to the narrative. I compromised by adding sections in italics where I clarify events and present information unknown to me as a child.

Dedication

This work is dedicated to my mother, my brother Tony, and my sisters: Helen, Geraldine, Phyllis, Chickey and Frances, and to the memory of my friend, Mark Stillman.

Prologue

I have chosen to tell you of my early life experiences through a child's eyes and voice to portray events as I saw them, in my innocence and limited understanding. Peter, the little boy, not the adult author, describes his family, friends and surroundings as they appeared to him at the approximate time he experienced them. As his narrative and education progress, his grammar and sophistication improve.

This random gathering of memories and events is like a family album, where the connections between the pictures and the stories they tell, often can only be surmised. These vignettes will introduce you to my family, relatives, family friends, and my childhood friend, Mark Stillman.

As this memoir begins, I am five years old. My mother has seven children to raise on her own. I am the youngest. My oldest sister Helen is sixteen. Geraldine is fourteen, Phyllis twelve, Tony eleven, Chickey nine and Frances seven.

The year is 1933. My mother is thirty-four. She has been separated from my father for three years.

The nation is in the midst of the Great Depression. My mother supports her seven children from a part-time sewing job and a meager Relief check. My aunts and uncles are practically the sole sources of our hand-me-down clothing and an occasional bottle of homemade wine. But financial help from relatives is impossible, because they too live on marginal incomes.

Rent consumes half of our monthly income, and the remainder never lasts to the end of the month. We are not starving; we are not destitute. My mother somehow even manages to feed the many beggars who come to our door.

She is a genius in the kitchen. Delicious meals materialize from food most people would throw away. Vegetables and fruits on the edge of spoiling, she gets for free, or buys for pennies. Soup bones can be had from the butcher for the asking. We eat day-old bread, and free bread when she has the time to wait in the long lines for government supplies. Milk and ground meat are our primary sources of protein. We eat lots of macaroni. (That's what we called pasta when I was a boy). Hardly a day goes by that we don't eat a pasta dish.

Besides pasta, what we have in abundance is love for each other, a strong religious faith, dreams of a home of our own, and the belief that life with all of its uncertainties and suffering is still an awesome treasure.

Chapter One

Our Neighborhood and My New Friend

"You want to go for a ride on the trolley?" my brother Tony asked. Tony was in the fifth grade. I didn't even start school yet. My new friend Marky and me were playing immies by the side of the house. "Can Marky come?" I asked Tony. He was five going on six. I just turned five. He was almost a head taller than me and had a thin face that was mostly nose, and ears that poked out a little more than they needed to. He had pale brown eyes and light brown hair that wasn't curly like mine.

"I'll ask his mother if Marky can come," Tony said.

We had just moved to a flat on the second floor of a three-story building on South Orange Avenue in Newark, New Jersey. It was like two houses stuck together. On the first floor were two businesses: a Jewish Delicatessen and a store where they sold newspapers, candy

Besides Pasta

and ice cream. Marky's family owned the delicatessen. We lived on the second floor above their store.

Marky's mother said it was okay to ride the trolley with Tony, so the next afternoon we got on the trolley across the street from our house.

"You see that tall brick wall over there?" Tony asked.

Tony, me and Marky were sitting on the wooden seats of the trolley on the side close to the sidewalk. The bench Marky was on, was flipped toward the front of the trolley. Marky sat facing me and Tony. The trolley window was pulled up, but you couldn't fall out because there were three iron bars that ran across the lower part.

The wall Tony pointed to was a block long. "What's behind it?" I asked.

"A reservoir. Sometime we can take a walk along the top of the wall and get a good look down inside."

"Aren't you afraid to fall in?"

"You can't fall in. There's a tall wire fence."

"Do people swim in there?" I asked.

"The water's for drinking," Marky said. "Not for swimming."

I wondered if the water tasted better than what we have in our house. "Can we get a drink sometime?"

"The reservoir water comes right to our house," Tony said.

Lots of trucks came by our house. The junk man, the coal truck, the iceman, a truck with vegetables and fruit, and the milkman. Besides, there were a whole bunch of trucks that brought stuff to Stillman's store.

"I never saw a water truck come to our house," I said.

"The water comes in a pipe in the cellar," Marky said.

I wasn't sure if I was going to like Marky for a friend. He didn't like to wrestle or play cowboys as much as me. Sometimes he used big words I didn't understand. But we both loved the movies, listening to "Gang-busters" on the radio, watching the buses and cars, and shooting immies. So maybe he was going to be okay.

Tony explained how the water is pumped inside of pipes that run under the street. And how small pipes come off of the main pipes and go into each house. Marky kept shaking his head to tell me he knew all that already.

"There's Saint Antonitus Church," my brother said. "The school I go to is behind the church. See that brick building? That's the school you'll be going to, Peter."

The school was five windows high. I wondered if the school had an elevator or escalator stairs like Bamberger's department store. I liked going up on the elevators in the downtown stores but going down made my stomach feel like it wasn't catching up with the rest of me.

A few blocks up from the reservoir was a movie house. We had to run to the other side of the trolley to get a better look. I asked my brother what was playing. There was a giant picture of a gorilla standing on top of a building. He was holding a lady in one arm and grabbing an airplane with his other hand.

"*King Kong,*" Marky said. "I heard them talk about the movie on the radio. My father said the movie wasn't suitable for small children."

Marky didn't speak like any kid I knew. Once I asked him how come he knew so many big words. He said his mother and father read stories to him. Even the newspapers.

"Doesn't your mother read to you?" he asked me.

3

Besides Pasta

I told him she had too much work to do to bother reading me stories. I didn't want to tell him she couldn't read. Besides, she would always tell me stories that were better than just reading from some dumb book.

Pretty soon we saw a giant soda bottle on top of a brick building. The bottle was a mile high, bright green, with writing on the side like on a regular soda bottle.

I couldn't believe it. "Wow!"

"The famous Hoffman soda bottle," Tony said.

"That must hold enough soda to last a year."

"The bottle is filled with water," Tony said. "They use the water to make the soda."

Tony had dark curly hair, bushy eyebrows and a dimple in his chin. Nobody else in our family had a dimple in their chin. Besides me and Tony, there were five more kids in my family. They were all girls. Helen was the oldest. She was fifteen. Then came Geraldine, Phyllis, and my brother Tony. Then Anna, who we called Chickey. I don't know how she got to be named after a chicken. My sister Frances was next. I was the youngest. I hated it when they called me the baby of the family.

Tony was always telling me stuff. I guess he knew just about everything there was to know. Next, we passed a park. There were no leaves on the trees. The grass was brown. Through the trees I could see some kids playing in a ball field.

"That's Valesburgh Park," Tony said. "There's a nice playground there. I'll take you sometime."

When the trolley reached the end of the line, we were in a place called South Orange. My brother told me that was where all the rich people lived.

"So why don't we move there and be rich?" I asked. My brother looked at me funny. Then he laughed. Sometimes it takes older people time to catch on to my jokes.

"There's a Catholic seminary college in this town," he said.

"Will I go to school there some day?"

"If you want to be a priest."

I wanted to be a cowboy and live on a ranch. "Are there any schools around here where I can learn to be a cowboy?"

Tony and Marky laughed. Sure, I never heard of a school for cowboys, but where do they learn how to ride horses, lasso and brand cows? Okay, maybe that was a dumb question. Why would they have a school for cowboys in New Jersey? But I bet they do out west.

We stayed on the trolley as the driver went from the front of the trolley to the rear. But the trolley didn't really have a rear. The driver didn't have to turn the trolley around. He just walked to the other end, sat down and drove the trolley back the way we came. I wondered what would happen if there were two drivers and they tried to drive different directions at the same time.

We got to ride back without paying another five cents. This time I didn't ask so many dumb questions, because now I knew where we got our water and how the water got to our house and that you couldn't swim in a reservoir, that the Hoffman Soda bottle wasn't filled with soda, and that there weren't any cowboy schools in New Jersey. I had a really good time, but I still felt like crying. If you ask a dumb question, people laugh at you, but if I didn't ask dumb questions how was I supposed to get to know all things I didn't know? Marky was practically the same age as me and he knew so much more. Maybe he learned a lot of that stuff in kindergarten. He was already in kindergarten when we moved into the house on South Orange Avenue. But the Catholic school didn't have a kindergarten. I was going to have to wait a whole year before starting school.

Our flat was like a railroad car. All the rooms were lined up so that to get from the front living room to the kitchen in the back, you had to go through two bedrooms. There was a small room off the front hall at the head of the stairs. Mama said that at one time the tiny room may have been part of the hallway. But now it was connected to our flat.

"It's kind of like a caboose," Tony said when he first saw it.

"What's a caboose?"

"Something stuck onto the end of a train."

"But this room is stuck on the side," I said.

"It's a side caboose, okay?"

The house was on a busy street. Buses, cars and trolley cars passed right by our house. I liked watching the trolley go by. Our building would shake every time it passed. The trolley's metal wheels made loud clickity-clack sounds and shot sparks off the track. Helen said it gave her a headache. Helen should work in a library, because she couldn't stand noise. But I thought it was great. I couldn't wait to go for another ride. This time maybe Tony will take us downtown.

When the trolley passed, people sitting inside waved to me and my sister Frances. She was two years older than me and about as tall as Marky. Usually we just waved back, but sometimes if the trolley stopped to let someone off or pick up someone, we did goofy things like make faces and fall down as though we were shot. The people who rode the trolley began to recognize us. They would point with their fingers at us as though they were shooting. I would grab where I was shot and fall to the ground. My sister would bend down and pretend she was crying. Some of the people on the trolley clapped.

The trolley cost a nickel for grownups, but kids were free if they rode with a grown-up. The ride was more fun than the bus. The wooden seats, the thump thump noise, and the man who came around to collect money made me feel I was on a train, even though I was never on a train. If the trolley went south you would end up downtown where there were movies and tall buildings where they sold just about everything you could think of. One store my sister Helen always talked about was Bamberger's. She liked to walk through the store with her school friends, especially where they sold perfume and woman's clothes.

On practically every corner, men sold hotdogs, or giant pretzels, or baked sweet potatoes. The walk downtown took forever, but by trolley you got there in just a few minutes. If the trolley was pointed north toward the Catholic Church on Ninth Street, you'd pass the Valesburgh section of Newark like Marky and I did when Tony took us for our first ride.

Our landlady didn't like big families. She told my mother that a whole bunch of kids would wreck the place. When Mama was going to rent the flat, she lied about how many children she had. When we first moved in Mama made us take off our shoes in the house so we wouldn't make a lot of noise. I didn't mind the shoes part. Running as fast as I could and sliding in my socks was fun. There was linoleum on the floor and my mother used Johnson's wax. She said Johnson's was the best. I bet I could slide a mile if the house was bigger. But I didn't like having to be quiet all the time.

If we made a lot of noise Mama was afraid the Stillmans would complain to the landlady. But pretty soon we got to be good friends with the Stillmans and we stopped worrying about them telling the landlady how many kids mama had.

The Stillman family lived in back of the store. They had two girls and two boys. Paul, the older boy, was the same age as my brother Tony. Marky was the youngest. I didn't mind Marky being so much taller than me because he was a few months older, and if he slowed growing, even a little, I had a pretty good chance to catch up.

My brother Tony and Paul Stillman did neat things. There was a big metal icebox in front of the delicatessen. The milk deliveryman left the milk there because he got there before the store opened in the morning. One day Paul and Tony told Marky and me that they wanted to show us a magic trick. They showed us a couple of big nails.

"We can change these nails into swords," my brother said.

"But you have to say magic words to make the trolley come," Paul said.

Marky, me, Paul and my brother were standing in front of our house. Paul went into the street and laid the nails on the trolley tracks.

My brother was leaning against the metal pole that held up the trolley wires. Pretty soon he went and sat on the icebox. Paul sat next to him and they started banging their heels against the box and saying magic words. Just then you could see the trolley coming, even before you could hear it.

The trolley ran over the nails. After it passed, Tony ran into the street and brought them back. They were perfect little swords.

I realized the trolley squished the nails but I didn't know how they knew when the trolley would come.

"Didn't you see your brother lean against the pole?" Marky asked.

"Yeah."

"He felt the trolley coming."

How could he feel the trolley coming? I didn't want to ask a dumb question so I said, "Yeah." But I don't think I fooled Marky.

"The noise the trolley makes travels through the wires and you can feel the vibration when you touch the metal pole."

Sometimes Marky talked like a mad scientist. I would get tired of asking what he meant, so I usually had to figure it out myself. I remembered how in a cowboy movie an Indian had pressed his ear to the ground and could tell a bunch of horses were coming before anybody could see them.

We tried. We'd listen with our ears pressed against the pole and pretty soon the vibration would start. We would start to count and found that when we counted to ten a trolley would appear just like magic. But we couldn't do the nail part, because Mrs. Stillman could see us from the store and she said never to go in the street. Besides, my mother sewed by the front-room window and would be able to see us too. She said that if I should ever go into the street without her, if the trolley didn't kill me, she would.

Ethel and Florence Stillman were in high school. They seemed like grownups to me. Florence sometimes worked in the delicatessen and I noticed if she weighed things that Mama bought, she'd only charge for a pound even when the scale showed a little higher. We almost always bought on credit. Sometimes if my mother sent me down for only one thing, like a loaf of bread or a bag of sugar, Mrs. Stillman wouldn't write anything in her credit book. The butcher wasn't anything like the Stillmans. He would charge you for a pound even before the needle stopped moving. One day me and Frances went with Mama to *fa la spese*. That's Italian for going shopping for food. At the butcher's, she ordered a pound of ground beef, a quarter pound of ground pork and a quarter pound of ground veal.

"Cut away that fat," Mama said, "I'm not paying such high prices for fat."

"A little fat makes the meatballs taste good, Antoinette."

He cut away a little more fat before throwing the meat into the grinder. All three of us watched him really closely when he put the ground meat on the scale. He was so fat you couldn't see around him from any one spot.

"Ah, exactly one pound," the butcher said.

Mama looked at me and I shook my head to tell her he had his finger on the scale.

"If I have to pay for part of your hand Signor Salumerie, you'd better wrap up the finger with the rest of the meat."

He shook his head, but he did add a little extra meat.

Chapter Two

My Family

My Uncle Pete told us what Mama looked like when she was fifteen and first came here from Italy. "She had long reddish-brown hair, high cheekbones, sparkly light brown eyes, and a nose like an aristocrat."

I wasn't sure what an aristocrat's nose looked like, to me her nose seemed kind of big and narrow, not wide like mine and my brother's.

Three of Mama's brothers already lived in America at the time she got here: Uncle Joe, Uncle Jerry and Uncle Pete. They had arranged for her to marry my father. His name was Dan. Her brothers said that Dan came from a good family and had his own business. He had a shoe store where he sold shoes that he made and could fix up old shoes like new. My sister Helen said my mother told her that he seemed nice, but that she didn't want to marry him. She loved a redheaded boy back in Italy. But my mother's father didn't like the boy. He shipped my mother off to America to be with her brothers. I don't know what could have been so bad about the boy to make my grandfather do that.

"She couldn't do anything but marry him," my sister Helen told me. "She didn't speak English, she didn't have a job and her brothers couldn't take care of her." Helen stood in front of the mirror fixing her hair. She said she was jealous of me because my hair was naturally curly and she had to work hard to make hers keep a curl. "They probably believed they were doing a good thing, finding her a nice-looking man who had a good job."

Helen knew the most about our grandparents and cousins who still lived in Italy. She could speak Italian as good as Mama. When she and Mama didn't want me and Frances to know what they were saying they would speak in Italian. Once I recognized some English words. They were talking about Helen's heart condition.

"What's room attic fever?" I asked Helen.

"Your joints swell, but the worst part is what the disease can do to your heart."

"Does your heart hurt?"

"No. But if I run or carry things up the stairs, I get out of breath."

I wondered how she got room attic fever because none of the flats we lived in had an attic. I guess she must have caught it from somebody at school. The doctor said it gave her a leaky heart. But you couldn't notice any leaks just looking at her. That was just a joke. I knew the leak was inside. But I still wondered where the blood leaked to. And how does the blood get back to the right place?

She was bossier than my other sisters. I guess because she was the closest to being a grownup. She was even bossier than Mama. When I was just a crawling around baby, Mama worked part-time in a sewing factory. Back then, Helen looked after us kids. That's when she must of gotten to be bossy. I never learned to speak Italian because Helen spoke to us in English. Besides, by the time I was born my mother had been in America for a long time and she was beginning to mix-up her Italian with English. Except when she got mad. Then she spoke pure Italian. I believe Italian is a better language to get mad in.

I knew Helen couldn't work in a regular job because of her leaky heart, that's why we had to wait for Geraldine to finish eighth grade. After that, Geraldine was going to Saint Rose of Lima's high school, a two-year business school. She told me that she would learn how to type and take shorthand. Then she could get a really good job. My mother said that after Geraldine got a job as a secretary, we could go off of Relief. Phyllis and Tony were going to go to the same school. My mother said, that after they finished business school, with three kids working and her sewing job, pretty soon we could save enough money to buy our own house and not have a landlady always looking for rent money and wanting us to be quiet.

One day a big box filled with clothes and shoes was delivered to our house. Helen said that the Relief social-worker lady must have sent them. The clothes were clean but you could tell they weren't brand new. There were buttons missing and some of the clothes had patches. The clothes smelled like moth balls. My mother wouldn't let us wear them until she washed them and hung them on the clothesline. The next day she laid them on the kitchen table and folded them like in the store. They smelled like new. We made believe we were shopping. Helen and Geraldine were the store people. They made up stories about who owned the clothes before. We knew they must be rich people because otherwise they wouldn't ever give away such nice things. Most of the clothes fit pretty good except for me and my sister Phyllis. She was big for her age and I was small. I guess whoever packed the box was going by age and not size. My mother had to do a lot of sewing. The shoes were the worst problem because there were only two sizes. Too small and too big. That was a joke my brother Tony made up. There was a pair of patent leather shoes that looked like new. Mama said I had to save them for my First Holy Communion.

"Now this handsome cotton shirt looks just right for you, Peter," Geraldine said.

I ran my hand over the material. I liked the soft velvety feel. "What do you think?" I asked Tony.

"Looks like a girl's blouse to me," Tony said.

I tossed the shirt back on the pile. "I don't like purple shirts," I said.

If I let my sisters pick out my clothes, they would dress me like a girl. I always got Tony's opinion. We would go around and around until everything was bought up, excepting we used make-believe money. If there were things nobody wanted or didn't fit, my mother gave them to the Bread Lady. Mama said she would be glad to get them, especially the woolen winter sweaters and a black coat that would fit someone tall and skinny...the same size and shape as the Bread Lady.

There was a black coal stove in the kitchen and a large, almost square table that had a metal top that was white and had small red and white squares around all four edges Kind of like a checker board but only one row. Against the wall by the back door was an icebox with two doors on the bottom part where we kept the food, and one door on the top part where the iceman put blocks of ice. He only delivered ice in the summer. In the winter we used a window box to store food. The box was the size of an orange crate. In it we put meat, eggs, butter, milk, and anything else that had to be kept cold.

My mother's three brothers lived nearby and came to see us pretty often. I especially liked Uncle Pete. I would sit on his knee because his lap was taken up with his belly. He loved to tell jokes in Italian. When he laughed, tears ran down his cheeks. His laugh was like a tickle. Pretty soon everyone around him was laughing. I wished I could understand what he was saying. Sometimes I'd ask one of my sisters to tell me what he had said. But the stories never sounded funny in English.

Uncle Pete's breath smelled like wine, Uncle Joe's like Italian salami and Uncle Jerry's like tobacco. Uncle Pete made his own red wine. He almost always brought a bottle when he came to see us. For us kids, Mama put a little in a glass and filled it the rest of the way with water when we ate Sunday dinner.

When I was in first grade we went to a hospital where my father was a patient. We drove a long time. We saw fields with cows, horses and farms with giant rolls of hay.

"This is the country," Mama said. "It looks like San Andrea. The old country."

I wondered why Papa had to be so far away. I didn't remember seeing him ever before, so the visit to the hospital was like meeting

15

him for the first time. The building was made of red brick and covered with creepy green vines. It was surrounded by tall trees. There were shady paths with wooden benches and tables. The tree trunks were so fat I would have to have four arms to reach around.

Papa was big, but his belly didn't stick out like Uncle Pete's. He was just big all over. He reminded me of the guy who was always fighting Popeye over Olive Oil. I can't think of his name. But Papa didn't have a mean face. His short dark hair stood straight up on top. I never before saw anybody with his color eyes. They were green, but not like grass, more like the color of a green apple. I asked my sister Phyllis why none of us had green eyes. She was always reading books. I figured she would know.

"Mama has dark brown eyes," Phyllis said, "I guess the brown covered up the green part."

Papa's hands were strong and almost as big as baseball mitts. His whiskers scratched my face when he hugged me. His breath smelled like tobacco. He gave me presents when we visited him. Mostly things he had made of leather. I liked the smell of the leather. He made small leather bags with leather strings to close them. They were perfect for holding my immies He made wallets, belts, and pieces of leather with my name burned into the leather. Once he made me a holster and toy gun he had carved out of wood.

I liked sitting on his lap. He would sing songs, make funny noises and he could throw me high up in the air, like I was a feather. He'd pretend he wasn't going to catch me, then would grab me the last minute. After a while my mother would shout something in Italian and he would stop. He sometimes had tears in his eyes when we got ready leave.

After we got home, I looked in the mirror to see if I could find any specks of green that didn't get covered by the brown. I didn't find any.

I wanted to know why he couldn't come home. My mother said he was too sick to be out of the hospital. But he didn't seem sick to me. I asked my sister Helen.

"When you were still a baby, he had a nervous breakdown and had to be put in the hospital."

I didn't remember any of that. "What's a nervous breakdown?" I asked.

"A person is trembly all over. They're afraid to do anything. He drank wine to keep from shaking, but that made him even worse. He broke things. He was mean to Mama."

"How was he before?"

"He was nice."

"What made him have a breakdown?"

"The Depression was starting. He had no customers in his shoe store. He couldn't pay the rent. Maybe that's why. I don't know. There doesn't have to be a reason."

I was scared to think something like that could happen for no reason. There always has to be a reason. A person just has to figure out the reason. That's what I think.

Maybe I made him have a nervous breakdown. Mama said I cried more than all the rest of the kids put together. Helen said I would wake up screaming in the middle of the night. Nothing they did would make me stop. She said I practically drove her crazy. I still wasn't sure what a nervous breakdown was but wondered if all my crying made him have one. That night when I went to bed I cried for a long time. I

17

wanted my father to come home and read to me and tell me things and open his shoe store again. Whenever I went into a shoemaker's store the smell made me think of my father. I would feel like crying. Whatever was the matter with him must have been pretty bad to make him be in the hospital ever since I was a baby.

Helen said that even if he got out of the hospital, my mother didn't want him to come live with us. She said that if we weren't Catholic our mother would have divorced him. I knew that if a person wasn't Catholic, they can get a divorce and get married again. Once you got married by a Catholic priest, that was it. The rule is that you only get one turn, unless the other person dies. Then you could get married for a second time. But because Mama was forced to marry Papa, I didn't think that should have counted. To be fair she should have another turn. Marky had a father; they had a store and didn't have to be on Relief. If I could write, I would send a letter to the Pope and ask him to change his rule.

Peter Rizzolo

Geraldine   Frances   Chickey   Helen

        Me   Tony

Chapter Three

The People and the Stores on Our Block

In our neighborhood you couldn't tell what country you were in if you closed your eyes and just listened to grownups talk. Only the kids spoke English. I couldn't understand most of the grownups even when they did speak English. Only the people on the radio and in the movies didn't have an accent. Unless the movie was a Western or about rich people, who all talked like Ronald Coleman or Bette Davis. I guess school teachers probably don't talk with an accent, but I didn't know, because I wasn't in school yet and none of my friends were teachers.

My brother, Tony, could imitate lots of different accents. I could too, but I wasn't as good as him. We could talk like cowboys, the guy who plays Dracula and even Charlie Chan. I got mad when my older sisters acted like they didn't recognize who we were supposed to be.

The candy store next to Stillman's was owned by a man who had black curly hair and big white teeth. My brother told me he was Greek.

His wife's name was Frances, same as my sister. She was nice, but mostly her husband waited on us.

"What's Greek?" I asked my brother.

"His nationality. You know, what country he's from. Just like your mother being from Italy makes her Italian."

"But what about us? Aren't we Italian?"

"Sure."

"But if I went to Italy, they would say I was an American because that's where I'm from."

Tony was doing his homework. "I didn't say you couldn't be more than one thing. You're Italian and American and also a pain in the neck. Don't bother me."

I thought about what he told me. When you saw a tree or a bird, and someone told you, "That's a maple tree," or "That's a robin," for some reason that made you feel better than not knowing. I guess the same was true with people. You were supposed to know what they were.

"A noun doesn't really tell you much about a person," Phyllis told me. "What you need are adjectives and adverbs."

"What are adjectives and the other thing you said?"

"They're words you use to describe things," she said. "You'll learn that in school."

I remember the first time I went in this kid's house, his mother said, "Oh, this is the little Italian boy you were telling me about." I felt kind of funny. She didn't even say Italian right. She said, "Eye-tail-yun." Why didn't he just tell her what my name was? I felt like saying, "You must be the Irish lady Tommy was telling me about." But I didn't say anything. Tommy was one of my neighborhood friends and I didn't want to hurt his feelings because of what his mother said.

My brother once told me you could commit a sin just by thinking bad things. I think that's another unfair rule. I know it's a sin to lie or do bad things or disobey your mother. But bad thoughts just pop up in my head; like to punch a kid or say bad words or tell somebody to go to hell. I heard grownups say those and lots of other bad words plenty of times. But thoughts are like the trolley ride where all of a sudden something's there, and you take a look. You didn't make the thing be there. Thoughts just pop up on the screen inside your head. If you don't say a bad thing or do a bad thing, thinking bad thoughts is like passing something in the trolley without getting off.

All that talk about naming things and thinking things came from me talking about the candy store man being Greek. When you walked in, his store, on the right there was a long glass cabinet with boxes of loose candy on glass shelves. On the floor on your left were piles of newspapers. On the wall behind the counter were shelves that held all kinds of cigars and cigarettes. In the back were magazines.

If ever my sister Chickey would come in the candy store with me and Frances, she would go in back and look at the magazines. She liked the ones with movie stars in them. The man kept looking back there at her like he was afraid she was going to stick one in her bloomers.

After my sister Frances and I got three cents deposit money from a milk bottle, we would go to the candy store. We took a long time deciding what to buy. The best part was telling a grownup to give me different kinds of candy, not things like beets or cauliflower or leftovers you couldn't recognize because they were all mushed together.

For five cents you could get a small bag full of candies. The store had gumdrops, dots, licorice, lollypops, jawbreakers, MaryJane's, chocolate-covered peanuts, kisses, and a million kinds of different colored stick-candy and chocolate candy bars with nuts and peanut butter. We only had three cents, so the man didn't fill the bag.

There were usually lots of grownups in the store. I wondered if they were buying candy for their kids or for themselves. But Mama said if we ate too much candy our teeth would fall out. One day I asked my mother, "Mama, how come the candy-store-man has such nice teeth? He must eat a lot of candy."

My mother was using a washboard in the kitchen sink. The bottom of the board was made of wavy metal and the top was wood with a small shelf where you could keep the soap, its two wooden legs rested on the bottom of the sink. She was scrubbing something that was covered with little bubbly clouds of soap. Sometimes a blue soap bubble would escape from the suds and float away. I liked to pop the bubbles between my hands.

Mama rinsed and wrung out a pile of clothes. She didn't say anything about the man's teeth. Maybe she didn't hear me because of the loud noise the running water made when it splashed against the metal washboard.

"Those aren't his own teeth," my sister Geraldine said. She was in the eighth grade. She was sitting at the kitchen table reading a book. "He ate too much candy when he was little and lost all the teeth God gave him. Watch when he laughs. They come out a little. He has to push them back in place."

I would hate to wear someone else's teeth in my mouth. And who would give away their teeth for him to wear? A dead person?

The next time me and my sister Frances saved up a few pennies, as usual we went into the candy store. I wanted to see if what Geraldine said about his teeth was true. Frances didn't like the same kinds of candy as me. I loved licorice and MaryJane's. She liked mostly chocolate. I kept looking at his teeth and hoping he wouldn't laugh too hard. What if they popped out and land on the counter?

"Come on, already, I have other customers," the man said.

"Hey, don't rush the kids," someone said, "They're making a big decision here."

I didn't know who said it, because I was afraid to take my eyes off of the candy store-man. And sure enough, when he laughed, he had to push his top teeth back in, just like Geraldine said. I looked at Frances. Her eyes were wide open. She must have seen the same thing I did.

There were grownups in the candy store were standing around talking and didn't seem to be buying anything. After we had lived at the South Orange Avenue house for a few months my brother Tony got a job working in the candy store. He made fifty cents a week. That had to be the best job in the world. He could sneak candy when the man wasn't looking and with the money he made, he could go to the movies anytime he liked. Sometimes when I would cry to go to the movies, Tony would give in before Mama, and give me a dime.

Tony told me that the Greek man did most of his business selling the numbers.

"Where does he keep them? They must be pretty good if all those grownups are buying them."

Tony just shook his head and didn't answer.

"How many can I get for a nickel?" I asked.

"The people *play* the numbers. They don't *eat* them. It's gambling. They come in the store to place bets."

I knew what a bet was but couldn't figure out how the Greek man could make money by betting with so many people. He couldn't always be right.

I liked to think about numbers. I could count to fifty forwards and backwards. Seven was my favorite number because there were seven kids in my family, and besides, everyone said seven was a lucky number. If our family was ever to be lucky, I should get the credit, because if I weren't born there wouldn't be seven kids. I don't know about six. It sounds like what you ask your dog to do when you want him to bite someone. Next year when I'm six, and grownups ask me how old I am, I'm going to tell them I'm going on seven.

By now you know I have a brother named Tony. Sometimes we'd wrestle or he'd carry me on his shoulders, but mostly he played with his friend Paul Stillman. Excepting for Tony, our house was filled up with girls. I was glad to have a brother and not be the only boy.

The Stillmans were Jewish. I think maybe I said that before. I wondered why they never went to church. I asked my brother Tony how come they didn't.

"There's no Synagogue around here. Besides, Jews don't believe it's a sin not to go to church. The Ten Commandments only say to 'keep holy the Sabbath.' Their way to keep it holy is to pray and rest."

Besides Pasta

I knew the Jewish Sabbath was Saturday and not Sunday. But I knew their store was open on Saturday. I asked Marky about that the next time we were playing in the back yard. We drew a chalk line on the cement and were seeing how far we could jump. We had it planned out so that we would land on a dirt patch at the back-end of our yard. With a stick we marked the place where we landed.

"I asked my father about that too," Marky said. "He said we rest on Sundays with the gentiles. We read the bible and say prayers at home."

I was getting ready to run to the spot we marked to jump from. I had to run as fast as I could because Marky had such long legs, he could jump pretty far without hardly trying.

"What's a gentile?" I asked.

"Anybody who's not a Jew."

"How can you lump everybody together like that? Don't the Arabs and Chinese and Africans have their own ways of praying?"

"I guess what I meant was Christians…their Sabbath is Sunday," he said.

I backed way off from the jump spot and ran so fast I almost lost my balance. My left foot landed on the chalk-line and I took off high in the air. I reached a foot farther than Marky's last jump.

"Not bad for a gentile," I said.

For his next jump he ran pretty fast. His big ears must have caught the wind just right, because he landed a few inches past my best jump.

He was sitting on his butt in the dirt with a big smile on his face. He said, "Not bad for a Jew!"

I wasn't too happy having him beat me, because between him, me and Frances I was always the champion jumper. "It's got nothing to do with your religion. It's your long legs and big ears."

He brushed dirt from the seat of his pants. "Why are you such a sore loser, Pete?"

It was true about his legs. But I felt bad for what I said about his ears. He told me once kids as school teased him.

"I was just kidding," I said, "For today you're the long-jump champion. But you just wait."

Above the Greek candy store on the same floor as us, was an Irish lady with two red-headed boys. The Fosters, who were half French and half something else, lived over the Irish family. On the third floor above us was an Italian family. They had three or four kids but they were older. I didn't even know their names. One of the Foster boys liked my sister Helen. He took her to the movies once. She was almost sixteen and everybody said she looked like a movie star. She thought that one side of her face was prettier than the other. When she talked to someone outside the family, she always turned her head so they would be looking at her good side.

After we were living there awhile my mother rented the tiny room off the front hall to a man. He was short and always wore a suit and tie and never said anything. He stayed in his room except if he had to go to the bathroom or at dinner time. My mother always passed the meat platter to him first. He took more than any of us. I guess because he paid and we didn't. But he only lived with us a couple of months. I don't think Mama liked that he ate so much. To tell the truth I was glad to see him go so we could have our flat to ourselves.

Down the street was a butcher shop alongside a store that sold vegetables. The people who owned those stores only spoke Italian. I

27

liked listening to my mother talking to them. They must have always been telling jokes, because they laughed a lot. I wished I knew what they were saying. I did know what *"Troppo Caro"* meant because my mother said that a lot. Funny how you learn to know what a word means without anybody telling you. Mama meant, "You're must be crazy if you think I'm going to pay that much." Italian is such a great language, because you can say so much with even just one word. Once when I was walking with my mother and a lady passed us. My mother whispered, *"puttana."* I asked her what *puttana* meant. Mama said that a woman who walks down the street with a cigarette in her mouth is a bad person.

One time I wanted to buy an ice cream cone from the candy store. There was a counter in back where the store owner kept the ice cream. That day, the man's wife waited on me. I only had three cents.

"How much for a vanilla ice cream cone?" I asked the lady. I already knew, but I wanted to try out *"troppo caro."*

"Five cents," she said.

"Troppo caro, troppo caro," I said. You had to always say it twice.

She laughed, but she still wouldn't sell the ice cream to me for three cents. Frances was with me. She gave me another two cents. The lady gave us a scoop of chocolate and a scoop of vanilla. We took turns licking. I took bigger licks, because I put in three cents and she only put in two.

The butcher shop had a wooden floor covered with sawdust. The store smelled like raw chickens and salami. While my mother waited her turn, I would spin on my heels to make clear circles on the floor. I wondered why they put sawdust down and where they got it. If nobody

Peter Rizzolo

was looking, sometimes I stuffed a handful of sawdust in my pocket. I used it to leave a trail when we played cowboys and Indians.

I watched the butcher cut the meat and slap the pieces with the side of his knife until they were as thin as the sole of my shoe. Except there was usually a hole in the sole of my shoe. To cover the hole, Mama cut out a piece of cardboard until she had enough money to have a new sole put on.

I liked to watch the meat come out of the grinder. I wondered if you could make spaghetti by putting dough in the meat grinder. My mother watched the butcher really close to make sure he didn't throw too much fat in the machine. I think I already told you about that.

Sometimes the butcher gave me a free slice of baloney or a hot dog. If Frances was with us, I would only get half a hot dog. My mother mostly bought soup bones and ground meat. Sometimes she bought a piece of hard salty fat that smelled like bacon, but you couldn't see but a speck of meat. She would cut the fat into tiny pieces. The smell when she fried the fat made my mouth water. It tasted sort of like bacon but saltier. Mostly she would throw the fried pieces in tomato sauce to give the sauce a meaty flavor.

The owner of the vegetable store would drag boxes of apples, oranges, plums, grapes, chestnuts, lettuce, spinach, string beans and a million other kinds of vegetables and fruit onto the sidewalk in front of the store. Bringing everything back inside every night must have been a big job. Sometimes the man would give me and my sister a small apple, usually one with a soft spot. He never gave me a plum or cherries or grapes even though I would be looking at them with my tongue practically hanging out.

Besides Pasta

Mama said green vegetables were good for me especially spinach and escarole. Spinach was okay, because everybody knows spinach makes you strong. But the stems were stringy and stuck in my teeth. I didn't like escarole. Once my mother made soup with escarole and I saw a bug in the soup. Mama looked. She said, "*Ecco, solamente pepe nero. Mangia figlio di Mama!*" I looked at Helen.

"She said it's black pepper. That you have to eat it," Helen said.

I knew Mama must need glasses because pepper doesn't have wiggly legs. I took a spoonful of soup with a bug in it and waited until Mama wasn't looking, then threw the spoonful of soup under the table. I wasn't the only one fishing out bugs. I started looking around and noticed Chickey, Frances and Tony were doing the same thing. After dinner when no one was around, Frances and I went into the kitchen and cleaned up the mess under the table. I noticed there was even some soup near Helen's place.

I liked the bakery best. The smell of all those good things was almost too much to take. Besides a candy store, a bakery would be my favorite place to work. The glass cases were filled with different kinds of cookies, cakes, pies, honey buns, and doughnuts. Behind the counter were shelves loaded with bread. Long skinny loaves, round ones, flat round loaves with a hole in the middle, fancy twisted loaves, and rolls. Some were crusty and others looked soft. I liked the crusty Italian bread best.

The lady in the bakery would sometimes give me an anisette biscuit that was so hard you could crack a tooth trying to bite off a piece. I sucked the biscuits like a lollypop.

If you didn't eat the Italian bread right away, in two days you could use the loaf to hammer nails. No matter how hard it got, Mama always figured out a way to make the bread soft enough to eat. She would grate the hard bread to add to meatballs or meatloaf or even in soup. Or she would put a little coffee in a cup, add some sugar and fill the cup with warmed-up milk. We'd dunk the hard bread in our cup. You had to be careful not to dunk for too long or the bread would get mushy and fall apart in the hot milk.

We hardly ever ate the soft white bread you could buy at Stillman's or the A&P.

"American bread is *porcherie*," Mama would say. "It is junk. You might as well eat paper."

Phyllis laughed when I asked her what "poor cherry" meant. "She meant that the food has no nutritive value."

I must have looked puzzled because she explained, "That means American bread does nothing to improve your health."

But by the end of the month when there was no money left from the Relief check, Mama would wait in the bread line for a long time to get two or three loaves of American bread. I liked toasting the bread on top of the coal stove. We had this metal thing that was shaped like a pyramid with the top cut off. You could lay four slices of bread on four sides of the toaster. When one side was toasted you turned the slices over to toast the other side. Even toasted, white bread wasn't as good as Italian bread but better than no bread. The bread line was where Mama first met the Bread Lady.

Chapter Four

The Bread Lady and the Circus Man

My mother's best friend was a lady who I never saw without a kerchief on her head, even in the summer. For all I knew, all the hair she had was the little bit in front that showed on her forehead. Mama met her in a bread line. Me and Frances were too little to leave at the house alone, so Mama usually took us with her when she went to get bread. A lot of people didn't have a job. To keep them from starving, Roosevelt gave away free bread. The bread line was a mile long, and sometimes you'd get tired of waiting. How many loaves you could get depended on how many kids you had. Except when they began to run out. Then you only got one loaf, even if you had a hundred kids. I think you had to have a card or something to show you were on Relief. One day the bread truck was late and after waiting a long time, my mother started to leave.

"I can't wait," she said to the lady behind us in the line. "My other children will be getting home from school." The lady looked at my sister and me.

"How many children do you have?" she asked.

"Five others. Four girls and a boy."

It was a cold day in November. I puffed smoke out of my nose like a dragon. I scrunched my lips and let the smoke out of the corners of my mouth. The lady smiled. Frances held one nose hole and blew smoke out of the other side. The lady laughed. She had a nice face.

"*Nevega*," My mother said as she looked at the sky.

That's another Italian word I knew. "Snow is coming! Snow is coming!" I told my sister. I started pulling my mother's arm to get her to go. Frances pushed her from behind.

"Where do you live?" the lady asked.

My mother tried to explain, but the way the lady looked at her I didn't think she understood. The lady wasn't Italian. Later I found out she was from Poland.

Even before we got home the snow began to fall. The flakes were as big as candy kisses. Frances and I caught them in the palms of our hands and watched them change into tiny puddles of water. My mother didn't like the snow. She said getting wet could give you a chill and you could get walking *newmonia* or even consumption.

Consumption was a big word that I knew because my mother was always saying we were going to get consumption if we didn't dress warm. But I didn't care. I loved the snow. The world turned white like a story-book Christmas, the way things must have been before people and cars messed things up. At night Frances and me would look out the front window as the falling snow covered the sidewalks, parked cars and the roofs of buildings. The light from the street lamps and the beauty shop sign across South Orange Avenue made the street sparkle like a cotton blanket sprinkled with a million tiny diamonds.

We were surprised the next day when the Polish lady came to our house with a bag full of bread. Her head was covered with snow and her nose was red as Helen's lipstick. I knew my mother was afraid the lady would get consumption, because she put a towel over the lady's head and sat her next to the coal stove. After that, the Polish lady brought us bread so that Mama didn't have to wait a long time in line. We started to call her the Bread Lady. She would stay and have a cup of tea with my mother.

"Read the tea leaves, Antoinette," the Bread Lady said one day after they finished their tea.

Mama shook the Bread Lady's cup to spread out the tea leaves. She held up the cup and looked.

She stared into the lady's cup. "Your daughter is going to meet a nice man. He has a good job. Someday they will get married and move into a big house and ask you to come live with them. You will have many grandchildren."

The Bread Lady laughed. "How many?"

Sometimes my mother would stare at the inside of the cup and shake her head like she didn't believe what she was seeing. She would shake the cup again and start over. I figured Mama and the Bread Lady were just playing a game. How could tea leaves know anything? But the Bread Lady looked serious and maybe believed what Mama was telling her.

One day Marky asked, "How come you don't have a father? Is he dead?"

"He isn't dead," I told him. "He's in the hospital from having a nervous breakdown."

Marky didn't answer right away. "I'm sorry," he said. "Maybe he'll get better and come home sometime."

I didn't tell him that my mother didn't want him to come home even if he was better. I don't know why she ever started bringing me to see him. One day I asked Geraldine how come we didn't go see him more times. She said the hospital was in the country and that we couldn't get there on the bus or trolley. But after Uncle Tony started coming around, she asked him to take us in his car so we could go see Papa.

I liked Uncle Tony. I knew he wasn't a real uncle, but that's what Mama said we should call him. He told me stories about the circus that he worked in when he was young.

"What made you quit working there?" I asked him even though I already knew the answer.

"I was on the trapeze. You know what that is?"

"I think so," I lied.

Uncle Tony had brought me a coloring book and crayons. I liked to color but wasn't good at keeping the colors inside the lines. Frances could color a lot better. Uncle Tony took the crayons and found a blank page. He drew a picture of a tent and two high-up swings. He drew a man hanging from the swing. I was surprised how good he could draw. He drew a clown and a fat lady looking up at the man.

"I was having fun swinging back and forth, showing off in front of the fat lady," he said. "I was doing great, but then I looked down at her and my hand slipped. I began to fall…."

Besides Pasta

"That must of hurt pretty bad," I said.

"Not that much, because I landed on the fat lady."

"Wow! You were lucky."

"I wasn't that lucky," he said.

He took my hand and let me feel the back of his head. There was a dent there big enough to hold a scoop of ice cream.

"After I bounced off the lady my head hit a stake."

"A piece of meat made that hole?"

"No. No. A metal spike that holds up the tent."

See what I mean about grownups? I put my fingers in the dent in his head. "What happened to your brains that used to be there?"

My mother was at the stove making zeppoles. You know what those are, don't you? They're globs of dough Mama drops in a pan of hot oil. They puff up into funny shapes and pretty soon turn the color of honey. You're supposed to eat them hot with powdered sugar sprinkled on them.

"Peter, your Uncle Tony likes to make up stories. I think he was born with that hole in his head."

I knew she was only joking because she started to laugh. "That's why you had to quit the circus?" I asked.

He nodded. He looked sad. I didn't think he was just making up stories. "Tell me again about the tall man."

"He was so skinny that if he stood sideways people would lean against him thinking he was a pole. And if he stood on his toes, he could peek into a second-story window. They had to put two beds together for him to fit and even then, his feet stuck off the end."

"And the fat lady...."

"She was pretty as a doll."

Peter Rizzolo

"Tell me again what you told me about the snow," I said.

"She was so light on her feet she didn't even leave a footprint when she walked on the snow!"

"But you said she weighed as much as a small elephant," I said.

"That's right, almost four hundred pounds. When I gave her a ride, I was afraid the car might tip over." He flipped his hand over and slapped the table. "I made her sit in the middle of the back seat. I had to put bricks in the front to keep the back end of the car from scraping the ground."

"You could buy a car without a roof. That way she could stand."

He looked confused.

"You said she was light on her feet."

"This is a smart boy, Antoinette," Uncle Tony said.

By that time my mother had made a pile of zeppoles. She let me put on the powdered sugar.

"How come the circus never comes around here?" I asked. I used a tablespoon to sift on the sugar. I liked to watch the sugar fall like snow onto the hot zeppoles.

"The next time the circus comes to New York, I'll take you and your mother."

"Can Frances and my friend Marky come?"

"Sure. Bring the whole neighborhood," Uncle Tony said.

My mother laughed. "You should write books, Tony. That way you would get money for telling lies."

My mother would roll her eyes when he told his stories. But she never went to a circus. So how would she know if he was telling the truth? And what about that hole in his head?

Besides Pasta

Uncle Tony owned a truck and used to deliver coal and something called Biancoline. You put it in the water when you washed clothes. He sometimes brought Mama a gallon. It had a nice clean smell, but if I took too big a whiff, it burned my nose. When Mama used it in her wash, the sheets and pillowcases turned out soft and white as the fur on a kitten's belly. After Mama used it, her hands smelled like Biancoline for a pretty long time.

We had a cat called Ginger. He had orange stripes just like a tiger. He must have been born before me, because I never remember getting him. Marky didn't believe Ginger peed on the regular toilet. But he really did, excepting he sat like a girl. Once when my friend Marky was there, I saw Ginger on the toilet. I yelled for Marky to come, but Ginger jumped off before Marky got there. I guess Ginger didn't like people watching when he went to the bathroom. I couldn't blame him, but I wished Marky could have seen him sitting on the toilet like a regular person.

I was talking about Uncle Tony. He always had a lot of money. I guess he was the richest person we knew. He would sometimes leave a couple of one-dollar bills underneath the sugar bowl on the kitchen table. My mother would slip the money in the pocket of her housedress without saying anything or thanking him. I knew she liked him because when he came, she would send me to the Stillman's delicatessen to buy four slices of ham and two Kaiser Rolls. She would make coffee and zeppoles for dessert. My brother said that Uncle Tony was "sweet" on my mother and that she liked him, but she couldn't remarry until after my father died. I never once saw them kiss or anything. If they did, he must have been a magician as well as a circus man.

My Uncle Tony had a truck and a car, so he had to be rich. His car was black with a spare tire on the passenger side by the front fender. The grill was as tall as me and looked like the teeth of a giant shark. I loved to see his car parked in front of our building. I would tell anyone who passed by, "That's my Uncle Tony's car. He was in the circus!"

My older siblings understood that Uncle Tony was a suitor of my mother's. Beyond the fact that he gave her money, they picked up on his love-sick glances and the double entendres. For several years he tried to talk her into divorcing my father. He was convinced an annulment was possible, since the marriage was not voluntary and my father was already suffering from mental illness at the time of their marriage. But after a few years, Uncle Tony gave up trying to convince my mother to marry him. He eventually married someone else and stopped coming to visit us on a regular basis. He did stop by sporadically for short visits or to take us someplace in his car. I suspect he was still fond of my mother and had grown to love us children as well. Many years later I was on the verge of being forced to drop out of medical school because I couldn't scrape together the tuition for my senior year. There were no student loan programs then. My hometown bank refused to approve a loan because I had no collateral. Two people lent me the money to continue. One was Uncle Tony and the other, the Bread Lady.

Mama's Zeppole Recipe

Mama used a well-seasoned, heavy iron frying pan. Once heated, it held the oil at a fairly constant temperature. She liked to use a gas stove because she could adjust the heat much better than with a coal stove or electric burner.

She didn't have a thermometer. But I cheated when I tried to reproduce her recipe. I found 325-335 degrees to be the ideal temperature. Any hotter and the inside of the zeppole didn't cook even when the outside was clearly overdone. At lower temperatures the zeppoles soak up too much oil.

Also, using a small amount of batter insures that the inside of the zeppole will be cooked. To cook larger zeppoles you'll have to add more baking soda and baking powder. But it gets tricky when you start changing things. Too much leavening leaves an unpleasant after-taste.

When do you turn over the zeppole? When the batter begins to bubble in the perimeter and you can see that the edge is getting a golden brown, it's time to flip the zeppole onto its back. Often, they flip over by themselves when they're ready. Cook them approximately a minute on each side.

Ingredients:

One cup + one heaping tablespoon sifted flour

Three tbs. of water

One egg

Three tbs. of sugar (a little more if you like them sweeter)

A tablespoon of oil

Peter Rizzolo

One-half teaspoon of baking soda

One-half teaspoon of baking powder

One-quarter of a teaspoon of vanilla (optional)

A pinch of salt

Mix all the dry ingredients. Make a well in the center.

Combine the egg (beat until frothy); add water, oil, and vanilla. Add the liquid mixture to the well and gradually incorporate the dry ingredients.

The batter should be sticky not runny.

Drop rounded teaspoonfuls of batter into the hot oil. Proceed as above. Place the zeppoles on paper towels and sprinkle generously with confectionery sugar.

Enjoy!

PS: If you are diabetic, have a weight problem, high cholesterol or all your male relatives died at an early age of coronary heart disease, I recommend you not get too good at making zeppoles.

Marky 1938

Chapter Five

Mama's Job

There was a coat factory a few blocks from where we lived. Mama carried unfinished coats home, where she hand-stitched the coat linings, and hems. After she worked on them, she brought them back to the factory. Mama said the hardest part was carrying the coats back and forth.

One day I asked my mother, "Why don't you use Tony's scooter?" I was six going on seven and had lots of ideas how to do things.

She thought I was joking, because she laughed. But I must have given her an idea, because the next day she brought home an old baby carriage somebody put out on the sidewalk for the garbage man to take away. One wheel was shaped like a potato chip and made the carriage dip up and down on one side. My brother banged the wheel with a hammer until it was almost round. Not perfect, but still a lot easier to push. When you pushed, the carriage moved sideways as well as up and down.

Peter Rizzolo

Mama started using the baby carriage. Now she could take a lot more coats in one trip. Even though I said to use a scooter and not a baby carriage, I should have gotten the credit, because I gave her the idea.

People always made jokes when they saw her with those coats piled a mile high on the carriage. One man asked, "You think your baby's warm enough lady?"

Sometimes I would go with Mama to pick up the coats. I would help her push the carriage. The sidewalk part was easy, unless you had to go uphill. Even going downhill, the carriage wouldn't go without pushing. The hardest part was taking the carriage across the street. The street stones looked like a million turtles stuck in cement and the carriage wheels kept getting stuck in the cracks between the turtles. The carriage shook so hard the coats kept falling off. Getting the carriage back on the sidewalk was the next hardest part. Sometimes a policeman or somebody we didn't know would help us.

When we got home, Mama would pile the coats on a table by the front room windows. On cold nights there was frost on the windows because she turned off the heat to save on coal. Mama wore a long woolen shawl over her shoulders and tied a cotton scarf over her head to keep warm.

I'm not sure exactly what all she did to the coats. She didn't have a sewing machine. She had to sew everything by hand. She showed me how to tie a knot at the end of a thread by licking my finger and twisting the thread into a ball. Sometimes she let me thread the needles for her.

Besides Pasta

She used a thimble to push the needle through the thick material. Once when Mama wasn't there, I tried to use the thimble. The needle slipped off the thimble and practically went through my finger. My mother once told me you could get blood poisoning from a nail or a cut. I sucked my finger for two days to be sure to get all the poison out. I didn't tell Mama, because she warned me plenty of times never to play with her needles.

She did her sewing at night after we all went to bed. Sometimes when I couldn't sleep, I'd get up, go into the living room, sit on the floor with my pillow and watch her work. There was a street light right outside our house. I guess that's why she worked near the window. The room was dark. When I scrunched my eyes, she and the coats were giant ink spots against the light from the windows. Sometimes the ink spots looked like a giant octopus or somebody sitting on an elephant. But when she stood, she reminded me of the statue of the Blessed Virgin that was on the dresser in her bedroom.

Sometimes I would sit on her lap as she worked. She would hum or sing quietly in Italian. I didn't understand the words, but I liked the sound of her singing.

The following day she'd carry the clothes back to the factory and bring home another bunch. As I said before, we were on Relief. That's what Roosevelt started to help people who were out of work. My mother hated to be on Relief, but with seven children to raise, she couldn't support our family without help. The Relief check couldn't have been very much because Mama was always out of money before the social worker came with the next check. She had to be careful how she spent it.

Mama would say, "If we don't have enough to pay the rent on the first of the month, the landlady will kick us out! What will we do then?" That was why she couldn't give us money for the movies or candy or new shoes or toys. Every birthday and Christmas I would ask if I could get a bike, a three-wheeler like Marky's. But I never did. My mother said they cost too much. Besides, I might go in the street and get run over. Marky let me ride his sometimes, but that wasn't the same as having my own.

Each family on Relief was assigned a social worker, who made monthly home visits. The woman assigned to us inspected the house and furnishings. She would threaten to reduce the size of the monthly check if she believed we were spending the money on frivolous things. Our windows always had clean curtains and crocheted valences Helen and my mother made from scraps of fabric Mama got for free from the coat factory. My mother crocheted doilies for the tables and arms and backs of our living room couch and side chairs. The social worker believed the curtains and crocheted things were signs of affluence; she would scold my mother for wasting the government's money when her other clients didn't have enough to buy food. The woman looked in our closets and dresser drawers to see if we were spending money on expensive clothes. She even looked in the icebox, which never had much in it. She would exclaim that Mama was obviously neglecting the children's health, using the Relief money to buy unnecessary things for the house.

The week my mother expected the social worker to come, she would take down the curtains, and put away the crocheted chair covers. She would scrub and wax the floors only after the lady came to inspect our flat. Mother lived in fear of a surprise visit. As a child I was oblivious of the humiliation these monthly inspections entailed. She usually came when we were still at school; after school I was usually outside playing so I hardly ever saw the social worker. But Helen told me years later how proud our mother was of our clean house and of the things she made, and of her children and how angry and frustrated she was to have that arrogant woman come into her home and poke into our private things.

After the woman left, Helen and my mother would have a cup of tea. Sometimes my mother would cry and not say anything. But usually she would tell stories about her childhood, growing up in Italy on a small family farm with lots of brothers and sisters. They raised chickens for meat and eggs and grew a large variety of vegetables and fruits. My mother was twelve years old when her mother died. Several months later, she and her sisters and brothers were shocked when their father returned from a short trip to France with a new wife and her two daughters from a previous marriage. My mother, still grieving the loss of her own mother, was not well disposed to get along with her father's new wife or her stepsisters. Even at a young age my mother possessed a strong will and volatile temperament. Her father, after enduring a household in turmoil, agreed to send my mother packing to America where three of her brothers had already escaped. Two years after my mother immigrated, her two younger sisters came to America. They all settled in the First Ward section of Newark, New Jersey.

In the last quarter of the nineteenth century, people living in the southern provinces of Italy immigrated to America to escape both natural and man-made disasters. So many came and settled in New

York that jobs became scarce. Going in search of work, they discovered that there was work to be had across the Hudson River in Newark, New Jersey. Hundreds settled in a half-mile square section of the city that was later to be called Little Italy. Saint Lucy's Church was the center of community life. From the late 1890s to the onset of the Great Depression, Little Italy was a thriving, community, bound together by a pioneering spirit, a common cultural heritage, and a strong religious tradition. These energetic, passionate people did not look to the government for support. It was from this stock that my mother came. For her, dependence was anathema.

The social worker didn't know how lucky she was that my mother was able to control her famous temper. After finishing their tea, she and Helen put the curtains back up, brought out the doilies and seat covers and scrubbed and waxed the floors.

With seven children, there were lots of clothes to wash. For years, my mother used a corrugated scrub board. One day she saw a Maytag Ringer washing machine in a second-hand store. The man said she could have the washer "as is" for four dollars. She agreed to pay him fifty cents a week. Uncle Tony loaded the Maytag onto his truck and drove to our house. Mama had him put the washer in the cellar. He had to use car parts from a junkyard to get the thing working. Mama was overjoyed. The only problem was that she was frightened to death of the cellar. She believed a man was murdered there and that his ghost lurked in its dark recesses. But she couldn't risk having the social worker find the washing machine. But the many hours of scrubbing she saved by using the Maytag more than compensated for the terror she had to endure in the cellar.

Chapter Six

The Stillmans and Us

Paul Stillman and my brother could make toys out of things people threw away, like old inner tubes. To make a gun all you needed was a big nail, a piece of wood from the end of a wooden box, a clothes pin, and scissors to cut the tube into fat rubber bands. Our homemade inner tube gun didn't look like a six-shooter, but if you were hit by the rubber you were still counted as being killed. The idea of the game was to get killed fewer times than anybody else.

From an old pair of roller skates, you could make a scooter. Paul and Tony took a little piece of rubber from the wheels so they could turn better. Then they nailed half of the skate to the front of a board and the other half to the back. They turned over the board and attached a wooden box on the front. Then they nailed a piece of wood across the top of the box for handlebars. I couldn't make one for myself, but my brother sometimes would let me ride his on the sidewalk. No matter how hard you pumped, you couldn't go fast except downhill. Once the scooter got going, the only way to stop was by dragging your foot along the sidewalk. I remember this one time I was racing Marky. He was using his tricycle and I was riding my brother's scooter. Marky was way ahead until we reached the top of a hill. He must have thought he already had the race won, because he slowed down as he went down the hill. I pumped really hard a few times and the scooter started going so fast my cap blew off. I looked to see where it went and ran the scooter into the curb. I went flying into the air and landed face down into a patch of dirt alongside the sidewalk. Marky came running to where I was sitting on the dirt, holding my nose and crying. He handed me his handkerchief. Then he went and got my cap. My knickers were torn and I could feel a bump growing on my forehead.

"I was catching up," I shouted after him.

"I have to get my bike," he said.

He had left his bike at the bottom of the hill. By the time he got back, I was checking the scooter. Tony would be mad if I broke his scooter, especially since I didn't ask him if I could use it. One of the handle bars was split.

"I have some black tape," Marky said. "We can put glue in the crack and use tape to hold the handlebar together until the glue dries."

"Yeah," I said. "And if Tony doesn't use his scooter for a couple of days, he won't be able to tell."

When I got back to our house Tony and Paul were in the back yard playing catch. He came over and looked at the bump on my head and felt my bruised nose. He didn't say anything about the broken handlebar.

"I meant to tell you," Tony said, "I oiled the skate wheels last night. You have to be careful going downhill."

Besides Pasta

Our building was really just two houses stuck together. A brick wall ran down the center of the basement from the front to the back. There were openings in the wall so you could get from one side of the basement to the other. Because the wall was so thick, the openings were like tunnels. A grown-up would have to stoop to go through. The floor was dirt, packed hard as wood, black from coal dust. I was never in a real cave, but that's what the tunnels reminded me of.

Each family had its own furnace and coal bin. There were three furnaces on each side. On our side, our furnace was the middle one, so you had to walk pretty far into the cellar to get to the furnace. The basement was dark, damp, and scary, especially the tunnels. I was sure there were rats, spiders, and other icky things in there.

My mother said that the man had been murdered on the other side from where our furnace was. She said his ghost was still there. The man who was killed was my sister Frances' Godfather. His name was Paulie. She said he owed money from gambling. My sister Phyllis told me that Paulie was hit in the head and put in his car. Then they ran Paulie's car into a tree to fool people into thinking it was an accident. She said my mother went to the morgue to identify him because Frances' godmother refused to go. When we sat around the stove, my mother would tell of going to see his body.

"A policeman came to the house and drove me to the morgue."

"How old was I?" I asked.

Phyllis, Helen and Frances were sitting in front of the stove tossing orange peels on the hot stove-eyes. That's what we called the round disks you could take out to add coal to the stove. We liked the smell the burnt peels made. Geraldine, Chickey, and Tony were in the living room listening to the radio. I didn't care about the radio, even if

Gangbusters was on, because what my mother was telling us really happened.

"Frances was only two years old," Phyllis said. "You weren't born yet."

"I went into a room that was cold as an icebox," my mother said. "On a table was a body covered with a white sheet. The man pulled down the sheet. I started to shake. I crossed myself and said a prayer."

"You know this man?" the policeman asked.

My mother told us that she couldn't talk. Paulie's head was turned sideways and he was staring right at her.

"Is this Paulie Polombo?"

She nodded her head.

She told us there was a cut on the side of his head that you could fit your whole hand in. "You could see the white bone. There was a sharp dent in the bone."

"Mama told Paulie's wife that his dying was no accident," Phyllis said. "That the men who killed him probably used an axe. Then Paulie's wife told a lot of other people."

"The men who did that terrible thing to Paulie were getting nervous," Mama said, "because pretty soon a couple of them came to the house and told her to stop spreading lies if she knew what was good for her and her family. Mama made us promise never to tell anybody outside the family.

I couldn't wait to tell Marky. He was the First Person in the Blessed Trinity, so he really was part of the family. Sort of.

"Did the cops ever catch the guys?" I asked Mama. On *Gangbusters* bad guys always got caught.

Besides Pasta

"No," Mama said. "That's why Paulie's ghost won't leave the basement."

Even without the story about Paulie, the cellar was scary. Something must have died there, a mouse, a cat…something. The only windows were where the coal trucks stuck in a metal sliding board and shot coal into the bins. The windows were so dirty they might as well have been painted black. To turn on the bulb that hung from the ceiling, you had to feel for the chain in the pitch dark.

Banking the furnace was mostly my brother's job. Before going to bed he would shovel a thin layer of coal ash on the hot coals. He usually made me go down with him. He said he wanted to teach me not to be afraid. But I think he was scared to go alone. Sometimes he couldn't find the chain right away. And the longer he took, the more scared we got. Pretty soon both of us would run out of there without shoveling any coal. My mother would get mad, especially at night-time because if you didn't bank the furnace, you would burn a lot coal. The fire might even go out. She would go down herself. But Mama was part to blame. She was the one who told us scary stories.

One time, my brother and Paul Stillman put a white sheet on a coat hanger then hung the sheet from a pulley in the basement. They passed a string through a hole in the floor in the Stillmans' apartment. When they would let go of the string, the pulley and the sheet would go sailing down the cellar toward our furnace. One night when my mother went down to bank the furnace, they released the pulley when they could hear that she was shoveling coal. The sheet went sailing toward her. She screamed so loud that Paul and my brother almost fainted themselves. She came tearing up the stairs saying a headless ghost attacked her. Tony was afraid to tell her what really happened, that they were just playing a joke on her. She would have killed him. But I don't think she would have believed him. I never saw her so scared.

My mother was a great storyteller and now she had another story to tell. We would sit around the coal stove in the kitchen. She would tell stories half in English and half in Italian. The ghost without a head was her favorite. She was sure Paulie's ghost haunted our cellar. We couldn't hardly keep our faces straight because we all knew what really happened. Each time she'd add a little something. After a while I began to believe her, even after my brother pulled up the linoleum and showed me the hole in the floor of the Stillmans' pantry. Paul had plugged the hole with chewing gum, but you could still tell where the hole was.

One day there were workmen in the basement fixing the furnaces. The whole place was lit up brighter than we ever saw before. Marky, Frances, and I played hide-and-go-seek. At first, we were afraid to go through the tunnels. But I knew Paulie's ghost wouldn't bother us with all those workmen around. The most fun was playing "King of the Hill" in our coal bin. Marky would get on top, then me and Frances would knock him down. Then I would be King. If Frances got on top, she would be Queen. After a while everything was black with soot except our eyes. When we went upstairs and Mama saw us, she screamed. She grabbed me and Frances, and dragged us into the bathroom, and took off all our clothes.

"Are you crazy, going in the coal bin?" she said.

The tub was filling with hot, steamy water. My knees were shaking, but I still had to laugh because Frances looked so funny. She was all black excepting the parts where her clothes were.

53

Besides Pasta

"It's not funny," Mama said. "What if the coal man came and you got buried in coal?"

"We would have heard him. We could have jumped out of there," I said.

"And what about your deaf sister? Mother of God, she could have been killed. And even if you weren't buried in coal, breathing in all that dust could give you consumption."

There were lots of things that could give you consumption. A chill, wet feet, if you ate with dirty hands, if you walk on a place where an old man spit, sitting in the movies on a rainy day, lying in the snow, if you were too skinny, if you didn't take cod-liver oil, and if you didn't finish your plate. Now I had to remember that coal dust was another thing that could give you consumption.

Besides consumption, my mother was dead scared of snakes. I guess they must have had a lot of them in Italy, because a snake usually had a part in just about all of her stories. She said that sometimes snakes would take over a whole house. In Italy there were gypsy men who made their living by clearing snakes out of people's houses. They would sprinkle the house with holy water, burn candles and incense, and say things in a language no one could understand. Pretty soon the snakes, one by one, would leave the house.

Mama's stories were great, but Helen won first prize for storytelling. If she saw a movie, she would remember everything every character said. And not only that, she told us what they looked like and what they were wearing. Once she told us how wonderful the flowers smelled in a Nelson Eddy and Jeanette McDonald movie.

"You can't smell flowers in a movie," I said.

She laughed. "I'm not kidding. I could actually smell the roses."

Once, I got to see a movie after she had told us the whole thing from beginning to end. I went with Marky and my sister Frances. I whispered to him what I thought was going to happen next. I didn't tell him my sister told me the whole story. He was amazed. He said I should be a writer. But then my sister Frances spilled the beans.

After the movie Marky and me sat on the icebox in front of the delicatessen. I was telling Marky how mad my mother got about us playing in the coal bin. About how she was worried we would get sick from breathing in the coal dust.

"My mother said it wasn't a wise thing to do. She didn't get mad. But she made me promise not to play in the cellar again."

"She didn't yell at you?"

"She never yells at me."

"So how do you know when she's mad?" I asked. "Hey look at that Packard. It's just like my Uncle Tony's."

"I know. You tell me that every time you see a Packard."

"So how do you know when she's mad?"

"My parents don't get mad," Marky said.

"Wouldn't they get mad if somebody stole something from the store?" Just then a trolley went by so he had a little extra time to think of a good answer.

"That's different. We were talking about them getting mad at me. They wouldn't like it if someone stole from the store. I guess they would call the cops if that ever happened."

"What if you spill something or dropped a plate."

"She would have me clean up the mess. But she still wouldn't yell at me. She gets a sad look on her face. Sometimes I wish she would yell at me."

"Maybe we should switch parents for a few days."

Marky laughed. "I'm not saying she wouldn't yell at you."

"You want to play immies?" I asked.

"I don't have any marbles on me."

"I'll lend you some of mine. I don't want to play for keeps."

"How come? he asked. "Will you get mad and yell at me if I win all your marbles?"

"I'm getting mad already and we haven't even started to play,"

"It'll be getting dark pretty soon. Let's just skip playing marbles for now."

"Okay," I said. I guess he didn't realize I was only making a joke. "See you tomorrow," I said. I ran around the back of the house and raced up the porch stairs two at a time. I was feeling guilty about saying we should switch mothers. I didn't care that my mother yelled a lot. I wouldn't want her to hold it in and just be sad when I did something bad. When I asked Phyllis why Mama yelled at me so much and Mrs. Stillman never yelled at Marky.

She said Mama couldn't help having a quick temper. She's from Italy and that's the way God made Italians.

Peter at age six (1934)

Chapter Seven

Going to School

In the first grade, all the boys were taller than me. Only one girl was shorter. Her name was Martha. I was grateful that God had put her in my class.

Marky went to the public school on Fourteenth Avenue, and I went to Saint Antonitus on Ninth Street and South Orange Avenue. Most of the kids who went to Catholic school went to the public-school kindergarten first, but I didn't. I don't know why. I didn't like Marky going to kindergarten because I had to wait until he and Frances got out of school to have someone to play with.

There was always some kind of working man digging in the street, climbing up poles, painting houses or hammering stuff. I liked to watch them work. Sometimes the men would talk to me and tell me what they were doing. This one man could hammer a nail all the way in with only three hits. He had a wooden box with a handle. The box was filled up with all his tools. He would tell me the names of his tools and what they were supposed to do. He even let me take a turn

Peter Rizzolo

hammering. After a million hits the nail hardly went in at all, and I would always bend the nail. He said I just needed a little practice, but he could see that I would make a good carpenter.

Whenever I found nails on the ground where the men were working, I would put them in my pocket. Pretty soon I had a bunch. My brother had an old rusty hammer he found somewhere. I got a wooden box from the vegetable store and had fun banging nails into the ends of the box. I had to use two hands because the hammer was heavy. Pretty soon I could get one all the way in. If I couldn't be a cowboy when I grew up, my next best thing was being a carpenter. I'd have my own box of tools and lots of nails. I could build whatever I wanted, even a house. But I guess first I'll have to go to school to learn my ABC's and reading. That's what the building man said when I asked if he could give me a job.

By the time I started first grade, all the other kids knew their alphabet and other stuff from going to kindergarten. Between that and missing a lot of school, I must have seemed stupid. I remember my first-grade teacher better than all the rest. That's because I had her twice. Her name was Miss Kehough, but all us kids called her Miss Keyhole. Once, I told a kid named Joey, who was my best first grade school friend that I could climb up the steam pipe that ran up the wall of our classroom. One day, when Miss Keyhole stepped out, Joey pointed to the pipe and gave me this look like he thought I couldn't do it. You couldn't climb the pipe in the winter because you would burn your hands. After checking that the pipe wasn't hot, I shot up hand-over-hand until I reached the top. Before I had time to get down, Miss Keyhole came back in the room. All the kids were snickering and

59

pretty soon she noticed that I was gone. Some of them were looking at me. She followed their eyes. Then she let out a scream that scared me so much I almost fell off the pipe.

"Peter, you come down here this minute!" she shouted.

I did. Then she dragged me to the front of the classroom, laid me face down on a desk, pulled down my pants and hit me on my backside with a ruler. I started to cry, not just from the hurt, but because the whole class got to see my underwear. I don't know if going to jail keeps people from doing bad things, but Miss Keyhole's ruler sure worked for me. After that I always got an A- in deportment. She said she gave me the minus because she was sure I did bad things when she wasn't looking. She was right. Sometimes when she wrote on the blackboard, I couldn't help sticking out my tongue and making faces. A lot of the kids did. But she never saw me, so I still didn't think she was fair to give me a minus.

But I was talking about Marky. He used big words and could read already when he was only six. Marky, me, and Frances, who was almost eight, played together after school until our mothers called us for supper. We played with other kids sometimes, but the three of us were like the Blessed Trinity. Marky was the Father, I was the Son, and Frances was the Holy Ghost. She wasn't invisible like a ghost, but she was kind of quiet. I guess that was because she couldn't hear very good. When she was four, she fell off a second-floor porch and cracked her head on concrete. The doctors said they didn't know why she wasn't killed. But her hearing was never good after the fall. My mother said that God took special care of Frances because she was so little when she was born. But He must not have been paying attention when she fell off the porch.

Frances couldn't go to a regular school because she couldn't hear the teacher. She went to a school for kids who couldn't hear or talk. She could talk as good as me, but all the other kids there couldn't. She had to learn sign language. She hated it, especially the name: "School for the Deaf and Dumb." Phyllis said that "dumb" means someone who can't talk. But I still thought that was a dumb name for a school.

Marky was smarter than me. I know that because I stayed back in the first grade and he got promoted. Mama said I stayed back because I missed over a month of first grade. I had newmonia and the doctor wouldn't let me go to school. I had to stay in bed, which was even worse than having to go to school. I looked through old magazines. I traced figures on cardboard and cut them out and held them up to the wall next to my bed. The light from the window made shadows on the wall. I made their shadows dance and talk to each other.

My room was right beside the kitchen. The smell of coffee and stuff Mama was cooking made me hungry. I wanted to go and peek in the pots. When she made tomato sauce, I loved the smell of onions and garlic being fried in olive oil along with tiny bits of bacon fat. If I weren't sick, I would have gone in the kitchen and fished out pieces of fried fat and put them on a piece of crusty Italian bread. Sometimes she would let me dip my bread in the sauce. When she was frying meatballs, she would skwoosh one and give the meatball to me for a snack. Just plain, with no sauce.

But with me being sick I couldn't go in the kitchen. My mother wouldn't let anybody come near my bed but herself. I never remember having a bed all to myself before. I didn't like not having my brother in the bed with me. But I guess she was afraid he would catch my newmonia. She made me lots of soup and something she called "beef tea." I liked regular tea with plenty of milk and sugar, but beef tea was a whole lot better.

She would bring mustard plasters from the drugstore. She put them on my chest to kill the newmonia. They were the size of a sheet of paper. She put one in front and one in back. They were held in place with cloth straps. I liked mustard on hotdogs, but the mustard plasters were heavy and burned my chest when she first put them on. But the heat did feel good after the plasters cooled down a little.

Most of the time I had no one to talk to. I'd sing loud so my brother and sisters wouldn't forget I was there. After a while I began to sing quietly because everyone was sick of hearing me. They said I sang off-key. I didn't know what keys had to do with singing. My favorite song was "Pennies from Heaven." I tried to imagine a place where pennies fell from the sky like rain and you could buy candy or go to the movies whenever you wanted.

The doctor came to see me once a week. He was worried because of my oldest sister Helen's leaky heart. He would listen to my chest a long time. My mother always tried to give him money before he left and he would say, "Now, now, Mother, you need that more than I do." He told her to be sure to give me the cod-liver oil the nurse at school had given me. I liked the doctor, but I hated the cod-liver oil. I don't think he ever tasted cod-liver oil, because if he did, he would never ask anybody to take the stuff. The taste was bad enough, but the smell was even worse. And you couldn't get the taste out of your mouth for a long time. After I started back in school kids said I smelled like a fish.

Peter Rizzolo

When one of us was sick, my mother had this idea that raw eggs were better than cooked ones. She would punch a hole in both ends of an egg. I would have to suck out the insides. She'd stand there and watch to make sure I finished every bit. I wondered why she punched a hole in both ends. I tried once just making one hole but found out I couldn't suck out the insides with just one hole. My brother Tony explained to me that the second hole was to let air in the eggshell because otherwise you would be sucking against a vacuum.

"So why doesn't the eggshell collapse? I asked him. "Like when you squeeze one end of a straw and suck hard on the other end?"

"Because an eggshell is much stronger than you think," Tony said.

I believed Tony, but I also knew that if you dropped an egg it would break in a million pieces.

Even worse than sucking raw eggs, Mama made me wear a wool vest under my shirt when I started back to school in the middle of the winter. The vest felt good on the way to school, but when the radiators began to hiss and the classroom got warm, I began to itch like crazy.

"Peter! Will you please sit still?" Miss Kehole would say. "You must have Saint Vitas Dance!"

I didn't know what that was, but sometimes my mother said the same thing. I didn't understand why they'd name a dance after a saint.

The wool vest itched so much that I couldn't help scratching. Once, the teacher sent me to the nurse to check me for fleas. The nurse told me to wear the vest on top of my shirt, but my mother said the wool had to be next to my skin. That I could still catch a chill if the vest was on top. And if I caught a chill, I would get consumption.

Besides Pasta

I don't know why, but after she washed the vest a few times the itching wasn't as bad. I guess a person can get used to anything. But when spring came, I was still glad I didn't have to wear a woolen vest, suck raw eggs or take cod-liver oil.

My favorite game besides "catch," "kick-the-can," and "it," was "immies." We'd smooth out the dirt with our shoes, pick out all the stones, and dig a hole the size of half an orange. I was the marble champion of the Blessed Trinity, but we didn't play for keeps because if I won all the marbles I'd have no one to play with. When I'd play other kids at school, there was always somebody who was better than the rest. He would end up with all the marbles. I never brought more than three marbles with me to school. And I never brought my best ones.

Sometime we'd play girl games like "hopscotch," "jump-rope" and "jacks." The Holy Ghost was the champion of those games. She was born ahead of time and weighed just over a pound. Like all the rest of us she was born at home. The doctor said there was no way she could live. Her eyes weren't even open. My mother put her in a cotton-filled shoebox and set her on a shelf over the coal stove in the kitchen. There was even a story about her in the newspaper. It told how Mama kept her alive by feeding her milk with an eyedropper. How the doctors said it was a miracle that Frances lived to be a perfectly healthy baby. There was a picture of Mama holding Frances wrapped in a blanket. All you could see was Frances' tiny face.

But when Frances was around four years old, someone left the back door open and she climbed onto a box on the second-floor porch. Mama saw her just before she fell but couldn't get there in time. Frances almost died. The doctors said her skull was cracked in two places and it was another miracle she was still living. It wasn't until later that we found out that the fall busted something inside her ears.

It wasn't so bad her being deaf. I just talked louder to Frances. If she could see my lips, even if I wasn't speaking loud, she could almost always figure out what I said. She could run faster than Marky, but she couldn't catch me. I liked to play "tag" because I would never be "it" for very long. Besides games, our favorite thing was going to the movies.

The Congress Theatre cost ten cents for kids on Saturday afternoons. You could see the news, previews, two movies, a funny-picture and a chapter of Buck Rogers, Flash Gordon, or Dick Tracy. Sometimes they would have movie stars there in person. Once, the Singing Cowboy, Tex Ritter, came to the Congress. He didn't have his horse, and all the kids wanted to know how come. He said the horse was at his ranch. That his horse didn't like the city.

Tex was wearing his white cowboy hat, fancy black shirt with silver buttons, and a silver holster with a six-shooter that must have been as long as my arm. He sat on a stool right there on the stage and played his guitar and sang a bunch of songs. I would have paid ten cents just to see Tex, even without the movie.

We loved the movies just about better than anything. When the lion would roar or the lady with the torch would come on the screen, my insides would start to shake just thinking about what might come next.

Saturday afternoons the movie would be packed with kids. Spitballs, gum wrappers and popcorn would be flying all over the place. The film broke at least once every Saturday and always at the best part. We stamped our feet and shouted at the man in the projection booth until he got the movie going. His was the best job in the world, because he could watch all the movies free and get paid for just sitting there. But he probably wasn't having fun when the film broke and everybody was screaming at him.

Frances and I didn't get to go every Saturday like a lot of kids in our school. In our family a dime was a lot. My mother would say that she could buy a loaf of bread, a bottle of milk or a half-pound of baloney for ten cents.

My sister Helen made any movie she saw sound so good that we'd cry and cry until my mother gave in. After Helen went to see *Alice in Wonderland*, she told us how Alice walked through a mirror into another world. I couldn't wait to see the movie, but before I got to go, they stopped showing it. There was no way to see the movie someplace else because the Congress Theatre was the last place for movies to go.

Another way we got to go to the movies was from the three cents deposit on milk bottles. When we saved up eight bottles, we had enough for two movie tickets and a little money left over for candy. My mother wouldn't let us keep the deposit money when she ran short of food money. Me and Frances drank as much milk as we could so the empty bottles would pile up faster.

One day I went to Stillman's delicatessen and said my mother wanted two bottles of milk. Then I went out back and poured the milk into a garbage can. Then I took the two bottles to Stillman's to collect the deposit. I don't know how Mr. Stillman knew what I was up to, but he told Mama. They say you shouldn't cry over spilled milk, but I did when my mother got through with me. I was glad she didn't pull down my pants like Miss Keyhole did when she hit me. The spanking didn't hurt that much because I was wearing heavy corduroy knickers. But it must have hurt Mama's hand. I noticed she had tears in her eyes. I wasn't mad at her for hitting me because I lied and wasted all that milk.

One day, the landlady, Mrs. Conti, came and told my mother that she was raising the rent two dollars a month. My mother said she couldn't pay any more. But the lady still raised the rent. Pretty soon Mama found another flat on Thirteenth Avenue. But a few months after we moved, our old landlady from South Orange Avenue came by and asked my mother to come back.

That night, at the dinner table, Mama told us what happened. I had the feeling she would be repeating that story for a long time. When she took the part of Mrs. Conti, she got this look on her face as though she was a queen talking to one of her subjects.

"Antoinette, you were a good tenant. I'm sorry you left," Mrs. Conti said.

Mrs. Conti was a widow who owned the building. She always wore a hat and gloves and high heels. Mama said she acted like the *padrona di casa* in the old country. Always with their nose in the air.

"I was paying too much rent for a second floor flat," Mama said.

"Show me where you can get a nice flat in a good neighborhood for twelve dollars a month. I tell you what, Antoinette, if you come back, I won't raise the rent as long as you choose to live there."

Mama set tea cups and saucers on the table. She poured Mrs. Conti and herself a cup of tea. Mama told us that she figured the woman couldn't find anyone to rent her place and that's why she came by.

Mama didn't answer the lady. "Drink your tea, it's getting cold."

Besides Pasta

After they finished their tea, Mama sat there looking in her own tea cup like she was reading the leaves. The woman had heard about Mama reading tea leaves.

"What? What do you see there?" the lady asked.

"The tea leaves say I am with a woman who has a good heart."

"Antoinette, you are too kind…here look in my cup."

Mama swirled her cup to spread out the leaves. Then she studied them for long time. She had a worried expression on her face.

Mrs. Conti sat on the edge of her chair. "You see something bad?"

Mama said she bit her lip to keep from laughing.

"I see *molti personi volgari* (many vulgar people). They will drive away your other tenants. You will have to go to court to get rid of them. You will have to spend a lot of money on lawyers before you get them out of your house."

Mrs. Conti took out a handkerchief and fanned herself. "You cannot see all that in those leaves."

Mama took another look in Mrs. Conti's cup. "*Personi volgari* will come. You can be sure of that. When I was there you could eat off the floor. I got rid of all the cockroaches."

Mrs. Conti tried to laugh but she sounded more like a mouse with her tail caught in a trap.

"Would you care for another cup of tea?" Mama asked.

She fluttered her handkerchief. "No, no more tea." She sat staring at Mama. "Okay, I guarantee the rent will stay the same…for at least five years."

"Why take the trouble and expense to move for the same rent I paid before. I will pay ten dollars a month and the same guarantee not to raise the rent."

"My God. I come here offering you a chance to come back with no raising of the rent...I...I cannot! What will the other tenants say if I only charge you ten?"

"Every flat is different. Ours was over a store. I had to fight more cockroaches than the other tenants."

Mrs. Conti let out a big sigh and finally agreed to let us have our old flat for ten dollars a month. Mama told us she was already thinking what she would do with the extra two dollars.

"You can buy a hat and white gloves and walk with your nose in the air," I said.

Pretty soon everyone at the table was suggesting what Mama should do with the extra two dollars a month.

Chickey said she wanted to take music lessons. Helen wanted to buy new curtains. Phyllis said we should buy a set of encyclopedias. Frances said she wanted to take drawing lessons. Geraldine and Tony didn't say anything. But I knew no one really believed they would get what they asked for because Mama never had enough money to pay for the regular stuff, like food and new shoes. Mama had the last word. "We save the money and pretty soon we will have our own place. No more *patrona* with her nose in the air." I wondered how long it would take to buy a house from saving two dollars a month. It seemed to me I'd be as old as Moses by the time we had enough. In the meantime, I was pretty excited about moving back to South Orange Avenue. I couldn't wait to see the look on Marky's face when Uncle Tony's truck pulled in front of his father's delicatessen with all our stuff piled in back.

Mrs. Conti didn't really know who she was up against in doing business with my mother. I loved going along with Mama when she shopped. She never paid the regular price for anything. She would ask how much a thing cost, then shake her head and say, "*Troppo caro, troppo caro.*" She would take my hand and start to leave the store, but before we got out, the grocer or butcher would call her back and drop the price to what she was willing to pay. She acted like she was doing them a favor taking the meat groceries off their hands.

Peter Rizzolo

Mama's Meatball Recipe

Of course, the most important ingredient is the meat. It all started with a trip to the butcher's. She never bought the already ground meat. She picked out what she wanted and watched him cut it up and toss the meat into the grinder. Usually the meat was beef and pork. Sometimes she had him add a little veal.

She cut the crust from stale Italian bread and at times American white bread, and then soaked the bread in milk. She wrung out the milk and with her hands, she broke the moistened bread into small pieces before placing the bread into a bowl with the ground meat. She added the other ingredients and with her hands gently mixed it all to a homogeneous consistency, then formed the meat into golf ball sized globs. She browned them on all sides in olive oil before placing them into a tomato sauce where they would simmer for at least an hour.

Ingredients:(serves eight)

One and a quarter pounds of fresh ground beef

A half-pound of fresh ground pork

A quarter pound of fresh ground veal

One large egg

Six slices of bread

Three tablespoons of parmesan cheese

A half teaspoon of black pepper

One large clove of garlic, finely diced and sautéed

Three tablespoons of fresh diced parsley

Salt to taste (Mama tasted the raw meat mixture...I would strongly advise against that)

71

Chapter Eight

First Grade the Second Time

Our family was happy to be back on South Orange Avenue. The Stillmans were real glad to see us. I had missed my friend Marky and didn't ever want to move away again. By now he was already in the second grade and I was in the first grade for the second time. There wasn't anything I could tell him that he didn't already know; excepting the Catechism, which I knew by heart and he didn't know anything about. One day I told him about Jesus and how he died on the cross to save us from going to hell. He said he didn't believe in hell. I wasn't surprised because he never memorized the Catechism.

"My teacher said that even though Roman soldiers nailed Jesus to the cross, the Jews asked them to crucify Him."

The Jews didn't believe Jesus was the son of God and the second person of the Blessed Trinity. I wanted to know what Marky had to say about that, with him being Jewish.

"I'm sorry they did that," Marky said. "But I'm sure my father had nothing to do with crucifying Jesus."

I guess he was making a joke, because he must've known Jesus died way before his father was born. "I don't really care if the Jews did or not," I said. "I know you wouldn't let them if you were there."

My mother always said that Marky was going to be a doctor when he grew up. Mrs. Stillman told her that their son Paul wanted to be a scientist, so Marky, being the only other boy, was the one who had to be the doctor. I was surprised one day when he said that maybe he wasn't going to be anything when he grew up. We were standing outside on a narrow patch of dirt where we usually played immies. Next to where we were standing was a driveway, and on the other side of the driveway was an iron fence. The dirt beside the house was hard and smooth from us always playing there.

"You can't not be anything. Even a bum is something."

There were a lot of bums who came around. They would carry out the garbage or sweep leaves off the walk. My mother would bring food on the back porch for them. The bums must have had a lot of friends, because we hardly ever had to bring out the garbage ourselves.

Marky was leaning against the house with one foot propped on the wall. His eyes were shiny like he was going to cry.

"I started going to the doctor…."

"How come?"

"I had blood in my urine."

He was the only kid I knew who said urine instead of pee or piss. "Must've hurt when you peed."

"No, it didn't. And I saw blood just that one time."

73

Besides Pasta

"I had a nosebleed once," I told him. "That didn't hurt either. My mother put ice on my head and pretty soon the bleeding stopped. Maybe you should've sat on a block of ice." I thought my joke would make him laugh. He didn't.

"At first the doctor said there was probably nothing to worry about, when I urinated for him, the urine looked normal."

"He watched you pee?"

"I urinated in the bathroom in a small bottle the doctor gave me."

I was on my knees punching the dirt with a rock, trying to make a hole. I looked up. "Why did he want your pee?"

"He put a drop under the microscope and looked at it for a long time. He said there was still some blood there but not enough to see with the naked eye."

By now I had a hole dug about as big as an orange. I never saw a worm in that dirt. I guess they gave up digging there because the dirt was so hard. I was smoothing out the edges of the hole. "Did he say how come?"

"He said the red blood cells were leaking out of my kidneys because my kidneys must have been damaged. He said a strep throat could damage a person's kidneys."

I didn't know what a strep throat was, but I didn't like the sound of it. Marky had a sort of long neck with a bump in the middle. Maybe that's what they call a strep throat. A lot of things could make a person leak someplace. I knew all about room-attic-fever making your heart leak. Now I had to worry about strep throat giving me leaky kidneys.

"I have to bring the doctor some of my urine once a month," Marky said. "Sometimes he lets me look in the microscope."

What did having a little blood in your pee have to do with not being anything when you grew up? I dug in my pocket and pulled out my snake-eye shooter and a couple of other marbles. "You want to play immies?"

I already told you about the first time I was in the first grade and how I climbed the steam pipe and what Miss Keyhole did to me. And how Joey could always make me laugh by making faces and sometimes just by looking at me. But Joey got promoted and wasn't in my class anymore so I could pay better attention to the teacher. Pretty soon I could recite the alphabet, write my letters and even my name. I couldn't read the Catechism yet, but I already knew a lot of the questions and answers by heart because I had to get ready for my First Holy Communion.

"Do you know who made the world and everything single thing in the universe?" I asked Marky one day. We were sitting on the icebox in front of his father's store, watching cars and trolleys and buses fly by.

"The Bible says that God made the world in seven days," Marky said.

"That's right," I said, even though I didn't know how long God took to make the world. What was the difference if he took a week or even a whole month? "Do you know where God is?"

"He probably moves around a lot," Marky said. "He could be almost anyplace right this second."

"He's not *anyplace*, God is everywhere!"

Marky laughed. "I don't see how He can be everywhere."

"I don't know how, but that's what the Catechism says." We watched a trolley come down the street. Sparks were flying off its front wheels. "Look," I said, "There's nobody on the trolley."

"Just the driver and God," Marky said.

"Yeah," I said, "and He doesn't even have to pay!"

I liked teaching Marky the Catechism. He had a hard time with the part about there being three persons in God. The Father, the Son and the Holy Ghost. The teacher said we couldn't understand the trinity because that was a mystery. I raised my hand and asked Miss Keyhole, "What is a mystery?

"It's something you can't fully understand or explain," she said.

David Plunkett raised his hand.

"Some people are too stupid to understand mysteries," Plunkett said. He pointed to me and laughed.

"Thank you, David. It's not nice to call people stupid. Ignorant is a better word."

I didn't understand the difference between stupid and ignorant, but I was afraid to ask. After school I asked Marky if he knew the difference. He said if you're ignorant that means you never learned about something. But if you were stupid, you're too dumb to learn. There was that word dumb again. I guess a lot of words meant more than one thing. That could be confusing, but they had to do that, because there were more things than there are words. A lot of jokes come from the double meaning of words. I liked to make up jokes from words having more than one meaning. When anyone talked about a tow-truck, I could picture a giant toe with wheels going down South Orange Avenue. Or the time I was helping my mother make ravioli. She was smoothing out the dough with a rolling pin. With a spoon, I was making little piles of ricotta cheese on top of the dough. Then she folded over the dough, and with a glass she cut circles of dough around each pile of cheese. Then I pressed down the edges with a fork.

"What if you don't have enough dough, Mama?" I asked.

"I can make more if I need to."

"Good! Can you make me a quarter so me and Frances can go to the movies?"

Mama smiled but I could tell she didn't get my joke. It isn't funny if you have to explain.

At school I was learning to sound out words. The thing that makes sounding hard is that some letters are like the *Invisible Man*. Like the word *knee,* what's the use of the k? And why do you need two es? If everything was spelled according to how the word sounded a person could learn to read and write a lot quicker; we wouldn't need to be going to school practically our whole lives.

Being in the first grade twice turned out not to be so bad. The best part was that I had an extra year to grow. Most of the boys were still bigger. But now there were two or three that were the same size as me. One of them was Tommy Walker. We got to be best school friends. He didn't live in the same neighborhood so we mostly played at school. During recess or after school when we duked up sides for games, even though I was a year older and could run and throw better than most of the other kids, I was always picked last and when the sides weren't even, I wouldn't get to play.

One day when David Plunkett was picking sides for his team, he had to pick me because I was last.

"I don't want that little wop on my side," he said.

I knew I was little but I wasn't a wop, whatever that was.

"Shut up, Plunkett," Tommy Walker said.

Plunkett said, "Shut up, you shanty Irish." Then he punched Tommy in the face.

Tommy's nose started to bleed. I kicked Plunkett's leg as hard as I could, then I started to run. He chased me around the playground. He never would of caught me, excepting one of his friends tripped me. Pretty soon Plunkett and his friend were punching me. I was never in a real fight before. I was sure they were going to kill me. Tommy told me later that I started to kick and punch so hard and fast that pretty soon Plunkett's friend ran away and Plunkett was lying on the ground crying.

"What's the matter with you, Rizz? I was only fooling around," Plunkett said.

My heart was pounding so hard I could feel the banging against my chest.

"Giving Tommy a bloody nose wasn't just fooling around."

Miss Keyhole just then came up and saw Plunkett on the ground. There was a purple bump on his leg.

"He did it," Plunkett said. "He kicked me for no reason." He pointed to me.

"He started the fight. He gave Tommy Walker a bloody nose," I said.

She told Plunkett to go the nurse's office. She grabbed my arm and dragged me to the principal's office.

"I'm terribly disappointed in you, Peter," Miss Keyhole said. "I thought you learned your lesson last year. This is a private school. We don't have to tolerate troublemakers here."

I had never gone to the principal's office. But I did know what Sister Teresa looked like from seeing her in the halls. Sometimes she visited our class. She was so mean looking she could of played Frankenstein in the movies and wouldn't even need any makeup. All she needed was those two knobs on the sides of her neck.

"Sister," Miss Keyhole said, "Peter attacked another student. Practically broke the student's leg. The boy, David Plunkett, said the attack was unprovoked."

"Thank you, Miss Kehough. Go check on David. I'd like to hear Peter's side of the incident."

She waited for Miss Keyhole to leave, and then she told me to sit down. She talked in a quiet voice. "I was looking out the window and saw the boys trip you. I could see they started the incident. David Plunkett was obviously lying. But Jesus said that if someone strikes you, you should turn the other cheek. Do you know what that means?"

"That you shouldn't hit back. But Jesus never said what to do if he hit your friend. He gave Tommy Walker a bloody nose."

"You should have reported that to your teacher. If you had, David Plunkett would be sitting here, not you."

"Plunkett called me a wop. And he called Tommy a shanty Irish."

"That's not a nice thing to say, but it's only his way of making him feel as though he's a better person than you. You should have told him he shouldn't call people names and that you would pray for him."

Besides Pasta

I didn't know what to say because I couldn't picture myself telling some kid that I was going to pray for him. He'd probably punch me a good one. Sister Teresa was writing something on a piece of paper.

" Take this note to Miss Kehough. And for the next two weeks, Peter, I want you to attend daily Mass. Pray for all people you know who do mean things. Ask God to change their hearts. He listens to children."

I'm sorry I said she looked like Frankenstein. True, she wasn't pretty, but she was nice. She had a kind smile. I did go to Mass every day for the next two weeks, and I liked going better than Sunday Mass. There were only a few people in the church. I couldn't understand what the priest was saying during the Mass, except when he read the Gospel. I liked the smell of the candles and the sound of the bells the altar boys rang when the priest held up the host and the cup of wine. I decided I wanted to be an altar boy, but I couldn't because I still had to make my First Holy Communion.

"I guess Tommy must be your best friend if you stuck up for him like that," Marky said when I told him what had happened.

"I would have done it if someone hit you in the nose." Then I told him what Sister Teresa said about turning the other cheek. "But even if I don't hit back, I'm not gonna just stand there and let him hit me again."

"Me neither," Marky said.

When I first met Marky, he didn't like to wrestle, but now we wrestled a lot. We never once had a real fight. But I didn't like his cousin. One time I almost got into a fight with him.

Marky's cousin lived a few blocks away. His parents owned a store that sold clothes. He sometimes came to play with Marky. His name was Herman. He was in the second grade, same as Marky. I think he was jealous of me and Marky. He liked to antagonize me. I know that word, because Helen would always tell me not to antagonize my mother. Like when I asked her for money or wouldn't finish my plate or wouldn't go to bed at night. Herman was always bragging. He had a two-wheeler, spy glasses, and a shoe box filled with baseball cards. He wasn't anything like Marky and I hated when he came around.

"I know where your father is," Herman said. "I heard Mrs. Stillman say he's in Overbrook."

We were in the driveway. Marky and I were drawing on the cement with pieces of coal. Herman was standing there, watching. He never wanted to get his hands dirty.

"He's in the hospital." I didn't know what Overbrook was.

"That's a hospital for crazy people," Herman said.

"My father's not crazy. He had a nervous breakdown."

"So why is he locked up in the State Mental Hospital?"

"Shut up, Herman," Marky said.

I wanted to punch Herman in the nose, but I remembered what Sister Teresa said. Besides, he was Marky's cousin.

"I feel sorry for you, because you're ignorant," I said. "You don't even know what a nervous breakdown is."

"I'm ignorant? You're the one who stayed back."

I could feel heat coming from my face. The good part of my brain got turned off by the bad part. I walked over to where he was standing. I kicked him in the leg so hard I hurt my big toe. He started to cry and called me a bastard. He ran in the house to tell Marky's mother on me.

Marky never said anything. I think he was glad I kicked his cousin. I don't think he liked him, either.

The next day my toe swelled up and turned black. But I didn't care. I figured I was going to have to go to Mass for another two weeks for kicking him. But I wasn't sorry, because Herman didn't come around so much after that, and when he did, he never said anything about my father.

I didn't really know if my father was still in the hospital. We went to see him a few times when I was in first grade but he and my mother would always have arguments. They would shout at each other and I was afraid he was going to hit her. He was a lot bigger than her. I remembered Helen saying my mother was afraid of him.

The last time we went, he got so mad he started yelling. Mama was crying. Two men came and took Papa away. The doctor said we shouldn't go see him anymore. I knew he had two sisters because Geraldine told me that sometimes he would go stay with them. So, if he did get out of the hospital, that's probably where he was.

I guess I was getting used to not having a father, because even though I still felt sad not having one, I didn't cry anymore when I thought about him.

One Saturday me and Frances asked Mama if we could go see *The Invisible Man.*

My brother Tony was in the kitchen putting sugar and butter on a thick slice of Italian bread. He laughed and said it's impossible to see an invisible man. My mother laughed, too.

At first I didn't get it, but then I knew what he meant.

"That's the name of the movie. And you can too see him. I saw the coming attractions. He dresses up in clothes and his clothes aren't invisible. And he has this thing wrapped around his head. With only his eyes showing, except there's nothing there."

She did let me go. I loved the movie. After seeing *The Invisible Man,* me, Marky and Frances played games where one of us was invisible. Cheating was easy because you could still see the person, but you were supposed to pretend you couldn't.

"You think a mad scientist could ever make someone invisible?" I asked Marky. I was breaking paint bubbles on the side of the house. I chipped off the paint with my fingernail.

"Maybe," Marky said. "You can see through some things."

"Like what?"

"Water."

"That doesn't count. You can still see water."

" What if you filled a bottle with water right to the top? Could you tell if there was water in the bottle just by looking? Or did you ever look in a really clean fish tank? The fish look like they're floating in air."

"People aren't made out of water so what good is that? And you said 'things,' so what else?"

"Air," Marky said. "You can't see air, but you can feel air if you blow on your hand. And air can blow out candles on a birthday cake, or even blow down a house when there's a tornado."

" Okay," I said, "So all a mad scientist has to do is to figure out how to make a person out of air and water."

"People are already mostly water. That what my teacher said."

I didn't know anything about that. I was tired of talking. "Let's pretend we're invisible G-men and go spy on the numbers-man."

Besides Pasta

That's what we started calling the owner of the candy store. Spying was one of our favorite things to do.

The best part about the first grade was getting ready for Christmas. We drew Santa Clauses, Christmas trees, made Christmas cards and even painted pictures on the classroom windows. There was a Christmas tree right in our classroom. We got to decorate the tree with things we made.

We sang "Silent Night," "Away in a Manger" and a bunch of other songs. The whole class got to go to the church and see the manger where Mary and Joseph and the three Wise Men were bigger than us. Jesus wasn't in the manger, because he still wasn't born.

Before Christmas recess we each got a box of hard candy. The box was like an animal crackers box with a string for a handle. The box had Jesus, Mary, Joseph, and the Wise Men painted on the outside. The candies were all different colors, shapes, and flavors. My favorites were root beer and cherry. I would try to guess what flavor the candy was by closing my eyes and smelling a piece. I found out that you can't tell the flavor just by smelling. But you could tell what you were smelling was Christmas candy.

The worst part of first grade was Promotion Day. At two-thirty in the afternoon, the teacher started calling out the names of the kids who were promoted to second grade. After she called your name, you went and stood in the hall. The kids who didn't get promoted didn't get their names called. They just stayed in the room.

I don't know how Miss Keyhole decided who to call first, but I was still sitting there by the time most of the kids were in the hall joking around and making a lot of noise. She had to keep going out there to

Peter Rizzolo

tell them to be quiet. My knees were shaking so bad that even if she did call my name, I don't think I could have walked out of the room.

There were just five kids left and I was afraid to look at anyone else because I was holding back from crying, and if any of them were crying I knew I couldn't keep from crying, either.

"The next person to be promoted is Peter Rizzolo," Miss Keyhole said. She smiled. "I'm going to miss you, Peter. Now get out of here."

My knees were still shaking, but I probably won the prize for getting out of there the fastest.

Chapter Nine

My Aunts and Second Grade

Besides having four brothers, my mother had two younger sisters. Aunt Tessie, who looked like my mother, was married to a tailor named Peter Dambrosio. She had a boy, Michael, and two girls, Dolly and Vera. They were a lot older than me, but I still liked to sit and listen to Dolly and Vera talk with my brother Tony, and my sisters, Geraldine and Phyllis. Tony and my sisters would tell them funny things that happened at school. Things came out that I never heard before. When they were around, I felt like I had seven sisters instead of only five. I showed them pictures I had colored and how I could write my letters.

"Your lettering is so good, Peter," Vera said. "A lot better than I could do in the second grade. I don't see how you print so well with your hand upside down like that."

That was the worst thing about being a lefty. Everyone had to say something about it. I threw, ate, brushed my teeth, colored, and wrote my letters with my left hand. And don't ask me how come, because I don't know. The next worse part was that nobody else in my family was a lefty and I don't know why I had to be. I wondered sometimes if I was born like that or if I just learned to be a lefty by accident. I asked Helen once because she used to take care of me when I was a baby. My mother was shopping and Helen was stirring a pot of soup on the coal stove. I could smell the chicken soup, but I could also smell celery and tomatoes. Helen always put a million things in her soup.

"You always used your left hand," Helen said. "You would grab a spoon with your left hand and bang the table like it was a drum. I would hand you something from the right side and you would reach over with your left hand and grab it."

"So, it's not my fault if I was born to be a lefty."

"There's nothing wrong with being left-handed," Helen said. She was cutting carrots into small blocks and throwing them into the soup.

"So why did Sister Patricia try to make me change? For a whole week she made me write my letters with my right hand. My hand shook. It gave me a headache. The writing was so bad she had to give up trying to switch me."

Phyllis was sitting there reading and I didn't think she was listening. "I read where a lot of scientists are left-handed," Phyllis said.

"I don't want to be a scientist."

"You don't have to be a scientist. What I mean was left-handed people are smart enough to do the kind of work scientists do."

"Marky's smart and he's not a lefty. His brother Paul is the one who wants to be a mad scientist and he's not a lefty either."

Phyllis picked up her book and left the room. I think she gave up on trying to explain what she meant. I went over and looked in the pot.

Besides Pasta

The soup smelled really good, but I saw a couple of chicken feet poking out of the carrots, tomatoes, and celery. The rest of the chicken must have been drowning. Except I knew the rest of the chicken was someplace else and not in our soup pot with his feet.

I liked chicken feet about the same as cod-liver oil, beets, raw eggs and escarole.

Sister Patricia, my second-grade teacher, wore a black dress that came all the way down to her black shoes. She wore a black cloth over her head and her face was inside a kind of white box with crinkly edges. It's hard to describe exactly. She wasn't tall and skinny like Miss Keyhole; with all the stuff she wore you couldn't be sure if she was fat or skinny. She didn't look any older than my sister Helen. She had blue eyes and freckles and, if I was to guess, I'd say she was Irish. I bet her hair was yellow, but with the way her hair was tucked inside her clothes you couldn't tell. She had a soft voice. To make us be quiet, she would beat her ruler on whatever desk she was standing by. Because the smaller kids sat in the front of the classroom, she banged on my desk plenty of times. She would never look exactly where she was hitting, so I was always careful not to keep my hands on top of the desk when she came near me. She never once hit anybody, but seeing how good she could bang, nobody was crazy enough to do anything to get hit for.

The next best part of second grade was going on field trips. There were thirty kids in our class and some of the parents would come in to help Sister so nobody would get lost or killed crossing the street. My favorite trip was to the museum. The Indian part was the best. There was a giant teepee you could walk inside. Only a few of us could go in there at a time. There were statues of Indian men, women and kids. They all looked like they were busy doing things. The guide said the Indians made everything they needed. Some of the men Indian statues were practically naked with only a little rag in front. The guide told us that the Indian was wearing a "lion cloth." When our guide wasn't looking, David Plunkett peeked underneath the Indian's lion cloth. Later, when I told Marky about the visit to the museum he laughed and said it's a loin cloth not a lion cloth.

The women and little girl Indians wore long dresses and leather jackets. The girls' black hair was tied in pigtails.

The teepee was filled with stuff they made. Bows and arrows, tomahawks, spears, rope, pots, blankets, and fancy shirts covered with colored beads. You weren't supposed to touch anything but I couldn't resist touching stuff. The statues looked so real I wondered if there were dead people inside. One of the Indians looked right at me. His black eyes were so real he gave me goose bumps.

My Aunt Mary, one of Mama's younger sisters, didn't look anything like my mother. Her skin was darker; she wore bright red lipstick and had painted-on eyebrows. She wore fancy clothes and high heels and her hair was always fixed up like a movie star's. She used a perfume that smelled like Easter flowers. Sometimes if she came by when I was still in school, I could tell she had been there because she left the Easter flower smell in the house.

She chewed gum and said bad words even in front of the kids. She knew a lot of people who were bastards because she was always talking about "those bastards."

Besides Pasta

"Come here, bedroom eyes, and kiss your Aunt Mary," she said to me.

I was shy about kissing anybody excepting my mother. I didn't know what made me hold back, because I really liked my Aunt Mary. The house was filled with electricity when she was there.

"One of these days you'll be sorry you passed up kissing me. There are men who would die for the chance."

Aunt Mary wore short dresses and would sit with her legs crossed, the way women do in the movies. I know my mother would have killed my older sisters if they wore lipstick and such short dresses and crossed their legs like that. I never saw Aunt Mary smoke, but sometimes if I went to the bathroom after she did, the window would be wide open and you could smell cigarettes. My mother acted like she didn't know. But as big as my mother's nose was, how could she not know? I believe she didn't say anything because Mary was her sister. Mama knew she was a good woman even though she smoked. Mama said Aunt Mary was a good mother and went without things to buy her children nice clothes. She had two boys, Sonny and Jimmy and a daughter Phyllis Ann. Her husband was Irish. His name was Danny.

Once when Aunt Mary came over, I was crying for money to go to the movies. A pirate movie was playing and Marky's mother already said he could go. My mother was used to my crying, and she knew how long I would cry before stopping. But Aunt Mary probably thought I would go on forever.

"Antoinette, how can you stand this little pain in the ass?" She reached into her purse and took out a dime. "Here, Peter, now get the hell out of here before I change my mind."

"You going to be here when I get back?" I asked.

"I hope not," she said. "Come and give me a kiss or I'll take back my dime."

I knew she was only fooling, but just in case, I went over and gave her a kiss. Then I kissed my mother because I didn't want her to be jealous. I ran downstairs to find Marky.

Christmas was my favorite time of the year. The best part was thinking about the music, the way they decorated the trolley poles, the things we did at school, and all the toys in the store windows. Geraldine or Phyllis would take me, Frances, and Chickey downtown on the trolley, and we would go through a bunch of stores, or sometimes we just looked in the windows. Bamberger's always had a giant Christmas tree in the window with a million lights, colored balls, candy canes, tinsel, fake snow, and glass angels. Under the tree was a pile of presents wrapped in fancy paper and bows. I was beginning to think Santa Claus was a made-up person, but Sister Patricia said he was real. His name was Saint Nicholas. He loved to give presents to children. In some of the stores there were men dressed up like Santa Claus, but I was already eight years old and too big to sit on their lap and tell them what I wanted for Christmas. Besides, telling them never worked. I always only asked for the same things. A pair of cowboy boots, roller skates, and a bike. I got clothes, marbles, tiny toy cars and trucks, and games like dominoes and checkers. I'm not saying I didn't like the things I got, because I did. But I never asked the make-believe Santa Claus for them, so he had nothing to do with my gifts.

I hated to go back to school after Christmas. Everybody talked about what they got. One day during second grade recess our class was on the playground. I tried to avoid Plunkett, but he and some other kids came right up to me and Tommy.

"Hey, Rizz," Plunkett said, "What did you get for Christmas, a prayer book? What are you praying for anyway? To not be a midget when you grow up?"

He was talking extra loud to make sure a lot of kids heard him. Some of them started to laugh. He knew I had to go to daily Mass after that time we had a fight. I wasn't going to tell him what I got for Christmas. After what he said, I wanted to say something mean to him but I couldn't think of anything that didn't have curse words in it. I didn't want to spend the rest of the year going to Mass, so I didn't say anything. I knew he was just trying to get me in a fight because he was mad about me kicking him. He was wearing leather boots that came halfway up his leg, so he probably wasn't afraid of being kicked. He was practically the tallest boy in our class and if I couldn't kick, the fight wouldn't be fair.

Tommy Walker was standing there, and I knew if he said anything Plunkett was going to call him a shanty Irish. Everybody was staring at me to see what I was going to do. Just then Sister Patricia blew her whistle and said recess was over.

"Saved by the bell, Rizz." Plunkett said.

Sister was standing pretty far away from us so I didn't think she knew what was going on between me and Plunkett. But when I got near to her, she winked at me. She never had done that before. She could have just gotten something in her eye. Or maybe for that day God was on my side. If you turn the other cheek, like you're supposed to, God can probably figure out a way to keep you from getting hurt.

Chapter Ten

Toby

I was the first one home from school. My mother was rolling out dough in long ropes about as thick as a pencil. Then she cut the dough ropes into pieces about as long as my pinky. She showed me how to take my thumb and press a piece so the dough curled over my thumb. Hers looked just like the cavatelli you buy in the store.

"Mama, mine aren't coming out good. They stick to the board when I skwoosh them."

"You're pressing too hard." She took my hand and pressed my thumb against a piece of dough. "You see, like this."

Pretty soon I was making perfect little cavatelli. They were just balls of dough, but I liked them better than any other kind of macaroni, except Mama's homemade ravioli.

At school we were drawing pictures of Easter bunnies, eggs, and baskets. We colored them, cut them out, and put them in the basket.

Besides Pasta

After we printed our names on the baskets, we hung them from the top of the blackboard.

"A kid in my class brought in a baby rabbit today," I told my mother. "Sister Patricia let us take turns holding the rabbit. I asked the kid where he got the rabbit. He said his father bought him at a pet store."

"When I was little, we had chickens," Mama said. "I used to feed them. When I was your age, my job was to collect *le uova*.

I knew *uova* meant egg in Italian. Sometimes for breakfast Mama would ask me: '*vuoi un uovo'*."

By now my mother had made a big pile of cavatelli. We put them on a cloth on the kitchen table.

Frances came in and began to help me spread out the tiny dough balls so they could dry. She liked to eat raw dough. She snuck a couple of pieces.

"Stop that!" my mother said. "Dough will make you sick."

Eating raw dough was one of the few things that wouldn't give you newmonia, or consumption. But Mama said that once you swallowed dough the yeast keeps working and would make the dough in your stomach blow up like a balloon and even split you open if you ate enough.

"Can I have a pet rabbit, Mama?" I asked.

My mother put a big black frying pan on the stove.

"The landlady doesn't even like us having a cat. Besides, a baby rabbit will make a nice meal for Ginger."

"We can keep him in the bathroom," Frances said.

"Yeah," I said. "Then he won't mess the house."

"So, what happens when Ginger needs to use the toilet?"

I didn't think of that. We always had to leave the bathroom door open so Ginger could get in and pee.

That night at supper time I told about the rabbit I saw at school. Chickey was all excited about getting one.

"I'll feed the rabbit and clean up its messes," Chickey said. "Please, Mama, can't we have one?"

We talked about the bathtub being the best place to keep a rabbit, but then there was the problem with Ginger.

Tony was starting in on his second plate of cavatelli. "There's an old torn window screen in the cellar," he said. "I can take off the old screen and cover the frame with chicken wire. We can lay that over the tub and use a rock to keep the screen in place. That way the rabbit can't get out and the Ginger can't get in."

Tony had a good idea. I didn't think Mama knew what to say. We were all waiting. I knew what she was going to say. I tried to imitate an Italian accent. "How are we supposed to pay for a baby rabbit? You think money grows on the trees?"

Everybody laughed, even Mama. "We will see," she said."

I never again asked Mama about the rabbit. Because I knew that whenever I asked for skates or a bike, she would say the same thing. And I never got them either.

In my basket on Easter morning there was a gingerbread man like Mama made every year. He had a hard-boiled egg stuck in his belly and his eyes were two black jelly beans. Each one of us got a gingerbread man, and Frances and Chickey and I got a basket besides. The basket had colored eggs, jelly beans, and a tiny chocolate-covered marshmallow bunny. But I wanted a real bunny, not one you could eat

Besides Pasta

and then have nothing left to play with. I broke the arm off of my gingerbread man and started chewing on his fingers. The bread tasted like ginger snaps.

"Don't you have to go to the bathroom, Peter?" Tony asked. He was sprinkling a cracked-open Easter egg with salt.

I shook my head. Chickey jumped up and ran in the bathroom. I heard her yell, "Oh, it's so cute."

I ran in and saw she was holding a fluffy ball of white fur. He had a pink twitchy nose, and ears that stood straight up. The rabbit's eyes were like shiny black marbles. Leaning against the side of the bathtub was the chicken wire cover Tony must have made.

"It's not yours," Chickey said.

"I know," I said. "It's not yours either. Let me hold him."

By now Frances had come into the bathroom. "What are we going to call him?" she asked.

I looked in the tub. There was straw in a wooden box and beside the box was a dish of carrots and lettuce. Ginger was rubbing against Chickey's leg. He was looking at the baby rabbit, just like the rest of us.

We decided to name the rabbit Toby. Everybody in the family loved Toby. There was nothing not to love except the way the bathroom smelled. At first Ginger would sit on top of the chicken wire cover staring down at Toby. He was a big cat. He'd stick his paw through but couldn't reach Toby, not even his ears.

It was Helen's job to keep the bathtub cleaned out and to put clean straw in Toby's box. I got the straw from the vegetable store. Some of the fruits came packed in straw. The man said that I could get as much as I wanted.

I got to hold Toby while Helen cleaned the tub. If my mother wasn't home and Ginger was outside, I would let Toby run around the house.

We all threw food in the tub and Toby ate so much that pretty soon he was as big as Ginger and a lot fatter. One day when I let Toby run loose, Chickey let Ginger in by accident and he went right after Toby. Ginger hunched his back, puffed his tail, showed all his teeth, and hissed. Even though Toby had bigger teeth than Ginger, he didn't have claws and I don't think the fight would have been fair. But Toby didn't run. He tucked back his ears and stared at Ginger. I think Ginger was surprised that Toby didn't run away or act scared. I got between them, picked up Toby, and put him in the bathtub. When I got back in the kitchen, Chickey was holding and petting Ginger. I petted Ginger too because I didn't want him to think I liked Toby better.

Promotion day from second grade wasn't scary because I wasn't worried about staying back. I couldn't read and spell as good as most of the other kids, but every time Sister Patricia asked a question, I was almost always the first one to know the answer even though I never raised my hand except if I had to go to the toilet. Sister could read my mind because she could tell if I knew the right answer just by looking at me.

I already knew that Marky was promoted to fourth grade because the public school finished a week before us. I couldn't wait to tell him that I was promoted to third grade. When I got home from school, I saw him sitting on the icebox in front of his father's store. He was reading a book. I sat on the box next to him. The day was hot. I was all sweaty from running home from school. Sitting on the icebox under Stillman's umbrella was a nice cool spot to rest. The umbrella wasn't shaped like a regular umbrella. Every morning Mr. Stillman turned a wheel on the side of the building and the long flat umbrella came down. During a heavy rain me and Marky liked sitting under the store umbrella. We pretended we were in a cave under a waterfall.

"What are you reading?"

"*Swiss Family Robinson*."

"What's it about?"

"This family is shipwrecked on an island all by themselves."

"I got promoted to third grade."

Marky closed his book. "Anybody stay back?"

"Yeah, a kid named Plunkett. I felt sorry for him. He started to cry."

"Wasn't that the kid you had a fight with?"

"Yeah."

"My father says there's going to be another big war."

"You mean with Hitler?"

Marky looked at me like he was surprised I knew about Hitler. "My father has cousins in Germany," he said. "They're afraid of Hitler. He blames the Jews for Germany being so poor. My father thinks his cousins should leave Germany."

"When my uncles visit, they talk about Hitler and Mussolini. My uncle Jerry said he got gassed in World War I. He almost died from it. He told my mother she was lucky her sons were too young to go in the Army. He was worried because his sons are older, and if a war started, they would have to go.

"My father," Marky said, "thinks my brother Paul may have to go fight the Germans.

"My uncle Pete said we shouldn't get mixed up in any more wars. He said the Germans didn't wait long after the last big war to start in fighting again."

"My father said that if Roosevelt gets elected again that he'll do something about Hitler."

" I have to go upstairs, so my mother will know I'm home. You want to come up? We can play with Toby."

My mother was glad to hear that I was promoted. She gave me a glass of milk and a piece of bread and butter for a snack. She asked Marky if he wanted a glass of milk.

"I'm not supposed to drink too much milk."

"How come?" I asked.

"The doctor said there's something in milk that puts too much of a load on my kidneys."

I loved milk. I felt sorry for him if he couldn't drink milk. I was glad I didn't have leaky kidneys.

"What do you drink?" my mother asked.

"Water and fruit juices."

I knew we didn't have any fruit juice in the house. She poured him a glass of water and gave him a slice of bread and butter. She heated up some left-over pasta fagioli. We both had a cupful. Marky said it was the best thing he ever tasted. I wouldn't go that far, but it was good, especially when you added plenty of stinky cheese.

The radio in the front room was turned on and Tony was listening to the news. I heard the announcer say something about the Lindbergh baby. Grownups talked and argued about the kidnapping all the time. Even the kids at school knew. They arrested a German carpenter who lived in New York. They found a box of ransom money in his house and a ladder that was the same as the one used to get in the window where the baby was sleeping. The man said somebody gave him the money to hold, that he didn't kidnap the baby. Some people believed him and some didn't.

Marky and I were sitting at the kitchen table eating our snack. When we finished, we went into the front room, sat on the floor and listened to what the man on the radio was saying about the kidnapping.

"I'm glad nobody kidnapped me when I was a baby," I said.

Tony laughed. "Nobody would kidnap you for a ransom. They only kidnap rich kids, so they can get money from the parents. What would Mama give them? A plate full of zeppoles?"

"Do you think Hauptmann kidnapped the Lindbergh baby?" Marky asked my brother.

"Maybe he wasn't the one who took the baby, but he was in on it. I don't believe he would hide that box of money without looking inside."

The radio announcer said, "This, ladies and gentleman, is going to be the trial of the century. Lindbergh is a national hero. The kidnapping and murder of his son has shocked people throughout the world. The trial will be held in the county court house in rural Flemington, New Jersey."

It seemed to me that everybody had been talking about this for my whole life. "How old was I when the baby was kidnapped?" I asked.

"You were three. The baby was the same age as you," Tony said.

I was going on eight. I counted on my fingers. I couldn't believe they took four years to catch the guy. Grown-ups argued about who was guilty. They would shout and get red in the face. My sister Phyllis didn't believe the German guy was guilty. My Uncle Pete said he was sure the maid was in on it.

"The baby's picture was in all the newspapers," Tony said, "He was chubby and had curly blond hair."

I knew what was coming next because I heard that story before, but Marky never did so I didn't say anything.

"One day Mama took Peter for a ride in his baby carriage. A policeman stopped her. He had a picture of the Lindbergh baby, and he was looking at Peter and then at the picture.

"But Peter has brown hair," Marky said.

"He was blond until he was four, then his hair started turning brown," Tony said. "Same as me."

"Tell the rest, Tony," I said.

"The policeman took Mama to the police station. They took her fingerprints. They asked her a bunch of questions. She didn't have anything with her to prove Peter was her baby."

"What happened?" Marky asked.

"A G-man came and gave her the third degree," I said.

"G-man!" Marky shouted.

Tony laughed. "Peter just made that up. The police let her go when they found out that Peter had a big burn scar on his right arm. The kidnapped baby didn't have any scars."

I was looking at Phyllis to see if she was going to tell how I got the burn on my arm. How I went into a coma and almost died from blood poisoning. But Phyllis didn't say anything.

"Peter was sitting in a highchair," Tony said, "and Phyllis was carrying a pot of hot coffee...."

"I tripped," Phyllis said. "Some of the hot coffee spilled on Peter's arm."

Marky looked at me. "That must have hurt really bad."

"I don't remember."

"Mama smeared on butter then covered the burn with a towel. After a while the whole arm got swollen, and Peter was put in the hospital. He started burning up with fever and went into a coma for three days from blood poisoning. The doctors said he was going to die. Mama was going crazy because they said she should have brought him to the hospital right away."

"When I told Sister Patricia about how I got the burn and all, she said God made a miracle because I wasn't supposed to die yet."

Nobody said anything because the man on the radio started talking about Hitler. I wondered who besides God knows when a person is going to die? I hoped my guardian angel didn't know. If she did, she might not be paying attention to keeping me from getting hurt. Maybe that's how come I got burned.

"Let's go do something outside, Marky."

"Okay," he said.

After we were outside, I asked him if he wanted to race to the corner and back. The loser would have to pay for a nickel's worth of candy, and the winner got to pick out what to buy. I noticed Marky doing tricks with a nickel while we were listening to the radio. I didn't have a nickel, but I knew I could run faster than Marky. But if I tripped and he beat me, I would have to owe him. Once I did fall but got up and still won the race.

Peter Rizzolo

Mama's Pasta Fagioli Recipe

There was always a pot of beans soaking on the kitchen stove, or at times in the bathtub. I have no idea why she placed the soaking beans in the bathtub. The Cannellini bean's smooth soft texture and delicate flavor blends favorably with the acidic tomatoes, al dente macaroni, and pungent pork rind. Even the individual vegetable flavors retain their independence. She never overpowered the other ingredients by using too much garlic and other spices. She used a single clove diced and sautéed in same olive oil in which she had sautéed the onions. She threw in parsley just before serving.

8 oz. of presoaked Cannellini beans (or 12 oz. can of beans)

Two stalks of celery

One clove of garlic

4 oz. of bacon rind or pancetta

2 oz. of Parmesan cheese

One cup of macaroni

One medium onion

Salt and black pepper to taste

Two medium fresh tomatoes

Drain the water from the soaking beans. Sauté the onions in olive oil. Dice the garlic and add to the pan, being careful not to overcook. Add the sautéed onions and garlic to the pot of beans. Add the two tomatoes, chopped in irregular chunks, the celery and two cups of

Besides Pasta

water. Simmer for about for thirty minutes. Dice four ounces of pork rind or pancetta. Fry until the fat is translucent and the meat browned. Remove with a slotted spoon and place in the pot with the beans. Add macaroni and cook on medium heat until the macaroni is al dente. Add two tablespoons of chopped fresh parsley just before serving. Sprinkle each serving with freshly grated Parmesan cheese.

Chapter Eleven

The Summer of '36 and Long Branch Island

The best thing that happened to me that summer was going to the beach for. the first time ever. Mama took me and Frances and Chickey. Uncle Tony still delivered coal and Biancoline to our house. After serving him a bowl of pasta fagioli and pile of fresh zeppoles, Mama asked him if he would drive us to the beach. He agreed and said it was okay if Marky came with us. But Mrs. Stillman said my mother had enough children of her own to look after.

When the day came, Mama packed a brown paper bag with sandwiches, a gallon jar of lemonade, paper cups, towels, and three empty tomato cans. The cans were for collecting shells. We didn't have bathing suits, but Uncle Tony said we could rent them at the beach. I knew about the beach from school, picture postcards, pirate stories, and the movies, but I still couldn't wait to see it. On the drive there, Uncle Tony said that if you looked far out on the ocean, you could see fish as big as his car. He said the fish put on a show as good as any circus act by jumping in and out of the water.

"You mean out and in, not in and out," Chickey said.

Nobody laughed except me and Uncle Tony. I guess Mama and Frances didn't see what she meant. I was glad Chickey came with us. She hardly ever played with Frances and me. She didn't do things with her older sisters either. She mostly stayed in the house reading magazines and listening to the radio. People said I looked like Chickey. We both had brown hair and brown eyes and the same color skin. I think we weighed the same even though she was three years older.

Mama didn't like riding in cars. She said the bouncing made her feel sick to her stomach. She never went to the dentist either because if the doctor were to put his hand in her mouth she would throw up. A lot of things seemed to make her sick to her stomach. I remember Phyllis told me once that when Mama was carrying me around inside her belly, she was sick to her stomach the whole time. I guess everybody's different about what makes them sick. A lot of the stuff Mama likes, like snails, tripe, liver, and chicken gizzards make me sick just thinking about them.

The closer we got to the beach, there were fewer houses and a lot more trees. I noticed that the dirt turned into sand even though we were still far from the shore.

We saw a fruit and vegetable stand. Mama made Uncle Tony stop the car. She bought five peaches. They were the best I ever tasted. I had to be careful not to drip juice on Uncle Tony's car. I sucked on the pit for a long time, then pretending the pit was a hand grenade, rolled down the window and tossed it at a mailbox. The box blew up and left a crater the size of an elephant.

The name of the beach was Long Branch. When Chickey saw the sign on the highway she pointed to it. "This is where you turn, Uncle Tony."

Mama and Chickey were sitting in the front of the car. Frances and I were in the back. For a long time, I thought the name of the beach was really Longa Branch, because that's how Mama said it. I never before saw the name of the beach written.

Frances and I started to jump up and down. We were shouting as loud as we could, "Longa Branch, Longa Branch."

You notice I didn't say Frances and me? Sister Patricia insisted we speak correct English in her class. When she'd ask me a question, at first, I couldn't get out more than two or three words without her correcting my grammar. Then I started to practice at home. I would picture in my head how Ronald Coleman would say something. He's a movie star with an English accent who always plays a rich person. One night at dinner, my mother asked me if I wanted more peas and carrots. Instead of saying, "No. I'm kind of full, Mama," I said, "No thank you, Mother. I'm rather full." My brother and sisters laughed and then we all started talking like Ronald Coleman and Betty Davis. They still tease me about it. I learned you have to be careful when to use proper English. When you're in school is one place, and I guess if you ever were to become a rich person that's how you're supposed to speak.

We parked the car on the street right next to the boardwalk. We went on the boardwalk and looked at the ocean. The sand was white,

Besides Pasta

the water was green and sparkly, and the sky was the brightest blue I had ever seen. I had to squeeze my eyes almost shut to keep them from hurting.

Now I could understand why people who saw the ocean didn't think the world was round. It looked flat all the way as far as you could see.

The beach was crowded with people lying on blankets, sitting in chairs, under umbrellas, walking around, and splashing in the water. I couldn't see how even one extra person could fit. There was a tall lifeguard stand. Sitting on top were two guys with blond hair and white noses. I couldn't wait to get on the beach, but I have to admit I was scared. Nobody in my family knew how to swim. Mainly because we never went to the beach. My mother wouldn't let us go to swimming pools, because she was afraid we would catch polio.

Uncle Tony said he wasn't going to get into a bathing suit, so I had to go in the ladies' bathhouse with my mother and two sisters. They rented suits that were black and made of heavy wool cloth. The booths where people changed had doors, but a lot of women didn't bother closing the doors, and I got to see a million naked ladies. I couldn't wait to tell Marky. But to tell you the truth, I was thinking most ladies look better with clothes on.

The bathhouse was under the boardwalk. When you came from the shaded sand and walked onto the beach, the sand was hot enough to fry your toes. Frances, and Chickey and I jumped like drops of water in a hot frying pan. We kicked sand onto people's blankets by accident. The people started to holler at us to be careful. The sand got cooler as we got closer to the water and my feet felt really good when I got close enough for the waves to wash over them.

Peter Rizzolo

Uncle Tony met us on the beach. He had taken off his shoes and socks and had his pants rolled up to his knees. He was wearing a straw hat and a long-sleeved shirt. He had found a space to spread a blanket. On one side of us was a fat lady sitting in a chair under an umbrella. She was reading a book. On another blanket behind us, two ladies were on their backs with newspapers shading their eyes. In front of us a baby girl was sitting on the wet sand, crying. She didn't have any clothes on. A lady came out of the water and picked up the baby. I didn't blame the little girl for crying; I would cry too if I had to be naked and have everybody looking at me.

Sitting on the sand, the waves looked a lot bigger than they did from the boardwalk. I saw kids in the water and the waves were going over their heads. There was a rope that went pretty far out into the ocean. The rope was connected to a pole that was sticking out of the sand in front of the lifeguard's stand. People were holding onto the rope, yelling and laughing. I asked my mother if we could go in. She said we could, but we had to hold onto the rope and not go out too far. Too far for her was up to our knees. But we went out to where the water reached our bellies.

The water was freezing cold. We took a long time to get used to the cold. If you just stood in one place your feet would begin to sink in the sand. We went out a little bit at a time, holding onto the rope with both hands. I was in front with Chickey and Frances behind me. When the water was up to my waist Mama yelled and waved her arms. We couldn't make-out what she was saying, so we waved back and stayed where we were.

Besides Pasta

It was fun but scary when the waves splashed over me. We learned to jump just before the wave hit us, so our heads didn't go under. I was glad there were two lifeguards right there because I knew my mother couldn't swim, and I forgot to ask Uncle Tony if he could. I held on tight to the rope and pretty soon another wave came and knocked me off my feet. The salty, fishy tasting water got into my nose and mouth. We were all laughing. After a while we got brave and started turning our backs to the waves letting them wash over our heads.

When we were cold, and tired from having to hold onto the rope, we finally came out of the water. We raced to the blanket. Uncle Tony and Mama were sitting on the blanket drinking lemonade. I was hungry because all I had to eat all day was a peach. We ate eggplant sandwiches and drank lemonade and made jokes about the people passing by. I never noticed before how white Mama's skin was, especially her legs.

"You better cover your legs with a towel," I told her. "Sister Patricia told us that the sun at the beach is so hot your skin will cook in no time."

"Antoinette, maybe we should rent an umbrella?" Uncle Tony asked.

"Save your money," Mama said. "I want to stop at that vegetable stand on the way back home and buy some sweet corn."

I ate a whole sandwich, Mama's peach, and drank two glasses of lemonade. Frances dropped half of her sandwich in the sand. We fed the sandwich to the sea gulls. They didn't mind the sand. Pretty soon there were a million of them flying all around us looking for food.

Mama's hair looked almost red in the sun and was loose and blowing in the wind. Uncle Tony said she was the prettiest lady on the beach. She laughed and shook her head.

"Always making up stories, Tony," Mama said.

But he wasn't making up stories. Mama was the prettiest lady on the beach. People always said you never would guess she had seven children by looking at her. Mama didn't like to say how old she was.

"Mama, how old were you when you had me?"

She had to think for a minute. "Twenty-seven," she said.

So, in my head I added my age to twenty-seven. Her age came out to thirty-five. She didn't look that old, so I checked my addition on my fingers. I was right the first time. I mean correct.

We filled the paper cups with wet sand. Uncle Tony showed us how to make a fort by turning over the cup and smacking the cup on the sand. You had to be quick so that the sand didn't fall out when you flipped the cup over. We built a really great fort.

"You want to do this again sometime?" Uncle Tony asked.

Chickey, Frances, and I all three yelled "yes" at the same time.

There were no public swimming pools anywhere around where we lived. To learn how to swim you had to go to the YMCA. The boys didn't wear bathing suits; that's what some kids at school told me. Maybe they were just joking. When I was four or five, I was always proud to show off myself, like when I took a bath or changed my clothes. But nobody in the family paid any attention to me. One day after taking a bath I dried myself then ran through the house spinning the towel over my head like a lasso. I didn't know the Bread Lady had come into house while I was still in the bathroom. She laughed when

111

she saw me naked, but my mother yelled at me to get dressed and after the lady left, Mama said I wasn't a baby anymore and that at my age running around naked was a bad thing to do. I didn't run around without any clothes on after that, but I still didn't see what was so bad. I didn't know about the YMCA then, but if I did, I would have told her that even the big boys swim naked at the YMCA. But by the time I was seven I knew that it's okay if a boy sees your peezer and bare butt, but girls aren't supposed to. The rule was the same for girls. I knew girls didn't really have anything to show because I got a good look at that naked baby girl at the beach. But I guess to be fair they had to make the rule the same for both girls and boys.

I talked to Tony about going to the YMCA to learn how to swim and he agreed that everyone should be able to swim. The next day, when just me and Tony and Mama were in the kitchen, I asked her about taking swimming lessons at the YMCA. Mama was slicing eggplant and sprinkling the pieces with salt and stacking them up in a dish.

"The YMCA swimming pool is *troppo caro*," Mama said.

My brother Tony was in the kitchen with his head poked in the icebox. "I'll check and see how much," he said. "I think he should learn to swim."

"Besides," my mother said, "your uncle Pete said his neighbor's boy got polio from swimming in a pool. Now he's in a wheelchair."

My mother had the eggplant all sliced, salted, and piled up. Now she put a bowl on top of the pile and put a heavy stone on top of the bowl. By the next day the salt would suck all the bitter juice out of the eggplant. Then she would bread each slice and fry it in oil. You could eat the eggplant just fried, but my favorite way was when she added tomatoes and cheese and baked the eggplant in the oven.

I didn't know what to say about the polio. When Mama talked about consumption or polio you couldn't ever win the argument. I felt as though I was using a slingshot to fight a G-man who had a machine gun. I was too big to cry. But even if I did, she still wouldn't change her mind. Tony just shook his head and left the kitchen. I didn't know if he was disappointed because he couldn't find anything good to eat in the refrigerator or if he cared that much about me learning how to swim. I went downstairs to find Marky to see if he knew anything about polio. The word sounded more like the name of a game than a disease. Like Bingo, or Ring-a-Lerio. But polio wasn't a game because having to be in a wheelchair wouldn't be fun.

"Marky's in bed reading," Mrs. Stillman said.

It was the afternoon. I never knew him to still be in bed that time of the day. "Is he sick?"

"No. You can go back there and see him if you like."

I hardly ever went in the back of the store, where the Stillmans lived. There were only three little rooms. A kitchen and two bedrooms. Paul and Marky and Mr. Stillman shared one room and the girls and Marky's mother had the other.

The window curtains were closed and the room was dark except for a lamp on a table beside his bed. Marky was sitting in bed reading a book. I could see the title. *The Swiss Family Robinson*. He was already half-way finished. "How come you're in bed? I asked.

"Yesterday the doctor said I have to lie down for at least an hour every afternoon until he sees me next month."

Besides Pasta

His bare feet were on top of the covers and I could see that his ankles were all puffed out. His toes looked like little sausages. He must have seen me staring.

"They're not swollen in the morning, but by afternoon they start puffing up. Push your finger in by my ankle. See what happens."

I did. His ankle was like a marshmallow. My finger left a dent you could hide a marble in. "Wow. What happened to your bones?"

He laughed. "They're just deeper than they should be. The doctor said I have edema."

"What's edema?"

"Too much water builds up between my skin and the rest of me. The doctor said my kidneys aren't getting rid of water like they should."

"Does edema hurt?"

"No, but by the time I go to bed at night my shoes are so tight my feet hurt a little."

"You don't have polio, do you?"

"No, it's nothing anybody can catch. The doctor said the strep throat damaged my kidneys. That I have to be more careful what I eat and drink. I guess over Passover I ate too much salty stuff."

I knew what Passover was because Marky already explained that to me…about the king of Egypt and Moses and all that. I didn't know what salt had to do with his feet swelling. He didn't seem sick, so edema couldn't be so bad. I didn't want to ask him about polio anymore.

"Can you come outside pretty soon?"

"No, I just got in bed. You want me to read to you how the story starts?"

"Okay." I hopped on the bed and sat beside him. He had both pillows so I sat there with my legs crossed like an Indian. I leaned toward him, trying to follow what he was reading. But I couldn't keep up, so I just listened.

"This family is on a boat," Marky said, "A mother, father and four boys. '*The tempest had raged for six days, and on the seventh seemed to increase. The ship had been so far driven from its course, that no one on board knew where they were. Everyone was exhausted. The shattered vessel began to leak in many places and the oaths of the sailors were changed to prayers, and each thought only of how to save his own life.*'"

"Oath is a funny word," I said.

"And it's hard to say," Marky said. "Especially if there's more than one."

We started to try to say oath with an s on the end. The more we tried, the funnier the word sounded. We started to laugh. Soon Marky had tears coming from his eyes, like my uncle Pete did when he laughed.

Mrs. Stillman came in the room. She wore thick glasses and a few pieces of hair always hung over her glasses. I don't know why she bothered to brush the hair back with her hand. It always popped right back. I wondered why she didn't use a bobby pin.

She puffed up the pillow behind Marky. "Peter, Mark needs to rest. He'll be out to play a little before dinner."

"Can't I just finish this paragraph I was reading?"

His mother nodded. She kissed him on the cheek, and then left the room.

"Let me see, where was I?" Marky said.

"Where everybody's scared and praying."

"Yeah. This is the father speaking. '*Children, I said to my terrified boys, who were clinging around me, 'God can save us if he will. To him nothing is impossible; but if he thinks it good to call us to him, let us not murmur; we shall not be separated. My excellent wife dried her tears and from that moment was tranquil....*'"

"What does tranquil mean?"

"It's the opposite of nervous." Marky closed the book. "I guess I am pretty tired."

"Okay," I said. I wanted to hear more, but I knew his mother thought I should leave. "Can I borrow the book when you're finished?"

"It belongs to the library. You can check out a copy for yourself."

My sister Phyllis was always bringing piles of books home from the library. I could ask her to bring the book home for me the next time she goes. Or maybe I could go with her.

Mama's Eggplant Parmesan Recipe

Eggplant is tricky. Bitter, tough, or soggy are the three outcomes you must avoid. Mama managed to do that every time. Here's how.

Ingredients: (serves six)

Two medium-sized eggplants (about two pounds)

Six ounces of Mama's homemade tomato sauce

8 oz. of mozzarella cheese

2 large eggs scrambled

3 tablespoons of freshly grated Parmesan cheese

Peel and slice the eggplant crosswise into thin portions, about five slices to the inch. Sprinkle each slice with salt and stack on a large platter. Build into three piles. After you have the slices sprinkled and stacked, cover with another plate and place a stone or brick on top. Let stand for at least one hour or better yet, overnight. By the next day you will find that a brown liquid has drained from the eggplant. This process, according to mama, takes the bitterness from the eggplant.

Rinse the slices under cold water and blot the eggplant dry, then dip in the eggs and dust with flour or bread crumbs before frying in hot olive oil. If the oil is not hot enough the eggplant will soak up too much oil. When you place the slices in the oil it should immediately begin to sizzle and pop.

Besides Pasta

Brown on both sides, then place on paper towels to remove excess oil.

This sounds tedious but goes pretty quickly if you use a large frying pan. Now pour some tomato sauce over the bottom of a baking dish (9" x 12").

Layer the fried eggplant. Cover with 1/3 of the mozzarella cheese, tomato sauce and parmesan cheese. Add another layer of eggplant and cover with 1/3 of the cheese and tomatoes. Add the final third of tomato sauce to the top layer.

Bake in the oven at 350 degrees for approximately thirty minutes. Add the remaining mozzarella and parmesan cheese, place under the broiler for a minute or two until the cheese is melted and browned.

Chapter Twelve

The Radio 1936

I spent a lot of time the summer of 1936 listening to my favorite radio programs. One of the reasons I stayed in so much was that Marky was sick and was always in bed in the afternoon when the best programs came on. We got to play a little bit right after school before his mother called him in. That left me with nothing to do but listen to the radio.

I'd take a pillow from my bed and lie on our living room floor on my belly with my elbows on the pillow. Most of the time I'd stare at the radio. I don't know why, but what else was I supposed to do? My mother told me an Italian man named Marconi invented the radio.

One day Marky and I were pitching pennies against the side of the house. We were talking about inventions.

"Besides the airplane, the radio is probably the greatest invention ever," I said.

Besides Pasta

I had just tossed a penny that landed right next to the wall. The only thing that could beat it was a leaner.

"I think electricity was the greatest," Marky said. He tossed a penny that landed a foot from the wall, stood up on its edge and rolled to the wall. He had a leaner.

"That was lucky," I said. I was glad we weren't playing for keeps, but I still didn't like to lose.

"Electricity needs to go through wires," I said. "Radio waves can shoot all over the world." That's what my brother Tony told me."

"That's not exactly true," Marky said.

"Let's play immies." I knew I could beat him at immies. "What do you mean it's not true?"

"Most broadcast signals aren't powerful enough to go more than a few miles. We learned about it in science class."

I could never win an argument with Marky. But I think I had him this time. "Jack Armstrong has a short-wave radio and can hear people talking in China!"

"We weren't talking about short-wave radios."

"It's still a radio whether it's short or the regular kind."

"I don't know anything about short-wave radios," Marky said. He reached in the back pocket of his knickers and pulled out a few marbles. "I can only play a couple of games. It's almost time for me to go in."

"Phyllis told me she read in a magazine about a man who could hear the radio in his head."

Marky laughed. "I never heard of that! Can he change the station and turn the sound off when he wanted to?"

"No. He only got one station. They found out that the filling in one of his teeth was acting like a radio receiver."

"You expect me to believe that?"

"Phyllis said the silver in the filling was what was picking up the radio waves."

Mrs. Stillman poked her head out of the front door of the delicatessen and called Marky. She couldn't see us because we were around the corner of the house.

"If I ever need a filling," I said, "I'm going to ask the dentist to tune to WOR. That's the best station."

Marky had this look on his face like he thought I was just making it all up.

"I'd better go in. Let me know what your dentist says about that."

I didn't have any fillings. The one time I ever had a toothache my mother took me to a clinic downtown. On the outside, the building looked like a hospital. Inside, we were sent to the second floor where there were wooden benches along one wall. We sat in the third row. We had to wait our turn. I wasn't scared at first, but as we sat there, I could hear kids yelling and crying. Pretty soon my insides started to shake.

"Mama, my tooth doesn't hurt anymore." I wasn't telling the truth, but I wanted to get out of there. I didn't fool Mama.

"We waited this long, *figlio di Mama,*" she said. "The doctor should at least look at your tooth. Maybe he can give you medicine."

When my turn finally came, they made Mama wait outside. I had to sit in a chair like a barber's chair, except the dentist's chair leaned way back.

Besides Pasta

I closed my eyes because I couldn't stand looking at the dentist with his big face so close to mine.

"Look," he said to the nurse. "It's his molar...too far gone to repair."

I opened my eyes and saw this giant needle coming toward my mouth. I clamped my mouth shut. "After this needle takes hold, you won't feel a thing. Now open your mouth. You'll just feel a little sting."

He lied about the needle feeling like a little sting. The shot hurt a lot. My gum felt numb right away but my tooth still hurt when he grabbed it with his pliers. I tried to tell him I wasn't numb, but I couldn't with his hand in my mouth. He put his knee on my chest and yanked. Still the tooth wouldn't come out. He yanked again. I could feel the tooth come out part way. My mouth filled with blood. The third time he pulled, the tooth came all the way out. He dropped it into a basin on the floor. I looked down. There was a mess of bloody teeth in the bucket. I couldn't tell which was mine.

The nurse gave me something to put over the hole where my tooth used to be.

"You must bite down hard on that to stop the bleeding. And don't chew on that side for a couple of days." She helped me out of the chair and brought me to my mother.

I was thinking that I wouldn't chew on that side forever.

I saw the nurse lead this little girl into the room I just came out of. I should have told her to run out of there as fast as she could. And if I ever get a toothache again, I wasn't going to tell Mama. As bad as a toothache is, it's twice as bad getting it pulled.

I started telling you about my radio programs when the man with a radio in his mouth made me think of my tooth story.

My favorite programs were *Jack Armstrong the All-American Boy, The Lone Ranger, Dick Tracy, Tom Mix and Buck Jones.* They were all fifteen-minute shows except the Lone Ranger, which was a half-hour. I would listen to four or five shows every day. If there were two on at the same time, I had to go back and forth between stations. After a while I would end up listening to the one I liked better. *The Lone Ranger* was my favorite. I loved the music at the beginning and end of the show. After each episode, when the Lone Ranger and Tonto rode away, someone would always ask, "Who was that?" And the other person would say, "The Lone Ranger." And far away you could hear the Lone Ranger say, "Hi, ho, Silver." I always got goose bumps no matter how many times I heard it.

I knew the Lone Ranger and all the rest were just standing in front of a microphone pretending, and that a sound effects person was making noises to imitate guns firing, a fist smacking somebody in the jaw, doors slamming, and horses running. I knew I could never take the part of the Lone Ranger because no one could ever have the exact same voice as him. But I could be a sound effects man. I could already make the sound of horses' feet. When I tapped the top of a table with four fingers, one after the other, my tapping sounded like the Lone Ranger and Tonto riding their horses. Besides that, I could make a pretty good shot sound with my mouth. Marky tried, but his sounded like somebody sneezing. Frances would point her finger at me and say, "Bang! Bang!" I would laugh when she did that, because a sound effects person would never say "Bang! Bang!" to make a pretend shot.

Besides Pasta

My next favorite show was *Jack Armstrong, the All-American Boy*. I liked the way the show began. A chorus would sing, "We the Futzer Hudson High Boys show them how we stand…"

The first word wasn't really futzer, but even though I listened to them sing a million times, I still couldn't get what they were saying. Phyllis said that 'futzer' wasn't a word that she knew of. She listened one time and laughed. "Sure sounds like they're saying futzer."

I don't know why they called Jack Armstrong a boy. He was already in high school. He could drive a car, fly and have adventures in the jungle, and do just about everything you could think of and do it better than anybody else.

If you sent in box tops, you could get all sorts of neat rings. Ones that could tell the weather, or one that could turn into a dog whistle, or have a secret compartment, or glow in the dark. You could also get shiny sheriff badges, wristwatch radios, disappearing ink, a Lone Ranger mask, fake silver bullets, maps, and signed pictures. I could never send away for anything because Mama never bought the cereals she was supposed to. The only thing she bought was cream of wheat. I had to add a lot of sugar, because plain cream of wheat tasted like the white paste we sometimes made from flour and water. Besides, you could never get anything by sending in a cream of wheat box top.

At school kids would show off stuff they got from Battle Creek, Michigan. That's where all the millions of box tops were sent. The things the kids got didn't look anything like what they made you think on the radio. One thing was pretty neat though, a Dick Tracy wristwatch radio with a secret compartment you couldn't open unless you knew the secret. You could hide a message or money and nobody would know it. And even if they knew it, they couldn't open it.

You had to send in Quaker Puffed Rice box tops to get the Dick Tracy wristwatch radio. But my mother said that puffed rice is mostly air. She said air was for breathing, not eating. She said that if I didn't eat a good breakfast, I would get consumption. She said her two stepsisters died of consumption and a lot of other people in her hometown in Italy did too.

The whole family listened to radio shows that came on later at night. George Burns and Gracie Allen, Jack Benny, and Fred Allen. Phyllis liked Fred Allen the best, but I didn't get his jokes. I thought Gracie Allen was funny. My most favorite show was *Gangbusters*, but it came on late at night, and I would almost always fall asleep before the show ended. The next day I'd ask Tony to tell me what happened. But sometimes he didn't listen to the show either and made up the ending. I could tell he made up the endings. I cried because nobody woke me. But by the time I was in the second grade I was too big to cry about missing a radio show, and besides, Tony got pretty good at making up stuff.

The summer before the third grade flew by fast. Before I knew I even had a vacation, I was back in school. I couldn't believe I was in the third grade, almost halfway through grammar school. My third-grade teacher was Sister Martha. I liked my second-grade teacher, Sister Patricia, but I loved Sister Martha. During recess, she would sometimes play with us. She could throw and hit really good...I mean well. When we played stickball, she took turns being on different sides. One day she tripped and fell and sat there on the ground laughing. Her dress was pushed all the way up to her knees. She was wearing black stockings.

Besides Pasta

That night I told Phyllis about it. She said Sister Martha could get in trouble if the principal found out she was playing stickball with the children. I couldn't see why she should get in trouble. Maybe the principal did see her, because after that time she fell, she didn't play stickball with us anymore. But she did play *ring-around-the-rosy* with the girls, except she only pretended to fall down.

My favorite subject was arithmetic. Math seemed easy to me and I couldn't understand why so many of the kids didn't get it. I guess they didn't learn the rules for subtracting and adding and multiplying. It's like playing checkers. You can't play if you don't know the rules. Some people like to make up their own rules. That doesn't work with math.

I liked geography too. The book we used was full of pictures and maps of different places in the world. When we studied about Europe, I showed my mother the map of Italy. She pointed to the part she came from. She said the name of the town was San Andrea. I couldn't find it on the map.

Mama said in San Andrea, tomatoes grew as big as grapefruit and tasted ten times better than what we have here. She said she could look from her bedroom window and see a volcano. Sometimes she dreamed the volcano erupted and blew smoke and ashes and melted rock all over the place turning the whole town turned black.

"Is that why you came to America?" I asked her.

She shook her head. "My brothers were here. So many people were coming."

Helen had told me that my mother's stepmother was mean and she made my mother come to America to get rid of her. I didn't say anything about that because I could tell my mother didn't want to talk about it. When her mouth changed into a straight line, I knew I'd better change the subject.

Sister Martha was even worse about speaking perfect grammar than Sister Patricia, but she never corrected you herself. She would call on one of the other kids for the correct way to say a thing. You had to think before you opened your mouth to speak. There were two ways to talk, Sister Martha's way, and the way you did the rest of the time. When I couldn't remember the grammar rule for saying something, I would think of Ronald Coleman or Jack Armstrong and try to hear how they would say it. Soon I could forget about the rules and still be right almost every time. But I didn't like to correct someone else's grammar. The kid I corrected always gave me a dirty look. So sometimes I would make a joke out of it. Like the time Josh was sick.

"Peter, Josh said that he doesn't feel too good today. What do you think he really meant to say?"

"I'm not sure, Sister. He's not really that good any day."

Everyone laughed except Sister. She just shook her head and called on somebody else. But she kind of laughed with her eyes, so I knew she wasn't mad.

One day Sister Martha asked us if anyone heard President Roosevelt's fireside chat. Nobody said they had. She said he talked about Social Security. We didn't know anything about Social Security, so she explained all about it. If you work for somebody, the person you work for pays in a little bit and you pay in a little bit. She gave as an example: if a person made one dollar the boss would take out a penny from your pay and add a penny to it. The money would be sent to Roosevelt, who would save your money for you. Then when you got to be sixty-five years old, you could retire and get a check every month from Roosevelt or whoever was president by that time.

"What happens to your money if you die before sixty-five?" someone asked.

"That's a good question," Sister Martha said. "Roosevelt didn't say anything about that." She looked around the class. "What do you think?"

No one said anything, so I raised my hand. "I think the government will use the money to pay people who live to be a hundred. Because they would be getting more than what was put in for them."

David Maloney raised his hand. "That's stupid," David said. "Hardly anybody lives to be a hundred."

"Yeah," someone said, "A person's kids should get the money if the person dies before they can collect."

And that's the way the discussion went, until Sister changed the subject. Most of us decided we wanted to keep the penny ourselves and not have to give our money to the government. A war might come and the government would need the money to pay for tanks, battleships, and food for all the millions of soldiers and sailors.

Marky and I sometimes talked about growing up. This one Saturday afternoon we were playing in the small cemetery behind the Protestant Church. In just one week I would have my ninth birthday, and in three weeks it would be Thanksgiving. All the leaves had already come off the trees. The sun was covered by dark clouds. During the week, the man who took care of the church grounds always chased us, but Saturday was his day to leave early. We could stay as long as we wanted. We liked reading the names and dates on the cemetery stones.

"Here's a girl who was only five when she died," Marky said. "She was born in 1913 and died in 1918."

I was wearing two sweaters, knickers and heavy socks that came up to my knees but I still felt cold. "I guess thirteen wasn't her lucky number," I said, "I wonder what she died from."

"There was a flu epidemic in 1918," Marky said. "My father said millions of people died. He said the soldiers brought the flu to America from the war."

"It seems there are a lot of ways a person can be dead," I said, "besides being shot, or run over by a car, or having consumption."

"I can't picture myself grown up," Marky said.

"Me neither. I mean I can't picture me being a grown-up. I can picture you. You already look like your brother. Your ears are as big as his already…and they stick out just the same."

Marky acted as though he hadn't heard me. I guess I shouldn't have made a joke about his ears. They weren't that big.

He bent down and brushed dirt off of a flat stone. He didn't look at me when he started to talk. "I heard my mother and father talking," he said. "They thought I was asleep. They were whispering, but I could still hear them. My mother was crying. She said the doctor could be wrong and that she wanted to take me to someone else."

"Wrong about what?" I asked.

"I don't know…."

"But why was she crying?"

Besides Pasta

"There's a baby buried here," Marky said. "He wasn't even a year old." He looked up. There were tears in his eyes. "I don't know why my mother was crying. Could have been about anything. I think we'd better go. It'll get dark pretty soon. I don't want to be here in the dark."

I was scraping dirt off a grave marker with a small piece of slate I found on the ground. I was thinking about why Marky had tears in his eyes. Was he crying about that one-year-old baby he didn't even know? I felt guilty because I knew that a baby dying is a sad thing, but I still didn't feel like crying. Or was he crying about what his mother said? A shiver ran through my whole body, thinking about either one of us being buried in the ground and the date we died carved on a stone. We were both born in 1928. It's just the date on the right side we didn't know about. I heard once that there's a book in heaven that has the date you're going to be born and the date you're supposed to die. So, if Marky goes to a new doctor who cures him, does the person who keeps the book in heaven have to put in a new date? Because if there's no way to change the date, what's the use of praying and how can you ever have a miracle? I felt myself getting mad at God. He knows when bad things are going to happen. People keep praying and praying to Him and as far as I can tell, it's not going to do any good because God is not going to change the date. Because if He did, that would mean the first date was wrong. But we learned in Catechism that God is perfect, so how could He make a dumb mistake like putting in the wrong date?

I looked up and was surprised to see Marky was gone. I never heard him leave...he just disappeared. That must be how it feels when someone you know dies. They're there one minute and then they're gone. And you never see them again.

I was alone in the cemetery with hundreds of dead people. The mostly bare trees were spidery black against dark gray sky. The wind began blowing hard, like before a storm. Dead leaves were blowing all over the place. I stood and ran toward the cemetery gate. The rusty latch was stuck. I grabbed a rock and smacked the handle. Still the latch wouldn't give. I didn't like to climb the cemetery fence because the metal pickets were sharp and once, I cut my hand trying to climb over. Another time I tore my pants. I made the sign of the cross, climbed to the top, then jumped to the ground on the other side. I ran across the field that separated our house from the church property. I raced up the back stairs to the second floor and through the back door to our kitchen. I sat at the table trying to catch my breath. Tony was at the stove peeking into a steamy pot of tomato sauce.

"The bogeyman chasing you?" he asked.

Yeah, something like that," I said.

Besides Pasta

Mama's Tomato Sauce Recipe

Her basic tomato sauce was made with whole tomatoes, garlic and spices. She simmered the sauce for two or three hours. Meat could be added to the basic recipe (meatballs, veal or pork), even anchovies or squid could be added on Fridays or other days we weren't supposed to eat meat.

Ingredients:

Eight tomatoes (San Marzano are best; fresh or canned)

Three cloves of garlic, minced

A tablespoon of tomato paste

Two tablespoons of olive oil

Six fresh basil leaves

Salt and black pepper to taste

One quarter teaspoon of fennel seeds

Two ounces of Red wine (when we had some)

Mama placed the six roughly cut tomatoes in a pot, then added salt, black pepper, fennel seeds, basil and red wine. She placed it on medium heat. She sautéed the garlic in olive oil for a minute or two then added the tomato paste and basil, mixing them together until the paste began to bubble. She added this to the pot of tomatoes.

As it simmered for two hours, we took turns tasting it and offering suggestions. I liked fennel seeds; Helen liked hot pepper; there was never enough garlic for Chickey; Tony had a hard time deciding

Peter Rizzolo

what it needed, but he didn't seem to mind tasting some on a piece of
bread whenever he passed the pot.

Chapter Thirteen

My Ninth Birthday

For my ninth birthday, I got a rubber ball and a balsa wood airplane kit. I wasn't surprised because I told everybody that's what I wanted. Even though I really wanted a baseball mitt, skates and a two-wheeler bike. I knew that cost too much.

My mother baked a pound cake. She forgot to buy candles, so Tony lit a match and stuck it the cake. I made a quick wish and blew. I know you're wondering what my wish was. But a person's not supposed to tell; otherwise the wish won't ever come true. But I'll give you a hint. The thing has two wheels and a pair of handlebars.

The rubber ball, the size of a baseball, smelled like a new eraser. The ball didn't hurt to catch. And if you missed and got hit on the head, you wouldn't end up with a bump.

At school I watched the sixth-grade boys playing catch with leather mitts and a baseball. I liked the noise of the ball made when it smacked into the pocket of the glove. When one of them missed a catch, I'd run after the ball and throw it to one of the guys.

Peter Rizzolo

"Hey look, a lefty. Not a bad arm for a little squirt."

I liked showing off how far I could throw, so I didn't even care that he called me a little squirt. I had to laugh thinking about it. I pictured Mama being a catsup bottle and by the time she had me there just a little squirt left.

Marky and I played catch every day with my new rubber ball. We started out real close and gradually moved farther and farther apart. At first Marky wasn't very good at throwing or catching, but after practicing awhile, he could throw as far as I could. He could catch even better because he was taller and had longer arms.

If there was nobody to play catch with, like when Marky had to stay in the house, I'd play by myself by bouncing the ball against the house. After a while the lady who lived upstairs would stick her head out of her window and tell me to stop, the noise was driving her crazy.

Then I'd throw the ball underhanded as high as I could and try to catch it. At first the ball bounced out of my hands just about every time, but pretty soon I got so good that I could catch it with one hand. One day as I was bouncing the ball on the sidewalk, the ball hit the edge of the cement pavement and bounced into the street, coming to a stop right in the trolley track. I started to go get it, but a trolley was coming. All I could do was stand and watch my ball get run over. I heard a loud pop. After the trolley passed, I could see from where I was standing that the ball was skwooshed too bad to ever be fixed. I was nine years old and shouldn't be crying over a dumb skwooshed ball. But I couldn't help it. I sat on the curb and started to cry.

135

Pretty soon Mrs. Stillman came out of the delicatessen. She told me I shouldn't sit on the curb and why I was crying? I told her about my ball. She said the same thing my mother told me plenty of times.

"You shouldn't be playing with a ball in the front of the house, Peter." She took my hand and pulled me toward the store.

"I know." I wiped snot on my shirt sleeve.

"How would you like a root beer and a small bag of potato chips?" she asked.

Root beer was my favorite and her potato chips were the best in the world. "Can I buy on credit?"

"There's no charge. It's for being such a good friend to Marky."

I sat on the back-porch drinking root beer and eating potato chips. I was wondering what I was going to do now that my ball was dead. Pretty soon Frances got home from school. She sat next to me looking at my bag of chips. Frances had big eyes anyway, but the way she looked at the bag, I thought they might fall right out of her head.

"Okay, but just two. There aren't that many."

She smiled and dug in the bag. She came out with a handful.

"Hey! I said a couple." Then she started looking at my soda with those same big eyes. There wasn't that much left. I handed her the bottle.

"Take the bottle back for the two cents deposit," I told her. "I'll let you keep a penny." I didn't want to get the deposit money myself because if Frances took it back, Mrs. Stillman wouldn't think I was being greedy getting the soda for free and then wanting to get the deposit money besides.

Now that I didn't have the ball to play with, I started to build the model airplane. It was a single-engine Spitfire, like the ones that fought in the war. Except the motor was a thick elastic band and the plane was made out of soft wood and tissue paper. A small tube of glue came with it. The parts were stamped on a thin sheet of balsa wood. You had to cut them out with a knife. I used a razor blade I found in the bathroom medicine cabinet. Tony didn't shave yet, but my sister Helen had a razor she used to shave her legs.

Besides the parts you had to cut out, there were long strips of wood and plans that you laid the strips of wood on after you cut them to size. You held the wood in place with straight pins while the glue was drying. I liked the smell of the glue. After you glued up the frames, you glued the four sides together. By that time the glued-together pieces of wood were beginning to look like the skeleton of real plane. The wings were next. They were hard to get just right. Then I attached the tail and rudders. Two small wooden wheels came with the kit. They were for the landing gear. You had to make sure the wheels were even or the plane, on landing, would flop over.

The whole thing took a long time. Between playing outside, doing homework, and listening to my radio programs I didn't have much time left to build the plane.

Before covering the plane's skeleton with tissue paper, you had to connect the elastic band to the tail-piece and all the way to the front to the propeller.

The most fun was painting the plane and putting on the decals. A brush and a small bottle of dope...that's what the paint was called...came with the kit. The day I finished it, I ran downstairs to show Marky.

"Wow! The picture on the box doesn't look that good," Marky said.

"Yeah. I can't wait to fly it. Tony said he's going to take me to Valesburgh Park tomorrow."

"I'll ask my mother if I can come." Marky said. "Have you tried gliding the plane?"

"Only in the house. Let's glide it off my back porch."

We raced around back and ran up the wooden steps to the second-floor porch. The yard was narrow but long. At the back there was a wooden fence and on the other side some tall hedges. If the plane landed in the hedges, we could stand on the fence to reach it. I held up the plane just behind the wheels and shot my arm out straight and easy. The plane headed almost straight down, pointing straight for the cement pavement. But halfway there, the plane leveled off, rose and swooped to the right, heading for the field next to the Protestant Church. The side of our building cut off our view so that we lost sight of the plane.

"That was beautiful," Marky said. "But we better go before the minister's cat jumps on the plane."

We flew down the stairs, into the yard, over the fence and into the church yard. Across the field I saw the Spitfire lying upside-down in the grass. The minister's cat was hunched up a few feet from the plane. The wind caused the propeller to rotate. The cat jumped.

"No, don't!" I shouted. Marky yelled too. But we were too late. The sound of the plane scrunching under that fat cat made me sick. Captain Midnight ran away just as we reached the crumpled Spitfire. I picked up the remains as carefully as I could. The wheels and one wing dropped off and the whole underside was flat from where the cat had sat on it. Marky picked up the wheels and the wing.

"The Spitfire flew really great," Marky said. "You think you can fix the plane?"

"I don't know. Besides, I don't have anymore paper or glue or balsa wood. You have to have the right stuff."

"My brother used to make model planes. Maybe he has stuff left over. He never throws anything away. I'll ask him."

"Okay. But I don't want him to fix my plane. I will."

Looking at the busted plane made me think of a bird Marky and I had found in the grass by the cemetery. It was just a baby and we figured it must have fallen out of its nest. We couldn't figure out why the mother would just leave it there. We looked in the trees nearby but didn't see any nests.

"A bird with a broken wing can't survive," Marky said, "Its mother must know that. Why else would she leave her baby to be eaten by a cat?"

"It's not right for her to just leave a hurt bird there. I bet a bird doctor could fix her wing with a cast or something."

"Doctors can't fix everything," Marky said.

"How come you're saying that? They fixed the swelling you had in your feet. And when I had pneumonia, my doctor made me better. Mama said a lot of people die from pneumonia."

"The doctor said my kidney problem isn't something they could cure."

I was looking at the airplane thinking about how I was going to fix it. The scrunched body would be the hard part. The wheels, I could just glue back on. I had heard what Marky said, but didn't know how to answer. "Do you feel sick?" I asked him. "Like you have to vomit?"

139

"No. But I get headaches. And you know about how my legs swell up. I guess the worse thing is that I keep losing protein from my kidneys. Even more than I did at first."

"That's why the doctor checks your pee?"

"Yeah. I asked him what you call what's wrong with my kidneys. I made him write the word on a piece of paper."

We walked back to the house. I wanted to show the busted plane to Marky's brother.

"What did he write?" I asked, as we walked through the delicatessen. Mrs. Stillman was waiting on a customer and Mr. Stillman was working at the meat-slicing machine.

"Is Paul in back?" Marky asked his father.

"He went to the movies with Tony. He should be back soon," Mr. Stillman said, without looking up.

Marky and I went in back. I put the Spitfire on the table. We sat there looking at it.

Marky reached in his pants pocket and pulled out a wrinkled piece of paper and handed it to me. I looked, but the word was too big for me to read. Besides, I couldn't read the doctor's writing. "If you put a pencil in Toby's mouth, he could write better than this. I bet your doctor didn't have Sister Martha for penmanship. You should have asked him to print the note."

Marky stuck the paper back in his pocket. "The next time I go to the library," he said, "I'm going to ask the librarian to help me find information about my kidney condition."

I could tell he was worried. I didn't see how the librarian could read the doctor's writing. And would she even tell him if it was something bad?

The table was already set for dinner. There were napkins, spoons and forks and bowls on the table. Something was cooking on the stove. I didn't like the smell. I sniffed and made a face.

"Borscht," he said. "It's made from beets. I don't like it either. Once the borscht made my urine red."

"Your urine?" I said. For some reason I thought of Thanksgiving, which was only a week off. Last year my mother got a free turkey from the church. They weren't giving away turkeys this year. I didn't know what we would have. Maybe an extra-fancy meatloaf. My mother had a hundred different ways she could make a meatloaf.

"Maybe I can slip a little borscht in Mama's meatloaf and make everybody pee red on Thanksgiving," I said.

My busted plane reminded me of how the poor turkey looked by the time we finished eating. It made me sick to look at it. At least with meatloaf it doesn't look like a dead animal. I went to the stove. "Can I take a peek at your soup?"

"Sure."

I lifted the lid. The thick bubbly soup looked like blood...like something you would see in a witch's kettle. I wouldn't be surprised if tiny webbed feet and wiggly bugs floated to the top. I didn't wait to see. I snapped the lid
shut.

Chapter Fourteen

Thanksgiving 1936

Somebody was shaking me. "Wake up, Peter. Mama wants us all to go to the ten o'clock Mass."

I lay there rubbing my eyes. Helen was still in her nightgown. Her head was full of bobby pins.

"Now don't go back to sleep. It's already nine."

Tony was already up. Ginger was stretched out on the warm spot where Tony had been sleeping. I could hear everybody talking and laughing in the kitchen. From the smell of onions, garlic and parsley I figured my mother had started making a meat loaf.

The house was cold. The kind of morning you had a hard time pulling down the bed covers. I dragged the blanket partway over Ginger. He didn't open his eyes, but he started purring really loud. I looked out the window. The glass was covered with spidery threads of ice that were sparkly from the sun.

I lay there thinking what Paul Stillman said when he saw my busted-up Spitfire. "It would be easier to build another from scratch."

Marky and I talked about what to do. We decided the Spitfire should go down in flames like in the war movies. We put a small rock in the front part, set the tail end on fire and dropped the Spitfire off the back porch on the third floor. As the plane fell, the wind made the body of the plane explode in flame. By the time we got down the three flights of stairs and into the yard, there was nothing left but the smoldering propeller, wheels, and the elastic-band motor.

"Don't go back to sleep, Peter," Helen shouted from the kitchen.

I broke a record getting dressed, pulling on my knickers, long stockings and shirt in about a half a second. I had to pee really bad. I hopped from one foot to the other. I ran to the bathroom, but the door was locked. I knocked. "I've got to go!" I shouted.

"You're going to have to make more noise than that," Tony said. "Frances is in there."

I banged on the door and yelled. But she still didn't respond. Then I heard the toilet flush. She still didn't open the door. I was about ready to pee in my pants, when the door swung open.

"Hi," Frances said.

I flew past her and reached the toilet just in time. I looked in the bathtub and was surprised not to see our pet rabbit, Toby. Someone must have let him loose. Mama and Helen never liked him to be running around the house. Not that Toby was afraid of Ginger anymore, but what they didn't like were the messes he made under the beds and behind the couch.

I looked all over the house and still couldn't find him. I went in the kitchen where Helen, Phyllis, and Tony were helping Mama cook. I didn't see Chickey anywhere around. I figured she was outside taking

Toby for a walk. We used a piece of clothes-line rope for a leash. But you had to be careful of dogs, and not let Toby slip out of the noose.

My mother was checking pots and telling everyone what to do. Her apron was covered with flour and I could smell bread baking in the oven. I peeked in the pots. There was chicken soup in one, tomato sauce in another and cut-up potatoes boiling in another. In a frying pan Mama was browning meatballs and Helen was rolling out dough to make fettuccini. I could already see some drying over the back of a chair. My stomach was grumbling for something to eat, but I was going to receive Holy Communion and wasn't supposed to eat anything. The rule was that you couldn't eat anything after midnight. You could drink water until an hour before receiving.

"Where's Chickey?" I asked Mama. "Is she walking Toby?"

"Chickey and I went to the eight o'clock Mass," Geraldine said. "She's probably outside with him."

The other day, I was in the kitchen taking apart an old alarm clock, when I overheard Helen and my mother talking about selling Toby. Mama said that somebody would pay a lot for such a fat rabbit. She said we could buy a turkey and have enough money left over to take the trolley downtown to see the Thanksgiving parade.

Helen laughed. "As much as I hate the way Toby stinks up the place and cleaning up the mess he makes of the bathtub, I can't see selling him."

"I don't care about having a dumb turkey for Thanksgiving, Mama," I said. I had a million clock parts spread on the table and was trying to figure out why it wouldn't work. My mother shook her head but didn't say anything. I never thought about what she said, until Thanksgiving morning.

When we got back from church, the whole Thanksgiving dinner was sitting on the table. A pile of homemade rolls, a platter of meatballs, a pan of candied sweet potatoes, a bowl of peas and carrots, a giant oval dish piled high with fettuccini, and bowls of tomato sauce and grated cheese at both ends of the table. There was a cleared-out place in the center of the table. Something was roasting in the oven. The smell was so good you could almost pass out from hunger.

We sat around the table as my mother placed the roasting pan in the center. The legs were too short to be a turkey. It was shaped like a duck but it didn't have any wings. Everybody was staring. No. Not a bird. Maybe a baby pig? My mother made the sign of the cross and said a prayer in Italian. She started carving the meat while we passed the other stuff around.

Nobody wanted to ask Mama if we were having Toby for dinner. My mother stood and started going around the table, putting pieces of the carved meat on our plates. We picked at our food, but nobody took even a taste. It didn't smell anything like bacon or ham so it couldn't be a baby pig.

Usually everyone talked at the same time, but the room was so quiet I could hear my heart beating in my ears. I looked at my mother's plate. She didn't eat any, either.

My mother ended up taking Toby and most of the rest of our dinner to the soup kitchen on Fourteenth Avenue. My brother told me later that he found out that Mama had tried to sell Toby but couldn't. That the man who lived next door to us got Toby ready for Thanksgiving dinner. Helen said that Mama told her that she couldn't kill Toby herself. Mama cried when she told Helen. She said she was sick of always having to give us soup bones and ground beef.

In 1936, Roosevelt was running for president for a second term. For a long time before election day in November, everywhere I went grown-ups were talking about Roosevelt. There were banners flying from buildings, people handed out buttons, and posters were stuck on practically every telephone pole. One day the Democratic Party workers in our neighborhood blocked off Fourteenth Avenue and built a stand right in the middle of the street. The sides of the bandstand were covered with flags. A brass band played "My Country Tis of Thee" and a bunch of other songs. Men in suits and derby hats gave speeches you couldn't hear, because of all the noise. Men and women went through the crowd handing out balloons, banners, buttons, and signed pictures of President Roosevelt. There were stands selling hot dogs, sausages, ice cream, and pink cotton candy. Marky and I got thirteen FDR buttons between us by always sticking them in our pockets and acting like we didn't have one. I got a picture of Roosevelt with a big smile on his face and a cigarette in a gold holder sticking out of his mouth. We walked around popping balloons by holding a button in our hands and poking them with the pin on the back of the button. We laughed when the person would jump. Nobody got mad except a little girl, who cried when I popped hers. Her mother was holding her in her arms.

"Now look what you've done," the mother said. "You should be ashamed of yourself." The lady shook my shoulder.

"I'm sorry," I said. I reached in my pocket and took out a button. "She can have this." The little girl reached for it, but the woman pushed my hand away. She turned and walked off.

Marky ran and got two balloons from the bandstand. He ran after the lady and gave her the two balloons.

The little girl smiled and grabbed for the balloons.

One thing we all had to be thankful for was that Franklin D. Roosevelt defeated Alf Landon to remain president. My brother and my older sisters always listened to the radio news and talked about how Roosevelt promised to give people jobs so they wouldn't have to be on Relief. There was something called the WPA. Men could apply for jobs fixing the streets, the highways, railroad tracks...stuff like that. They would get paid fifty dollars a month by the government. Mama said that was more than twice what we got from Relief and from her job sewing coats.

The Sunday before the election, my uncle Peter came to visit.

"What will Roosevelt do," Uncle Peter asked, "when he doesn't have any money left to pay all the people on the WPA?"

"It's better to pay people for doing work than just giving out Relief money," my brother Tony said.

"And the things the workers need like uniforms, shovels, cement, and lumber will have to be bought," Phyllis said. "That will get the factories going again."

Uncle Pete shook his head. He always got red in the face when they talked about Roosevelt.

Besides Pasta

"The schools are being taken over by the Communists," Uncle Pete shouted. "You see what happened in Russia when the government takes over everything."

"Come on, Uncle Pete, there are no communists here."

"You don't think Roosevelt is a communist? Look what he's doing!"

I was tired of listening to them argue. I went downstairs to see if Marky wanted to play checkers. Checkers was the opposite of grown-ups arguing and getting mad at each other and never knowing who was right. In checkers somebody wins and somebody loses and you're still friends even if you're the loser. When I was little, I used to cry when I lost at checkers. I still don't like to lose, but I don't cry. Cards are different, because it's mostly luck if you win. Tony says games should be fun even when you lose. I guess he's right, but for me, they're a lot more fun when I win.

One thing that wasn't fun anymore was school. I did love Sister Martha, but she gave us way too much homework. When I saw my sisters and Tony doing homework, I never really thought about it. But now I got assignments every night in two or three subjects. The math only took a few minutes but geography, history, and English took a long time. You had to answer questions by finding the place in the book that told about it.

I got home from school at three o'clock and my radio shows came on at five. There was only a couple of hours left to play and start my homework. Then after dinner, if I ate fast, I had a little time to finish my homework before the grown-up shows came on at seven. I got to listen until eight and then had to go to bed, except for Friday when I could stay up as late as I wanted. But I usually fell asleep by nine.

We mostly got to play Saturday and Sunday. Saturday was the Jewish day of rest and Sunday was the Catholic day of rest...that's what I learned in religion class. But Marky and I were never tired so there was nothing to rest from. One Saturday Marky and I were playing spy on the Greek numbers man and were sitting on the metal milkbox in front of Stillman's. We watched people who were going into the candy store. We were looking for gangsters in dark suits and black hats. If we saw anyone who looked like he could be a gangster, I would describe how he acted, what he was wearing and what he looked like. Marky wrote everything about the man in our gangster file. If the man came in a car, I had to say the year and make.

"How come you never go to church on Saturday?" I asked Marky.

"My parents have to keep the store open. Besides there's no synagogue around here. You have to take the trolley and a bus to get to the nearest one."

"So how do you know so much about the Bible?"

"My father reads the Bible almost every night. And on Friday we have a Seder.

"Hey, a short guy in a suit just got out of a Packard. He's wearing a white hat, but he looks mean."

Marky glanced up, and then began to write in our spy book.

The man had already gone in the store so I had to tell him what to write from what I remembered. "He kind of looked like Edward G. Robinson. No cigar but the same fat face and thick eyebrows. He wasn't carrying anything but his chest was all puffed out. He could have had a gun under his jacket."

Besides Pasta

While we waited for the man to come out, I asked Marky, "What's a Seder?"

"We say prayers before we eat and have lighted candles on the table. After we eat my father reads the Torah."

"What's that?" I asked.

"It's what you call the Bible."

I felt jealous from what he said about his father reading to him at night. My mother couldn't, and my brother and sisters never thought to do it. Anyway, I was already too big for them to be reading me bedtime stories. I wasn't jealous of the reading as much as the fact that he had a father who was always there and who took care of the family. How could my father not care about me, and my brother and my sisters? He must not still be in the hospital, so how come he never comes around or even send me a card on my birthday? I guess Mama told him never to come back, but that wasn't my idea. And besides I never did anything for him not to like me. I got angry whenever I thought of the way he didn't care about us. I knew that hating someone is wrong. I was going to have to come up with another word to explain how I felt. I just couldn't think of one.

Just then the man came out of the store. He had a newspaper under his arm. He looked around and then his eyes came to rest on us. My mouth got dry and Marky stopped writing and closed his book. The man winked and got in his car. Marky wrote down the license plate number.

"Now he knows what we look like," I said.

"Maybe he was just some guy buying a newspaper."

"Well, just in case," I said, "we better wear disguises the next time we do this."

"And we'll have to spy from a different place. Maybe from the alley next to the beauty shop." Marky said.

"I don't know; you can't just be standing in an alley. You have to be doing something," I said.

"I found out about what was written on the paper the doctor gave me."

I didn't know what he meant. "Oh yeah. You asked the librarian to help you."

"It's called the nephrotic syndrome."

"What kind of sin is that?"

"That's not the way it's spelled. Look." He pulled a piece of paper from his pocket. He showed me.

I shook my head. "Why do doctors have to use words nobody understands?"

"If you have high blood pressure, swelling, and protein in your urine, then that's what you have."

I knew he had swelling and stuff in his urine. "I thought just old people get high blood pressure. My mother says my Uncle Jerry has high blood pressure from the war."

"My pressure just started being high. That's why I started getting headaches."

"But I thought you told me that strep throat damaged your kidneys."

"That's how it started, but strep throat is just one of the things that can damage your kidneys."

I didn't want to keep asking him stupid questions. I didn't even know what high blood pressure was or how they could tell he had it. I remember Mama telling me Uncle Jerry could die from a stroke if he didn't take care of his high blood pressure. That he had to stay calm and not let things make him mad. I did notice he didn't always argue about politics like everyone else in my family.

"You can have a stroke from high blood pressure?"

He nodded. "Yeah. I can't have even a speck of salt."

"What's salt got to do with blood pressure?"

"Salt makes your blood pressure go up."

Marky was acting like he wasn't worried. But he must be scared of dying from a stroke. "Doctors don't know everything," I said. "If they did, people wouldn't be dying all over the place."

"You're right," he said. He snapped our spy book shut. "To hell with the damn doctors."

He stood and kicked the icebox. If he hadn't been wearing shoes, he would have broken his foot. He went into the delicatessen, slamming the door behind him. I never saw him that mad. My heart beat like I had just run around the block as fast as I could. I was afraid that getting mad might make his pressure go up and cause him to have a stroke right there in the store. I was going to have to be careful not to say stupid things.

Chapter Fifteen

The Yankees and the Bears

Most of the grownups I knew were crazy about listening to baseball games on the radio and talking about the players. Especially my sister Phyllis.

The players had great names. Dizzy Dean, Lefty Gomez, Carl Hubbell, Lou Gehrig, and Joe DiMaggio. When Marky and I played catch, I would be Lefty Gomez and he would be Dizzy Dean. We made jokes about a catcher for the Yankees named Bill Dickey. I'm glad *he* wasn't my father.

Everyone was talking about a rookie centerfielder for the Yankees named Joe DiMaggio. In his first year he hit 29 home runs and batted 323. That same season Lou Gehrig hit 49 home runs and batted 354. DiMaggio had to get a lot better to catch up with Lou Gehrig. They called Gehrig the *Iron Man* because he never missed a game, even when he was sick.

Besides Pasta

My sister Phyllis could tell you the batting average of practically every player on the Yankee team. She knew how many games each of their pitchers won and lost, and even their earned run averages. She was in her second year at Saint Rose of Lima's Business High. By next year she would be able to get a job. My sister Geraldine already graduated Saint Rose of Lima's and was working for the social service office in Newark. Mama said that when Phyllis gets a job next year, we could get off Relief and move into a bigger flat.

I didn't like the idea of moving, but no one asked me for permission. My mother was the king *and* queen of the house. I can think of only one time she changed her mind once it was made up. That was about Mussolini. She used to say he was great, because he made the trains run on time. But she doesn't like him anymore because he was going to get Italy in another war.

"The Bears are a Yankee farm team," Phyllis said.

"You can grow baseball players on a farm?"

She laughed, "Sort of. Players start out in what they call the minor leagues. As they improve, they move them up to better and better teams. Most of them never get to be a Yankee."

"Why is everybody so nuts about DiMaggio? Lou Gehrig hit a lot more home runs."

"It's his first year with the Yankees. Rookies usually take awhile to get used to major league pitching, but DiMaggio started slamming home runs right away."

"Can we go see him play sometime?"

"It would cost a lot to go see the Yankees. Next season I'll take you to see the Bears play at Ruppert Stadium in Newark. I read they're going to have ladies' night on Fridays. Women can get in for ten cents."

Even ten cents was a lot to pay to see a bunch of farmers playing baseball. A movie only cost ten cents and for that you saw two pictures, a cartoon, and the Pathe news. You could even stay and see the whole thing a second time without paying any more money.

"What do kids have to pay?"

"Under twelve you get in free. After that you're going to have to wear a dress to get in for a dime."

I knew she was only kidding. But thinking of me sitting there in a dress made me laugh. "What do boys over twelve have to pay?"

"Same as grown men. Fifty cents."

That Christmas, besides asking for roller skates and a two-wheeler bike, things I asked for every Christmas, I asked for a baseball and a leather mitt. I didn't really expect to get skates and a bike so I wasn't disappointed. But I did feel bad about not getting the baseball and fielder's mitt. I didn't complain. I knew what little money Mama had. She had to pay the rent and buy food and clothes and things for the house.

Marky didn't have a mitt of his own. He used his brother's old mitt, and a thrown-away baseball that was just a bunch of string. Marky bought a roll of black tape in the hardware store. We wrapped the ball in tape. We took turns being the pitcher. At first the ball was sticky from the tape, but after a while the stickiness wore off from the ball always rolling around in the dirt.

The person being the catcher was always Bill Dickey. It was a right-hander's mitt, so when I caught, I had to take the mitt off to throw the ball with my left hand. I could wear the glove on the wrong hand, but the thumb was on the wrong side and the ball wouldn't stay in the mitt.

"What would you like to be when you grow up?" I asked Marky. We were playing catch in the backyard.

"My mother says I should be a doctor," he said.

"I think you'd make a good doctor," I said. I wasn't sure why I said that. Maybe the gentle way he held Ginger or the time he found a bird with the broken wing and tried hard to fix it, and how sad he was when the bird died.

"Before I go to medical school, I want to play shortstop for the Brooklyn Dodgers," Marky said. "What about you?"

"That's a good idea. First, I'll play centerfield for the New York Yankees, and after I break Ruth's home run record, I'll go to Seton Hall Seminary School and learn how to be a priest."

Once in a while Marky would grab his head and say he better stop playing because he had a headache. But he never talked about his high blood pressure after that. I didn't want to see him get mad again. I did notice that besides his ankles being swollen, sometimes his hands looked a little puffed up, like a baby's. I acted like I didn't notice.

January, February, and March of 1937 seemed like the worst winter there ever was. We went out every day after school and played catch in the backyard. We chipped in and bought a baseball from a kid for fifteen cents. The ball was like brand new. I loved the smell of the leather and the feel of the raised stitches on my fingers when I threw the ball. When I wasn't the one to use the baseball glove, I wore a thick mitten on my right hand.

"My mother said we might move this summer when school is finished," I said one day while we were playing catch.

"How come?" Marky asked.

"There's a place on Hunterdon Street, near Fourteenth Avenue. It's two floors and costs just a little more than what we're paying now."

Marky threw a ball to me really hard. It landed right in the pocket of the mitt. That was the one place the glove didn't have much padding. I took off the glove and rubbed the palm of my hand.

"I know where Hunterdon Street is," Marky said. "It's only a few blocks away. There's a church on the corner of Fourteenth Avenue and Hunterdon."

"Yeah. Saint Rocco's. There's a priest house next to the church. The house my mother looked at is next to that."

Marky threw the ball over my head. In the excitement to catch the ball I reached with my bare hand. Now both my hands hurt, and my feet were freezing besides.

"I hate winter," I said. "Let's go inside and look at your baseball cards." I knew Marky had to go take his daily afternoon rest in bed. But even with him in bed, we still could look at his baseball card collection. Marky knew all the stuff written on the back of each card just about by heart.

"I started seeing a new doctor at Beth Israel Hospital," he said when we were inside.

"How come?"

"My parents wanted me to. They said he's a famous kidney specialist."

"Maybe you can get him to autograph our baseball," I said.

I was looking at a Dizzy Dean card. He was wearing a uniform with a redbird on the front of his shirt. The card still smelled like bubble gum.

"He started me on a pill that's supposed to keep my legs from swelling. The doctor said the strep throat did a lot of damage, but it's done all it's going to do. My mother got a list from him of things I can and can't eat."

" What if you get another strep throat?"

"My mother asked him the same question. He said she should keep me home from school if any of the kids in my class are sick with a sore throat."

"No wonder he's famous. Telling kids to stay home from school."

I made a joke out of it, but I knew it must be bad if his parents were taking him to a famous doctor. The Stillmans weren't rich even though they owned a store. They sold a lot on credit and most of their customers were on Relief. Marky once told me his father was worried that the new A&P store down the street was going to take away his business.

"Can I take Paul's mitt upstairs? My mother can sew in some kind of padding in the pocket."

"I'll have to ask Paul when he comes home. He and Tony went someplace," Marky said.

"How does a person get to be a famous doctor?"

"You have to go to school for a long time to become a doctor. Then you have to be smarter than the rest of the doctors or find a cure for polio...something like that."

"I guess I'll have to be a famous baseball pitcher. All you have to do is have a strong arm and a good aim."

That winter was spent longing for spring. Marky had his tenth birthday and got a Rawlings fielder's mitt and a new Spalding baseball. When we played catch, I used his brother's right-handed mitt. We played in the backyard until our feet got so cold we couldn't stand it.

One day we walked downtown to Davega's Sporting Goods Store. We wanted to buy baseball caps and see what a Louisville Slugger bat would cost. I had twenty-one cents from milk bottle deposits and he had thirty cents from saving up his ten cents a week allowance. The least expensive hats were 39 cents so we didn't have enough between us to buy two. I thought to say, "*Troppo caro, troppo caro*" but the man didn't look Italian and wouldn't understand me.

"Let's buy one hat and share it," I said.

"Okay," Marky said. "But I'm putting in more money so I get to say what's on the hat."

I was trying on a navy-blue Yankee cap and looking in the mirror. I could just see myself on a baseball card...millions of kids in a few years wanting to trade their Lou Gehrig baseball card for the one with my picture on it. "I'm not going to wear a Brooklyn Dodger cap," I said. "I like the Yankees better." I handed the cap to Marky.

I had to laugh the way cap looked on him. It sat high on top of his head.

Besides Pasta

"Your head is way smaller than mine," he said. "If I have to wear a Yankee hat, at least it's got to fit."

We decided to buy the navy-blue Yankee cap that fit Marky's head. The hat came down to my eyebrows.

The man in the store laughed when he saw me try on the hat. "Okay," he said. "I'll give you a special deal. Two hats for fifty-one cents."

As we walked home from Davega's I was thinking how I didn't want Marky to figure he owned part of my hat just because he put in nine cents more than me.

"You were nine cents short of buying your Dodger cap. Right?"

We were standing on the curb waiting for a chance to cross the street. A trolley flew by, the two poles on top of the trolley sparked as ends of the poles bounced against the wires. People inside were reading newspapers; others were taking naps. Nobody was paying attention to us or wondering who we were in our new baseball caps. Someday they were going to be sorry they didn't jump right off that trolley and get our autographs.

I wasn't sure Marky had heard me because of all the noise the trolley made. The air was cold, and the wind was so strong we had to pull our caps down low to keep them from blowing off. I was glad to be wearing my heavy knickers and two sweaters. I wiggled my toes in my shoes to keep them warm.

"You're right. I was nine cents short," he finally said.

"Right. I ended up giving you nine cents to buy your hat. The man sold me my hat for only eleven cents. I know that doesn't seem fair, but that's what he did. In a way, I'm part owner of your hat."

He thought about that for a while, and then he laughed. "That's one way to look at it. The way I see it, we got two hats for fifty-one cents. That's twenty-five-and-a-half cents for each hat. You could say I put in four-and-a-half cents more than you."

How was I supposed to owe somebody half a penny? "The man never explained how he broke the price down, so don't worry," I said. "Just consider my nine cents as a late birthday present. Maybe you can treat me to a peach ice cream cone sometime. Hey, did you notice how much those bats cost?"

"The cheapest one I saw was a dollar and fifty cents," Marky said.

"Yeah I noticed," I said. "I asked the man if we could buy on credit. He said the store had a policy not to give credit. I told him the Stillmans sell us stuff on credit all the time."

"What did he say?"

"He said, 'Who the hell are the Stillmans?'"

The rest of the way home we kept saying, "Who the hell are the Stillmans!" We repeated the words in different voices; like Bela Lugosi, Ronald Coleman, and James Cagney.

Marky said out of the side of his mouth, "Now listen you bums, you give it to me straight, you hear? Just who the hell are the Stillmans?"

He sounded exactly like Edward G. Robinson. We were both laughing so hard tears came. Then I had to pee so bad I couldn't stand it. But there was no place to go where someone wouldn't see me. I don't know how people know a person has to pee, but they must because they never take their eyes off of you when you have to go. I walked really fast. I made Marky promise not to say anything funny.

Besides Pasta

"If you had a clothespin in your pocket," he said with a serious face, "you could slip it on your penis and not have to worry about having an accident."

I bit my lip and tried not to laugh. But the picture in my head of me with a clothespin on my peezer made me bust out laughing. You can figure out what happened after that.

Chapter Sixteen

Edgar Bergen & Charlie McCarthy

In 1937, the *Edgar Bergen and Charley McCarthy* radio show had everybody talking, especially about the dummy named Charlie McCarthy. He looked kind of weird because he wore only one eyeglass. I'm not sure why. I guess he could see okay out of the other eye and probably only had to pay half as much for just one glass. Pictures of Charlie in magazines always showed him dressed in fancy grown-up clothes: a tuxedo, bow tie and top hat.

He had a round face, like my school friend Tommy. He even looked a little bit like him, but I never told Tommy that. Who wants to be told he looks like a dummy?

Charlie was always sassing Edgar Bergen. But since Edgar Bergen was doing the talking, he was really sassing himself.

Besides Pasta

They said Edgar Bergen could make his voice sound as though it was coming from someplace else, even the next room. And he could talk without moving his lips. I practiced in front of the mirror. Some letters are impossible to say without using your lips. Like words beginning with b, m, and p; w was kind of hard too. You could fake it, but your voice came out like a drunk person's. I figure Edgar Bergen cheated a little because you couldn't tell over the radio if his lips were moving.

I liked Charlie's humor. Mostly he insulted people, especially Edgar Bergan, but not in a mean way. A lot of his jokes had to do with using words with double meanings. I wasn't the only one who liked him. Our whole family listened to the show every Sunday night. A lot of the jokes were about Charlie's head being made out of wood. This one night the guest star was W.C. Fields. He always played a drunk person in the movies. He had a gigantic red nose. I don't remember exactly what they said but this is pretty close:

W.C. Fields: "Charlie, is it true that your father was a wooden table?"

Charlie: "If he were a table, your father was probably under it!"

W.C. Fields: "Be quiet, you home-for-termites. You'd better stay clear of beavers!"

Charlie: "Is that a flame-thrower I see, or is it your nose?"

Charlie always got the best things to say. What I liked was hearing a kid wisecracking with grown-ups and getting the best of them.

Sometimes I would take Frances' one-armed Shirley Temple doll and pretend it was Charlie. I tried to throw my voice at the doll's head, but because I couldn't make the mouth move, I couldn't make it seem as though the doll was talking. And with Frances being hard of hearing, I had to almost shout. Not moving my lips was hard enough speaking in a normal voice. I could see she was trying to read my lips. She would never laugh at my jokes. One day she walked off right in the middle of my best act. I gave up on her stupid Shirley Temple doll. I decided that I needed a real Charlie McCarthy dummy for my acts to work. With him being able to move his mouth, roll his eyes and turn his head from side to side, I could make it seem that he was really doing the talking. The controls for moving the eyes and mouth were in the back. I had never seen what they looked like but it probably wouldn't be hard to learn to use them.

Every time we listened to the show on the radio, I would say that I wished I would get a Charlie McCarthy dummy for Christmas. But Christmas was still a long way off. School had just finished and we were getting ready to move to the house on Hunterdon Street.

I hated to move away from South Orange Avenue. I hated to change schools, and mostly I hated being a million miles away from my friends, especially Marky.

"It's only a few blocks from here," I told Marky. That was a lie. I didn't want to say exactly how far.

"We can take turns," he said. "Sometimes you can come up here and other times I can go down there. Is there a park in the neighborhood?"

"There's a field by the public school. It's only a couple of blocks from the house."

We were sitting on the icebox in front of the Stillmans' store. I was wearing my Yankee baseball cap. He had on his Dodger cap. I knew I had grown a little bit, because my feet could almost reach the sidewalk. I sat with my butt right on the edge so my feet could reach the ground like Marky's. The awning was down. Although the day was hot, we felt comfortable in the shade.

"Remember when I used to call this the big umbrella?" I said. "I bet you always knew the right name for it."

"I liked the 'big umbrella' better. My father said that this summer it's going to be my job to lower the awning every morning and raise it at night. I'm going to help out in the store like a regular job."

"Will you get paid?"

"We didn't talk about it. But I know he pays my brother and sisters when they work there."

"I'm going to miss this dumb old icebox, too," I said. "Uncle Tony's coming tomorrow with his truck to help us move. He said we might have to make two or three trips to get everything."

"I know, you already told me."

I watched an old man go into the candy store. "You going to spy on the numbers man when I'm gone?"

"It wouldn't be fun spying by myself," he said. "You always told me what to write in the spy book."

"Maybe you can come with me and Phyllis to see the Newark Bears play."

"That would be great. I'll have plenty of money from my job. If we go, I can buy the hot dogs and peanuts and sodas."

"You can bring your mitt and maybe catch a foul ball. Phyllis said if we ever did, she would get the whole team to autograph the ball.

"That would be great."

"I wish I could get a job this summer and save up to get a lefty mitt."

"There's a kid in my class who delivers the Saturday Evening Post. I think he makes a pretty lot of money," Marky said.

"You have to be a certain age?" I asked.

"I don't think so. But I think you have to get your own customers."

"Your father has lots of customers. Could he give me some?"

Marky shook his head and puckered his lips, pretending that he felt sorry for me. It was our "fat and skinny" act. I would say something stupid like the skinny one always did, and he would give me that how-could-you-be-so-ignorant look.

On moving day, we all helped load Uncle Tony's truck. He and my brother carried the heavy stuff like the icebox, the kitchen table, the Maytag, the living room couch, and the dressers. We filled paper bags with our own things. Helen made us write on the bags where things came from. That way, when we got there, we could put them back in the same place. We were lucky the day was sunny with no sign of rain, because the truck wasn't covered in back. Uncle Tony tied everything down with clothes-line rope to keep our stuff from flying off while he was driving.

After we loaded the truck for the third time, the people in the building all came out to say goodbye. Frances, Chickey, Mrs. Stillman, and my mother all cried. Marky wasn't there.

I was kind of glad Marky wasn't there because I didn't want to be a sissy and cry in front of everybody.

"Where's Marky?" I asked Mrs. Stillman.

"He's inside helping his father. He said to tell you to come in and say goodbye before you left."

Besides Pasta

My brother, Frances, and my mother got in the truck with Uncle Tony. As they drove off, Frances leaned out the window and waved to everybody. Helen and Phyllis started walking to the new house. Geraldine said she would wait and walk with me.

I went in the store and saw Marky taking cans of Campbell's soup from a box and stacking them on a shelf. His father was waiting on a customer.

"Hi."

"Hi," Marky said. He was wearing a gray apron and long pants and black canvas sneakers. He looked like a grown-up store person. There was a pencil and pad in the front pocket of his apron. He kept stacking the cans. The store smelled like tuna fish and pickles. I sat on a low stool and watched Marky work. I started handing him cans from the box. When he reached up, I noticed he wasn't wearing socks. The skin on his ankles looked tight and stuck out over the edge of his sneakers. I saw an old man on the trolley once whose ankles looked exactly like that. I wondered if his ankles hurt.

"Isn't it time for you to rest in bed?"

"I will. Right after I finish what I'm doing."

"My sister Geraldine is waiting for me."

"Does she like her new job?"

"Yeah, I guess so. She's always talking about things that happen at the office. I better go. Can you come down next Saturday?

"I have to work in the store on Saturday. I can come on Sunday."

Marky put up the last can and then started to flatten the box with his foot.

"I can't wait to show you the house. There's an attic on the third floor. It's as big as this whole store."

Peter Rizzolo

He stuck out his hand. I stood there looking at it. We never shook hands before. At first, I thought he wanted to show me something. When I finally grabbed his hand, he squeezed hard and pumped my hand up and down. For some reason we both started to laugh.

Chapter Seventeen

Our Flat on Hunterdon Street

Even though I missed South Orange Avenue, Hunterdon Street was more like a regular neighborhood. No buses or trolleys flew past our house; there weren't any stores on our block. A lot of the families had a whole house all to themselves. In the house we moved into, another family lived downstairs. They had a girl named Josephine, who was the same age as my sister Chickey.

Across the street from us the Baiocchis lived in a three-story house that they had all to themselves. They had three boys and four girls. The oldest boy was a doctor, but he still lived at home. I never knew what his first name was. Everyone just called him Dr. Baiocchi. There was a boy named Tim. Or maybe that was the doctor's name. I do know that the boy named Tony was the same age as my brother Tony. The girls were named Annette, Dottie, and Regina. Our two families took to each other like we were cousins. Dottie and Annette reminded me of my cousins Dolly and Vera. I liked listening to them talk with my sisters.

Peter Rizzolo

One day Phyllis and I were sitting on the floor in the front room listening to a baseball game on the radio. The announcer was talking about Joe Gordon, the second baseman for the Bears.

"He's a delight to watch, folks. So much grace, such pizzazz," the announcer said.

"What's pizzazz?" I asked Phyllis.

"A person with a lot of pep. Someone who's fun to be with or watch. Someone who creates excitement."

"Like Dolly and Vera and the Baiocchi girls?"

"Yes. They all definitely have pizzazz."

I knew I didn't have pizzazz because everyone said I was a good listener. That's a polite way of saying how come you're so quiet? Being a good listener is practically the opposite of pizzazz.

The youngest Baiocchi girl, Regina, was a year older and a couple of grades ahead of me in school. At first, I thought she was stuck-up because she always dressed in Sunday clothes and kind of ignored me. I couldn't blame her. I was shy around girls who weren't my sisters. Especially if they were pretty and were taller than me. She was pretty and taller and besides, she didn't like baseball, or playing marbles, or catch, or kick-the-can. And you can't wrestle with someone who's wearing Sunday clothes. Her favorite thing to do was read books and talk with my sisters Geraldine and Phyllis.

One day Regina and her sister, Annette, were in our front room talking to my sisters about books they had read. They were sitting on the bare wooden floor. Helen had taken the slip-covers off the couch and side chair to wash them. She said we couldn't sit on the couch and chair because we would wear out the upholstery. She was at the

171

window putting up a set of starched crocheted curtains that my mother had made. I was sitting on the floor kind of off to the side, listening. They were going back and forth about books I had never heard of.

"My favorite book is *Swiss Family Robinson*," I said.

I didn't say that was the only book I ever read that wasn't a school book. I guessed comic books didn't count. Everybody turned and looked at me. I felt like you do in the classroom when the teacher called on you. How your stomach knots up inside and you can't think what to say. I had only read half when the book was due at the library. I could have taken the book out again, but to tell the truth it was getting boring with nobody getting killed or anything really bad happening. Besides, I was tired of always looking up words in the dictionary.

"It was your favorite book?" Regina asked. "I thought it was boring. Everybody was so perfect and the ending was too...I don't know what."

"Predictable," Annette said.

"Yes, that's it," Regina said. "Didn't you think the ending was predictable, Peter?"

I shrugged. They went on to talk about other books. Regina didn't like any of the things I liked, and the only thing we agreed on, I messed up by saying it was my favorite book when it wasn't. After they left, I asked Phyllis to write down the names of her three favorite books that she read when she was my age. I was a slow reader and figured three was about all I could handle that summer with all the other stuff a person has to do.

The house had a big porch across the front that was about three feet off the ground. On one side, steps went down to the sidewalk. There was a long railing with fancy round spokes. Frances and I liked to sit on the railing and hook our shoes around the spokes and lean back until we could almost touch the floor of the porch. The lady on the first floor saw us and told Mama we were going to break our necks. It's funny that I never knew anyone who had actually broken their neck, even though there were a million ways to do it. If you ran down the stairs too fast, or played on the ice, or jumped off the porch, or climbed a tree, or left a ball on the floor. I was having trouble keeping up with all the different ways.

One day Chickey and her girlfriend Josephine, from downstairs, were sitting on the front porch steps reading magazines. I climbed up on the porch railing and spread my arms out like wings. I started walking along the railing. I had, plenty of times, and whenever I started to lose my balance I would jump onto the porch. I knew they were watching so I started to sway, pretending I was going to fall.

"Peter!" Chickey shouted. "You'll break your neck!"
I leaned a little too far away from the porch and couldn't jump onto the porch. Instead I fell over sideways, head first toward the ground. I shot my left arm out so my head wouldn't hit the hard dirt. My hand folded back and made a loud snapping sound. It felt like a grenade had exploded in my wrist.

My hand was hanging from my arm in an unnatural position. Like something dead was stuck there. The wrist bone looked as though it was going to poke through the skin.

Chickey screamed and ran in the house to tell my mother. My mother came running out of the house with a towel. I was sitting on the ground holding my dead hand and crying. I thought there was nothing for the doctors to do but cut off the dead part. I thought that any second the bone would poke through the skin and my hand would fall off. I closed my eyes. I couldn't look. Oh God, don't let them cut off my hand. My whole body shook.

"My God!" Mama said. "Thank God you didn't break your neck." She laid my arm on the towel. I held up my broken wrist with my other hand. Somebody ran across the street and get Dr. Baiocchi. He wasn't there. The priest from next door came out and looked at my wrist. My hand was starting to turn blue.

"You need to get to the hospital right away."

There was a whole army of people gathered around me by this time. I was getting more scared by the minute because of the way people were looking and shaking their heads and saying how they never saw anything like it. A man I didn't know said he would drive me to the Newark City Hospital.

At the emergency room, the intern took one look at my wrist and sent for an x-ray. The pain wasn't so bad if I didn't move my arm, but to move even a speck caused a pain like ten toothaches. The x-ray person kept moving my arm this way and that way. With every move the pain came back. I didn't want to be sissy, but I couldn't help screaming my head off.

When the x-rays came back the doctor told my mother that I had broken both bones in my wrist. He said I was lucky the skin wasn't broken. I didn't know what he meant. I had a cut on my thumb once that needed stitches. That didn't hurt anything like my broken wrist bones.

"We have to set the bones and put his arm and hand in a cast. It'll have to be in the cast for six weeks," the doctor said.

Six weeks! That was practically the whole summer. A nurse asked my mother to wait outside. She then brought me to a room with a table in the middle. I had to lie on the table. She put a strap around both my ankles and pulled tight. Then she put my right hand in a leather cuff. I didn't like being tied down. Why did they have to tie me down? What were they going to do? The nurse said I mustn't move while the doctor set my wrist. I promised her I wouldn't move if she didn't tie me up. She said she was sorry, but that she had to.

"Aren't they going to knock me out first?" I had seen operations in movies and they always knock a person out unless it's a war movie and then the person would usually die unless he or she was the star of the movie.

The doctor came back in with two men in white suits. One man leaned across my chest; the other man held my arm at the elbow. The doctor pulled as hard as he could, at the same time trying to squeeze the bones in my wrist back in place. I remember screaming from the pain, then I must have passed out because the next thing the doctor was doing was putting on a plaster cast. He said there was nothing wrong with my lungs. I had to lie there an hour for the cast to get hard.

"It feels really hot inside the cast," I told the doctor.

"That's normal. The plaster gives off heat as it hardens."

"Hot enough to burn my arm?"

"No. Just feels a little warm."

My mother came back in and sat with me. Her face was the same color as my cast and her eyes were red from crying. She leaned over and kissed me on the cheek. She held my hand.

Besides Pasta

Just the tips of my fingers and thumb stuck out from the end of the cast, and at the other end the cast went halfway up to my shoulder. They put on a sling and told my mother to bring me back the next day for them to check the cast.

The man who took us to the hospital didn't wait. We had to take two long bus rides to get home. On the way I told Mama how they tied me down and didn't give me anything to kill the pain. She said she could hear me screaming. People on the bus were staring at us because both me and Mama were crying. She was crying because she was remembering me screaming and I was crying from being mad about the way they tied me down and didn't numb the pain.

Once we got home, everybody crowded around and had to knock on my cast. Geraldine said how brave I was because by that time I was finished crying. But I knew I wasn't brave because I had screamed my head off and passed out.

"It could have been worse," I said. "I could have broken my neck."

Tony wrote on my cast, "It wasn't your fault! You were the fall guy." Then he signed it.

Pretty soon everyone started to sign it. Frances drew a pretty good picture of Dick Tracy. Chickey wrote, "Showing off doesn't pay." Most everybody just signed their name, but Mr. Bellini, an artist, who was renting our attic space, took me up to the attic and had me sit on a stool while he drew a bunch of tiny birds. Underneath he wrote, "Leave the flying to them." He signed it.

Everybody was having such a good time signing and drawing on my cast. I thought if I charged them a nickel each, I could practically make a business out of broken bones. But don't worry, I may be greedy, but I'm not crazy.

I understood now why Uncle Tony quit the circus after he fell from the trapeze. Falling and breaking bones is not the kind of thing a person wants to take a second turn at doing.

That night I woke up screaming from a bad dream. The doctor who was pulling on my hand pulled so hard the skin started to tear. Then there was a loud ripping noise and the doctor fell backwards onto the floor with my bloody hand in his lap. Blood came gushing out of the end of my arm.

Mama was holding me in her arms. She rocked me for a long time. I finally fell asleep.

The next Saturday when Marky came down to see me, he brought his fielder's mitt, and his brother's mitt for me to borrow. He also brought a baseball. I was sitting on the front steps. He sat beside me. He was surprised to see that I had my arm in a cast. I told him how I busted my wrist and how they put the bones back in the right place and how much it hurt. I left out the part about passing out.

"I can't believe they operated on your wrist without giving you ether or a shot of pain medicine," Marky said.

"My sister Phyllis said that nobody pays to go to the City Hospital and that the nurses and doctors who work there are so busy, after a while they don't really care how much it hurts."

"That's still not right," Marky said.

"She said it's because they always have millions of people waiting to see them and they have to fix you and get you out of there fast. She said that as soon as she gets a job, we can go off Relief and not have to go to the City Hospital."

"Maybe you can go to Beth Israel Hospital. My mother says they have the best doctors there."

I pulled the cloth sling back and tapped the cast with my knuckle. "It's as hard as a baseball bat. Let's go to the playground. I'll hit you fly balls."

He looked serious. "I don't know, Pete. I don't think you should."

"I was kidding," I said. "If I just bump the cast against something, I get electric shocks in my fingers."

But we did go to the playground. I threw him the ball with my right hand. He'd catch it and roll the ball back to me. I couldn't hardly throw with my right hand. Marky laughed and said I was throwing like a girl. I figured that girls don't throw well because they didn't practice as much as we did. I got as little better after a few throws, but I still looked awkward.

The day was warm and sunny. We were hot and sweaty. That added up to one thing…the ice cream store on Fourteenth Avenue. Marky's father was paying him thirty cents a week to help him in the store. He treated me to my favorite, a double-dip of peach ice cream in a sugar cone.

"I'm saving up," Marky said. "Pretty soon we can go back to Davega's to buy a Louisville Slugger."

I wished I had a job and made thirty cents a week. I could go to the movies every week for ten cents, give my mother ten cents to help pay the rent, and still have ten cents left over to save up for a lefty fielder's mitt.

But for now, nobody was going to give me a job with only having one arm to work with. I knew I was too young to have a regular job, but I could shovel snow and run errands.

I really liked the artist who lived in our attic. He painted the scenery for the Newark Opera. Mr. Bellini, who was about as tall as my brother Tony, had a long thin face and black curly hair that covered his ears. He smelled like a combination of cigars, pepperoni, and turpentine.

The attic had a fan in the window, but in the summer on some days the heat was so intense you could hardly breathe. One day I brought Mr. Bellini a bottle of lemonade Mama had made. He drank practically the whole thing without stopping. He wasn't wearing a shirt and his chest was covered with black hair. Even his back was practically covered with hair.

"Can I watch you paint?"

"If you like. But no talking. I must have quiet."

Practically every day I brought him something cold to drink. Usually just ice water. Sometimes iced coffee. Then I'd sit and watch him draw. The blank canvas turned into flowers, trees, mountains, and buildings that looked so real you felt you could walk right inside. He was a magician, making things appear from nowhere with nothing but his mind and hands.

Sometimes Mr. Bellini asked me to run to the store to buy him a stogie cigar. At first the man in the store wouldn't sell me the cigars. But he did after Mr. Bellini gave me a note saying the cigars were for him.

I liked the smell of the cigars. Once I put one in my mouth. I was careful not to get the end too wet. I didn't like the taste. Even not being lit, I practically threw up when I sucked air through the cigar. He usually gave me two or three cents for going to the store for him. Once he didn't have any pennies and had to give me a nickel. He said the nickel would cover the next time.

His paintings went from the floor to the ceiling and were half as long as the whole attic. He was painting a fancy stone house with trees and flowers and a fountain. On the floor were old cloths covered with specks and splotches of dried paint.

"This is for the garden scene in *Romeo and Juliet*," he said "Have you ever been to the opera?"

"No. But I saw Jeanette McDonald and Nelson Eddy in a movie…."

"No, no, no. It's not the same. For the movies they do a scene over and over and over. On the stage they only get one chance. That is what makes live theatre so thrilling to see and hear."

"My mother says that her father took her to Napoli to see the opera when she was a young girl."

He was wearing an apron that was stiff with paint. He was using a fat brush with a long handle. He had to stand on a ladder to paint the top parts. He was humming, and then started to sing in Italian. He sang pretty well, but not as well as Nelson Eddy.

"I wish I could draw," I said. Imagine getting paid for something that was fun. But I knew I could never draw that well. Besides, they mustn't be paying him very much with him being so stingy and having to live in an attic.

He made me wear one of his aprons that went all the way to my ankles. He handed me a brush and pointed to a blank place on the canvas.

"Paint in this space," he said, as he popped the lid off a can of gray paint.

My left arm was still in the dumb cast, so I had to paint with my right hand. He showed me how to wipe the brush on the side of the can so the paint wouldn't drip. I was nervous because I didn't want to ruin his painting.

"You shouldn't worry," he said. "I can always paint over it. Do not think. Just paint."

Behind us was a picture hanging on the wall. I could see that he was copying the picture. "This is where you are painting." He pointed to a place on the picture.

There were bushes and flowers. "I can't draw that."

He laughed. "You are painting the background. You will see. Just paint from here to here and don't worry. He started to sing in Italian. I couldn't understand the words but by then the melody sounded familiar because I heard him singing it before. He had a powerful voice for such a skinny man.

"Frances can draw better than me," I said when he stopped singing.

"Well, sometime I will have her help me. Would you like to go see an opera, Pietro?"

When *Romeo and Juliet* opened, Mr. Bellini gave Mama three tickets. Mama, Helen and I went. The opera was on a side street in downtown Newark. From the outside the Newark Opera House looked like a regular movie theatre, but the insides were a lot fancier and cleaner than the Congress where I usually went to the movies.

The seats were covered with red velvet and there was red carpet down the aisles. There were small balconies along both sides. The people in them were all dressed up. I could see why Helen was so fussy about what I wore. She and Mama had on their Sunday church clothes. Mama was wearing a pair of Helen's earrings.

Some of the people had tiny spy glasses. There were lights on the side walls, and overhead was a giant chandelier with a million sparkly chunks of glass that hung like icicles. The light was so bright, you could hardly look directly at the chandelier. Before the opera started, the lights got dimmer and dimmer, but never got altogether dark like a movie.

I reached under the seat and was surprised not to find any chewing gum. I felt under Helen's seat and there wasn't any there either. I wondered where grown-ups put their gum.

Romeo, who was still in high school, killed this guy in a sword fight. Then he had to run away because everybody was after him. He couldn't come back to get his girlfriend Juliet, because they would arrest him if he did. She was mad at him because the guy he killed was her cousin. But she didn't stay mad at Romeo. She loved Romeo.

Juliet couldn't stand him being gone, so she took medicine to fool everyone into believing she was dead. But she was only in a deep sleep. She had sent a note to Romeo to come get her, but he never got the message.

Helen could understand more Italian than me. I wouldn't have known what was going on without her telling me.

Romeo came back to get Juliet and saw her in the tomb and thought she was dead. When he started to sing, I recognized the melody because it was Mr. Bellini's favorite part to sing while he was painting.

Romeo killed himself and then Juliet woke up and found him dead. Then Juliet stabbed herself.

It wasn't right for Romeo to kill himself. First of all, it's a sin. It's against the Fifth Commandment. And even if killing yourself weren't a sin, he was stupid not to have waited a little longer. Even from where I was standing, I could see she was still breathing. He could have taken her to a doctor.

When the opera was over, my mother and Helen were crying. Then everybody started clapping, whistling, and shouting, "Bravo! Bravo!" I couldn't clap because I still had my arm in a sling. But I did shout *Bravo* as loud as I could.

I knew Romeo and Juliet weren't really dead, but I still got goose bumps when they came out and took bows. Somebody ran on the stage and gave Juliet a bouquet of flowers. I especially liked seeing the scenery behind them and knowing that Mr. Bellini painted all that in our attic. And that I did a small part of the painting. Right-handed!

I wish real life could be like the opera. Where after a person dies, you can come back with everybody cheering and screaming *Bravo*. And then start all over again and do things even better the next time.

One thing I'd like to do over was my walk-the-railing act. I wanted to get the cast off my arm, but I was afraid to go back to the City Hospital. My brother Tony said they cut the plaster cast off with a saw. Phyllis said they use scissors that look like hedge trimmers. The cast was hard as rock. I didn't see how they could use scissors. The cast was pretty loose and I wished I could just slip my arm out. But because of the bend at the elbow and wrist, there was no way to slip out. I was terrified to think of them using a saw. How could they tell how deep to cut?

Besides Pasta

When the day came to have my cast removed, my mother took me to the hospital emergency room. We waited a long time. when our turn finally came, they said we were in the wrong place and had to go to the bone clinic. At the bone clinic the nurse was real nice. She took off the sling.

"My, look at all the names on your cast. You must have a lot of friends. Who are the artists?"

"Mr. Bellini and my sister Frances. He draws pictures for the opera and Frances draws pictures from the funnies."

"It's a work of art! Almost a shame to take it off."

Mr. Bellini had drawn a picture of Juliet on the balcony. It took up practically half of the cast. It *was* pretty neat, but I didn't care, even if it was a picture of Joe DiMaggio. I couldn't stand having the cast on another minute. "Don't worry," I said. "Mr. Bellini can draw me another picture."

The nurse took me into a room and made my mother wait outside. She put my arm on the table on top of a towel. On a tray next to the towel was a small saw, scissors with a short cutting part and long handles and something that looked like pliers with flat pieces on the end.

"Now this is not going to hurt," the doctor said. "But you must sit still, so the saw doesn't slip." He yawned.

His blond hair was messed up and he looked sleepy. He picked up a pencil and drew a line from the top of the cast all the way to where my thumb poked out. Then he picked up the saw and began sawing on the line he had drawn. They took a long time to saw through the thick cast. The doctor was being careful, but I still jumped when the saw would go all the way through and scrape against my arm. Then he did the other side.

He picked up the pliers with the flat ends.

"I'm going to widen the cut I made in the cast."

He poked the flat ends in the crack and by pushing the handles the flat pieces moved apart, stretching the crack his saw had made. Then he picked up the scissors and cut the padding and cloth that was underneath the cast.

The nurse took off the top of the cast. The smell alone almost knocked me off the stool. She lifted out a skinny, pale, wrinkled arm that didn't look anything like my regular arm. Between the smell and the looks of it, I felt like I was going to throw up. The room started to spin and the next thing I remember is waking up with my mother standing there smiling at me. I looked at my arm. The color was more normal, and they must have washed it because it didn't smell.

They took a bunch of x-rays and the same sleepy doctor said the bones were knitting together just fine. He said for me not to feel bad about passing out, because that was from taking the cast off, and all the blood that should be going to my head rushing into my arm.

"Now, no more high-wire acts, you hear!" the doctor said. "I don't want to see you back here anytime soon."

Besides Pasta

Mama on the left with neighbor 1942

Chapter Eighteen

"Where's Ruppert Stadium?" I asked Phyllis.

We were making plans to see the Newark Bears play the Baltimore Orioles on Ladies' Night. Besides the Yankees, the Bears were my favorite baseball team. Everyone said that this team, the 1938 Bears, was the best ever. They even beat the Yankees in an exhibition game.

I was going to ask Marky, to bring his mitt, and his brother's mitt for me. Between the two of us we had a good chance of catching a foul ball.

Phyllis was drinking coffee at the kitchen table and reading a book. She already graduated from business high and was secretary for a minister who visited people in prisons. I didn't see why she still had to read so many books now that she graduated.

"Where's Ruppert Stadium?" I asked her again.

"It's Down-Neck." she said.

"That's a funny name for a place.

"I don't know how it got that name. It's mostly factories."

"Can we walk there?" I asked.

"It's too far. You have to take a bus to Penn Station and another bus from there to the ballpark."

I was drinking a glass of milk and chewing on a stale anisette biscuit. She started reading her book and turned a little bit away from me. I could tell she didn't want to talk anymore.

I started jumping around the kitchen throwing out my right arm, diving for the corners and reaching as high as I could.

"Do you mind, Peter?" she said without looking up. "I'm trying to read."

"I'm practicing catching foul balls."

"Uh...huh," she said. She still didn't look up.

After school Marky and I would meet in the park because we went to different schools. We'd play catch until it got dark. Sometimes we'd play in a pick-up game with kids who showed up. I'm lefty, so I couldn't play the infield except first base or pitch. But the other guys always had a first baseman and pitcher. I usually ended up in left field or ended up catching for both sides. Marky's favorite position was second base.

I went to see Marky to remind him about coming with us for Ladies' Night. Phyllis said we would be getting home late by the time we took two buses, so I had better ask Marky's mother if he could stay at our house. I was excited to see If his mother let him. That would be the first time he ever stayed at our house for a whole night.

I hadn't seen Marky since my cast came off. He'd be surprised how skinny my left arm got. I wondered if he might pass out like I did when

I first saw it. He shouldn't because my arm wasn't wrinkled and smelly anymore.

I was surprised Marky wasn't in the store when I got there. His parents were waiting on customers. Mrs. Stillman waved me toward the back. Paul was sitting at the table with a bunch of tools. He was working on a skate with wooden wheels.

"Hi, Peter. Have a seat," Paul said.

Paul didn't say anything at first. I was getting scared thinking that something bad happened. He looked really serious.

"Where's Marky?"

Paul laid down a pair of pliers he was holding. "He had to go to the hospital."

My stomach tightened up. I was afraid to ask what was the matter. "Did he have an accident?"

"It's his kidneys. He was having headaches. He started throwing up."

I couldn't see what your kidneys had to do with headaches and throwing up. I didn't know what to say. "I broke my wrist." I held out my arm.

"I was sorry to hear about that," Paul said.

"The doctor told my mother that the bones healed up good, but I hate my arm being so skinny and weak."

"Don't worry; the muscle will come back pretty soon."

"Yeah. That's what doctor said." I was thinking about what Paul said about Marky. I sometimes vomit when I'm sick, but that's not a reason to be put in the hospital.

Besides Pasta

"Marky has infected tonsils," Paul said. "The doctor said he has to have an operation to remove them so he doesn't keep getting sore throats. He said Marky's kidneys couldn't stand any more damage."

"A lot of kids at school had their tonsils out," I said. "One kid said he ate nothing but ice cream for a whole week after the operation." I did notice that Marky got tired twice as fast as me when we played catch. And he never wanted to race anymore.

"The bigger you get, the harder your kidneys have to work," Paul said. "Marky grew quite a bit this past year."

"Yeah, we're almost the same age and he's way taller than me. How long will he be in the hospital?"

"About a week."

Paul explained that foods like meat and fish are hard on the kidneys. I kept nodding my head because Marky once told me all about that. Paul said they were going to give Marky a special diet to keep the bad stuff from building up in his blood. Paul used bigger words, but I think that's about what he meant.

"I guess all that staying in bed didn't help."

"It helped some, but the problem is that his kidneys keep getting worse. At the hospital they don't even let him up to go to the bathroom."

Mrs. Stillman came in the kitchen and sat at the table. She took off her glasses and rubbed her eyes. She looked tired and like she might cry any minute. Paul told his mother that he was explaining about Marky being in the hospital.

"How do you like the new house, Peter?" she asked.

"It's okay. Phyllis is taking me to see the Bears next Friday. Did Marky ask you if he could come?"

"He did," she said. "He's very disappointed he won't be able to go. We brought him a radio so he can listen to the game. He said you could borrow his fielder's mitt." She smiled. "He said that if you catch more than one foul ball you have to give him one."

"Tell him the first one I catch will be for him. And tell him Phyllis said if I catch a ball, she's going to get Buddy Rosar, Babe Dahlgren, and maybe even Snuffy Sternweiss to sign it. Rosar and Dahlgren are both batting over 300, and Sternweiss steals second practically every time he gets on base."

She smiled, but her eyes were full of tears. What did Paul mean when he said Marky's kidneys couldn't take any more damage? I couldn't stand thinking about Marky being so sick. There had to be something the doctors could do. Paul's words kept going through my head. His kidneys can't take any more damage. I started to cry. Mrs. Stillman put her hand on mine. Then she pulled her chair closer and pressed my head against her chest.

"Pray for him, Peter. God is tired of listening to this old lady."

My head was filled up with all the things Marky ever said about dying.

"Here's a girl who was only five when she died," Marky said. "She was born in 1913 and died in 1918."

I was wearing two sweaters, knickers and heavy socks that came up to my knees but I still felt cold. "I guess thirteen wasn't her lucky number," I said. "I wonder what she died from."

"There was a flu epidemic in 1918," Marky said. "My father said millions of people died from it."

"I can't picture myself grown up," Marky said.

191

"Me neither. I mean, I can't picture me being a grown-up. I can picture you. You're already almost as tall as Paul. And your ears are as big as his already."

"I heard my mother and father talking," he said. "They thought I was asleep. They were whispering, but I could still hear them. My mother was crying. She said the doctor could be wrong and that she wanted to take me to someone else...."

"Wrong about what?" I asked.

"I don't know...."

"But why was she crying?"

"There's a baby buried here," Marky said. "He wasn't even a year old." He looked up. There were tears in his eyes. "I don't know why my mother was crying. Could have been about anything. I think we'd better go. It'll get dark pretty soon. I don't want to be here in the dark."

A shiver ran through my whole body, thinking about either one of us being buried in the ground, and the date we died carved on a stone. We were both born in 1928. It's just the date on the right side we didn't know about.

I told Mrs. Stillman I would pray for Marky and would ask the Sisters to pray for him too. After leaving Stillman's', instead of going straight home I went to the Convent on Eighth Street. The Sisters who teach at Saint Antonitus School lived there. I knocked on the door and asked the lady who answered, if Sister Patricia was there. Pretty soon she came to the door. She acted surprised to see me.

"How nice of you to visit, Peter."

"My friend Mark Stillman is in the hospital. His brother Paul told me there was something wrong with his kidneys. I asked Sister if she could pray for him."

"Of course, I will. I know who Mark is. I've seen him in the delicatessen on Saturdays."

I didn't think she would know him. It seemed like a good thing for her to have a picture in her head of who she was praying for. Before I left, we talked about my family moving and me having to go to the public school for the fourth grade. She asked me if I was still going to daily Mass. I told her yes and that we lived right next door to Saint Rocco's Church.

On the long walk home, I was starting to feel a little better, knowing that I got a holy person to pray for Marky. I decided not to talk about it with my mother or brother or sisters. I'm not sure exactly why. I just didn't want to. With me, Sister Patricia and Mrs. Stillman all praying, that should be enough. That's one of us for each person in the Blessed Trinity. I didn't want to pester God by having a million people praying all at once.

Phyllis and I got to Ruppert Stadium about a half-hour before the game was to start. It was a chilly night in early September, and the baseball season was just about over. I was wearing my navy-blue, Yankee baseball cap, a long-sleeved flannel shirt, knickers and stockings that came to my knees. It was kind of like a baseball uniform, except it wasn't the right colors.

It wasn't dark yet, but I could see from the outside that the lights were already turned on. When Phyllis and I got inside, we walked through a long dark tunnel. I could hear people shouting and could see the light at the end. We went up some steps and came out in the bleacher section near third base. The Bears' dugout was on the opposite side of the field and I could see a bunch of white uniforms in the dugout but couldn't make out who was who.

Men were dragging gigantic rakes around the infield and other men were laying out the chalk lines and cleaning off home plate. The grass was perfect, the greenest I ever saw. Around the walls there were billboards. There was one for Ballantine Beer. I took notice of it because Ballantine was the main sponsor of the Newark Bears' radio show.

Phyllis pointed to it. "They make that beer right here in Newark. The factory's near the ballpark."

Guys were going around selling roasted peanuts, ice cream, hot dogs, soda, and Ballantine Beer. The smell of the hot dogs and peanuts made my mouth water but I didn't want to ask Phyllis to buy me anything because she already paid for my ticket. The beer looked good the way it foamed up and ran over the edge of the cup.

"Can I have a beer?" I asked Phyllis. I was only kidding. I tasted it once when somebody left a little bit in a glass. It looks a lot better than it tastes. Anyway, I didn't want to get drunk and take a chance missing a foul ball. I sat there pounding my glove with my fist. The pocket was deep and soft. The smell of it reminded me of Marky. He would always oil it to keep the leather soft. I could picture Marky pounding a baseball in the pocket. The scared feeling I had when Mrs. Stillman held me and we were both crying, all of a sudden came back.

"What's the matter, Peter?" Phyllis asked.

Peter Rizzolo

"I was just wishing Marky could be here." I never told Phyllis or anyone at home about how sick he was. I kept thinking maybe it's all in my head and if I talk about it, something bad would happen.

Pretty soon the players came out and stood in front of their dugouts. They took off their caps and held them over their hearts. Everybody stood and sang the "Star Spangled Banner." The umpire shouted, "Play ball." The Bears took the field.

A bald-headed man with a big belly and beer foam on his top lip poked me in the ribs, "Hey kid, you want to go out there and play shortstop, Nolan looks a little tired to me."

"I'm left handed," I told him. "A lefty can't play shortstop. I like to pitch or play first base or centerfield."

He looked at my mitt. "That ain't no south-paw mitt."

"It's not mime…it's my friend Marky's. He's having his tonsils cut out and he let me use it."

"What are you gonna do with his tonsils?" the man asked. Then he poked me in the side and began to laugh.

I didn't get it at first. "I was talking about his mitt, not his tonsils. If I catch a foul ball, I'm going to have some of the ballplayers sign it and give it to Marky for a present."

"That's Marius Russo on the mound, kid. Now that guy has some kind of arm. His knuckler's a thing of beauty."

Pretty soon he and Phyllis were talking about who was the best base runner and who made the most errors. The man looked at my sister like he was surprised how much she knew about the players. The two of them never stopped talking. It was like having two radio announcers right there. But it was better than listening on the radio.

195

Besides Pasta

The man lit a fat cigar. I could see from the paper ring that it was a Philly. It smelled a lot better than Mr. Bellini's stogies.

In the second inning, Charlie, *King Kong* Keller, the Bears center fielder, hit a home run that smashed into the scoreboard in center field. By the top of the ninth inning the Bears were ahead; one nothing. By now it was really dark and there must have been a lot of clouds because you couldn't see the moon or stars. The darkness made the ballpark lights seem a lot brighter. Just three more outs and the Bears would win the game. When I shut my eyes, I could still see the field and the players clear as anything.

A bunch of foul balls were hit into the bleachers on our side, but none were close enough for me to catch. But I didn't care, because Russo had a three-hitter going. When he struck out all three Baltimore players in a row in the top of the ninth inning, everybody stood, shouted, and clapped as loud as they could. Nobody said "bravo" like they did at the opera, but they were just as excited.

Grown-ups and kids jumped on the field and chased after the players, as they ran toward the dugout. I guess they wanted to get the players' autographs.

Kids were running around the bases. I asked Phyllis if I could. She said okay. I gave her Marky's glove, hung from the wall and dropped to the field. I raced to home plate and stood in the batter's box waiting for the pitch. The pitcher was taking his time, so I stepped out and kicked dirt from my spikes. I stepped back in and held my bat high like Charlie Keller did when he hit the home run. The pitcher threw in a fast ball right on the letters. I smacked a line drive down the right field line and raced to first base. The right fielder bobbled the ball. I rounded first and headed for second base. The throw went wild. I didn't hesitate. I headed for third. By the time the third baseman got the ball, I was rounding third and heading home. I dove head first into the plate and reached around the catcher to avoid the tag. I stood on home plate, brushed dirt from my knickers, and then tipped my cap to my sister and the fat guy.

"What if I didn't catch a foul ball on my first trip to a professional baseball game? I couldn't wait to tell Marky that I ran the bases and scored a run on a double, an error by the right fielder, and some great base running. He'd probably smile and tell me that if he was playing right field, he wouldn't have bobbled the ball and he would have thrown me out at second base.

I'd say, "But I wouldn't try for second if you didn't make an error."

"So, all you would have gotten was a single."

"I would have stolen second on the next pitch."

"Not if I was pitching."

"You can't play right field and pitch at the same time."

Marky laughed. With me making jokes….and the blessed trinity working on his kidneys, pretty soon he'll be able to leave the hospital and we can play catch like we always did.

Besides Pasta

Mama's Potato and Egg Sandwich Recipe

Sometimes I took a potato and egg sandwich to school for lunch. It was better if you ate it right after Mama cooked it, but it was still good cold on buttered Italian bread cut lengthwise so you got more of the crust. She sometimes added sliced tomatoes. Never ketchup!

First, she peeled and cut one or two potatoes into tiny cubes. Then she fried the potatoes in olive oil until tender and a little crispy. She poured off most of the oil leaving the potatoes in the pan.

Then she added a little milk, salt, pepper, a pinch of dried oregano, and some parmesan cheese to the eggs before she scrambled them with a hand-cranked eggbeater. She poured the eggs into the frying pan, mixing the potatoes and eggs together with a wooden spoon as she fried them.

Her secret was not to overcook the eggs. That way they always turned out fluffy and delicious. Besides eggplant sandwiches, Mama's egg and potato sandwich was my next favorite lunch.

Chapter Nineteen

Fourth Grade at the Public School

From Hunterdon Street, I would have to cross quite a few streets to get to Saint Antonitus School. Mama was worried about all the traffic and there not being monitors at each street corner. That's why she decided to send me to the public school on Fourteenth Avenue. I only had to cross two streets to get there.

I had a different teacher for practically every subject, not just one teacher like at the Catholic school. None of the teachers knew me. And the worst part was that neither did any of the kids in my class. I don't know why the teachers had such a hard time with my last name. None of them said it right.

It seemed as though no one was in charge in the classroom. Kids got up and walked around whenever they felt like it. They all talked at once without even raising their hands. Kids left the room to go to the bathroom without asking permission. I was quiet and sat with my hands together on my desk. Pretty soon kids started calling me Saint Peter. Some kids called me "Pizza Rizz" because I had two Z's in my last name. Sometimes I felt like going to the blackboard and erasing everything and writing out in big letters, "Peter Rizzolo is my name. You can call me Pete or Peter…I don't care which."

Once I raised my hand and asked if I could be excused.

"What for Rizz?" a kid shouted. "You having dirty thoughts about Rosie?"

Rosie sat in the seat next to me. I heard she had stayed back once or twice. Her breasts were already bigger than the teacher's.

"Yes, you may be excused," the teacher said. Then she said to the kid who shouted, "Jerome, you could use some of Peter's good manners. And I think you owe Rosie an apology."

"No, he don't," Rosie said. "Peter's always looking at me." She sat up straight and shook her shoulders. She raised her eyebrows up and down and rolled her eyes. Everybody started laughing and talking at the same time. If I were a keg of ice, I would have melted in three seconds. My face was on fire.

When we went to recess, everyone pushed and shoved. After a while I stayed in my seat and just got on the end of the line. I especially hated gym class. We didn't have gym in the Catholic school, and even though I liked the idea of gym class, it wasn't any fun. The teacher would say, "Now we're going to have a freestyle period. Pick an event and play by the rules." Everyone would run and grab balls or ropes or whatever and start right in choosing sides. I never knew what they were doing or what the rules were. The gym teacher sat on a bench reading a book and didn't care that I didn't know what was going on.

I wasn't good at basketball. In fact, I never once even held a basketball before fourth grade gym class. They laughed when I dribbled or shot baskets. Pretty soon I gave up trying and sat on the bench watching. The teacher didn't care if I played or not; after a while he gave me the job to keep score.

They didn't know that I wasn't supposed to take gym because of my heart murmur, and I didn't tell them. When the weather was nice, we played tag football in a field next to the school. You weren't supposed to tackle because no one wore helmets or pads. But still, in just about every play I got knocked down and run over by somebody. I was always going home with bruises and torn clothes. My mother was upset, especially one day when I came home with blood all over my shirt from a bloody nose. My nose was swollen and it hurt when I pushed on it.

"*Mama mia*!" Mama screamed when she caught me trying to sneak past her as I headed for the bathroom. "Come here, Peter. Did you get into a fight again?"

"No, Mama. I got hurt playing football in gym class."

She went to the icebox, opened the top compartment and chipped off a piece of ice. She wrapped it in a hand towel and banged it on the stove to break the chunk of ice into smaller pieces.

She couldn't believe the teacher would let me get so beat up in a gym class. While Mama got the ice pack ready, Helen grabbed a face cloth and cleaned the dry blood from my face and neck. It hurt really bad when she tried to clean blood from my nose.

"Mama," Helen said, "you should go to school and talk with his teacher. This isn't the first time he's gotten hurt in gym class."

201

Besides Pasta

Mama had high cheekbones and when she had a mad look, she reminded me of the face on Indian pennies. I didn't know if she was mad at me for letting the kids at school always beat me up, or if she was mad at the school for letting it happen.

"It's okay, Mama," I said. "I won't let it happen again." In a way I wanted her to go, but I knew the kids would think I was a sissy if she did. I think maybe she understood that without me having to tell her, because she never did complain to the teacher.

Fourth grade math was easy. It was the same as I had in third grade at Saint Antonitus. I could usually get the right answer in my head quicker than the kids could on paper. The teacher said I had to write how I came to the right answer, otherwise she didn't know if I was just guessing. That was stupid, because even if a person was a great guesser, you couldn't guess right every time.

"Yeah!" Jerome said. "Saint Peter's just guessing. Can't even write it down."

"I know he can write," Rosie said. "He sends me notes all the time."

Besides me, Rosie got teased the most of all the kids in our class. I knew she was just trying to make the other kids like her by joining in with them. She was lying about the notes, but I didn't say anything. They wouldn't believe me anyway.

I was getting to be a better reader, but when I had to stand up and read in front of the class, I would see a word and my mind was like a blackboard with nothing written on it. One day I was called on to read and came to the word, *next* and I couldn't say it.

"Sound it out, Peter," the teacher said.

"Yeah, sound it out, Pizza," Jerome shouted.

Everyone started making a joke out of it.

"Pizza doesn't know what comes *next.*"

"You'd better call on the *next* person, teach."

"Maybe *next* time he's in fourth grade he'll do better."

I sat down and the teacher called on someone else to finish the reading. I knew the word was *next* and I don't know why I couldn't say it.

The only good thing about getting my nose broken playing touch football was that Mama decided to send me back to the Catholic school for the fifth grade, even though it was pretty far and I had to cross a bunch of busy streets. I couldn't wait to be back with my old school friends, especially Tommy Walker and Mike Patterson. Mike was really Tommy's friend but I liked him pretty much too.

Even though I hated the public school, it wasn't such a bad year. I was beginning to make some neighborhood friends, and I still had my favorite radio shows, especially *Jack Armstrong*, the *Charlie McCarthy Show*, and *Gangbusters*. Another favorite show was *The Shadow*. Lamont Cranston was the Shadow. He could make himself invisible.

Since Marky left the hospital, he had to take two kinds of medicine and had to be more careful what he ate. About one or two Sundays a month, I went up to see Marky or he came down to see me. One time he came on Saint Rocco's feast day. Fourteenth Avenue was closed off for about four blocks. There were stands along the sidewalks that sold hot dogs with "the works," sausage and peppers, roasted sweet potatoes, French fries, Italian ice and gelato, pizza, zeppoles, and sandwiches. There were a million kinds of cookies and Italian pastries.

Besides Pasta

To drink, there was soda, root beer, lemonade; and for the grownups, coffee, beer, and wine.

It was like a carnival with gambling games. You could win toys and stuffed animals. The only ride was a truck with a small merry-go-round in the back. There was a statue of Saint Rocco that had money stuck on it with pins. A bunch of kids were always standing around the statue, hoping the wind would blow off some money. But it never did, not when I was around. I had a dime saved up for the feast. My stomach was complaining about not having any sausage and peppers. But I didn't want to spend a whole dime on one thing.

"Why do they pin money on the statue?" Marky asked.

"It's to pay Saint Rocco to help keep people from getting a bad disease. That's Saint Rocco's job in heaven."

"What does he need money for in heaven?"

"The money goes to the church that's named after him. They need it to buy candles and to feed the priests. The pastor must eat a lot because he's pretty fat."

Marky knew I was just kidding around. When I told him about the Catholic religion, he would ask questions I never thought of. It would make me ask myself questions I couldn't answer. Later I'd ask my brother or older sisters.

"I learned about Saint Rocco in third grade," I said. "He lived in Rome a long time ago. He helped people who were dying from some kind of disease that made them turn black all over."

"The Bubonic Plague," Marky said. "I read about that. It was more than five-hundred years ago."

"You weren't even alive five-hundred years ago. How could you read about it way back then?"

He didn't get it at first, but then he laughed.

"Yeah, that's it," I said. "The Bubonic Plague. I think they got it from rats." I was hungry and didn't want to talk about rats and people who were turning black and dying. "You bring any money?"

"Thirty cents. I was paid yesterday," he said.

"I've got a dime."

"My mother said for me to be careful what I eat."

Marky ended up getting a root beer and a roasted sweet potato. I got lemonade and a hot dog with the works. I felt guilty eating it in front of him and would have given him a taste, but I didn't want to wreck his kidneys.

"The doctor said my tonsils were full of infection, and that it was a good thing he took them out when they did."

"Did it hurt?" I asked.

"They gave me ether, so I was knocked out by the time they operated. But it was really sore for about a week after the operation. The only thing I could eat was ice pops and ice cream."

"I thought you weren't supposed to eat ice cream."

"I'm not. I heard my mother and father arguing about it. My father said all that diet crap hasn't changed a damn thing. My mother started to cry. I was sorry I asked for ice cream."

We were sitting on a curb eating. We could hear organ music from the tiny merry-go-round truck. I was waiting for Marky to finish his sweet potato to ask him if I could look where they took out his tonsils. I had a good idea where they used to be because I had looked at my own tonsils in the mirror. Mine were as big as Jawbreakers and almost as red.

Besides Pasta

"You ever think about dying?" Marky asked. He folded the skin of his sweet potato and dropped it in the gutter.

"I do when I go to bed. The nuns taught me to say the bedtime prayer about if I die before I awake, I pray the Lord my soul to take."

"You really believe in God and heaven and living forever?"

"Don't you?" I asked.

"I want to. But a lot of people believe that when you die, you're gone. Just like when a tree or animal dies."

"They don't have a soul." I took the last bite of my hot dog

"In a way just disappearing is less scary than facing a God who's always mad about something."

"How do you know he's mad?"

"I don't know about Jesus, but Jehovah was always sending plagues and floods. He smote people he didn't like."

"He smoked them?"

Marky laughed. "Smote...it means to strike them dead."

I knew what smote meant, but I wanted to make him laugh. He must be tired of being sick, and peeing in a bottle for the doctor, and having his feet swell up every night. I looked at his ankles. They were swollen and hung over the edges of his sneakers. I wanted to tell him I was sorry he had to always be sick and thinking about dying. I never really thought about being dead. The only dead people I ever saw were in the movies. It wasn't fair if he should die before he got a chance to grow up and be what he wanted to be.

"I better get going. My mother said I had to be home before dark."

I didn't want him to go. "Can you come to the house first? I want to show you a card trick I learned."

"I better not. It's a long walk." I watched him make his way through the crowd. I wanted to run after him and tell him I was sorry he had to be sick and that every day I was praying for a miracle to happen. But I just stood there. I got goose bumps as I saw him get smaller and smaller until finally, I couldn't see him anymore.

Chapter Twenty

Fall and Christmas of 1938

Besides going back to Saint Antonitus for fifth grade, two other things I couldn't wait for were my birthday and Christmas. I really loved the idea of being ten years old. I can't really explain why. You're not a baby and you're not a grown-up; you're right in the middle. And you have a long time to figure out what to do by the time you're ready to have a regular job. I didn't like grown-ups always asking me what I wanted to be.

I liked the young priest, Father Ambrose, who lived next door to us. He was the assistant pastor of Saint Rocco's Church. But he was just a regular person when he wasn't in church preaching and celebrating Mass. Once, he took my brother Tony and Tony Baiocchi with him to hit golf balls at the driving range. Tony said Father Ambrose could hit the ball a mile.

Father Ambrose sometimes came to our house for dinner. Once he brought my mother a bottle of red wine. His favorite was mama's pasta fagioli, but this time she made minestrone soup, ravioli, and meatballs.

Peter Rizzolo

Father sat at the head of the table and said grace. I guessed he was about the same age as my mother. I wished he could be my father. If he were my father, and the kids at school once saw him, they would think twice about giving me bloody noses. But I knew he couldn't be a priest and my father at the same time. There was no use thinking about it.

He was a big baseball fan, and pretty soon the conversation at the dinner table turned to baseball.

"This spring I'm going to organize a parish baseball team. Seventh and eighth graders. I want to compete against some of the other teams in the area."

"I'm going to Saint Antonitus next year," I said. "Will Saint Rocco's be playing them?"

"I'm working that out with their manager. You can come out to our practices, Peter. Would you like that?"

I looked around the table. Everyone was busy eating and talking to one another. I didn't know what to say. I was only going into the fifth grade. Those seventh and eighth graders were a lot bigger than me.

"Hey, Peter, go for it," Phyllis said.

"I don't have a fielder's mitt or spikes."

"That's okay. Most of the kids don't have equipment," Father said. "At the church bazaar this spring I'm going to have a raffle to buy equipment for the team. If you help sell chances, I'll see to it that you get a mitt."

"What's the prize?" Tony asked.

"I haven't figured that out yet," Father said.

Besides Pasta

Mama noticed Father's plate was almost empty. She passed the platter of ravioli and meatballs to him. It would have been his third helping…and the first two were pretty big.

"No thanks, Mother, it's great, but I can't fit in another bite."

My mother frowned. "*Mange, figlio di mamma*, I don't want you to die from Consumption."

Father laughed. "It's more likely I'll die from over-consumption if I have another helping."

Everybody laughed. I could tell that my mother didn't get the joke.

"Next time you come to dinner, Father," Tony said, "Mama will make her famous pasta fagioli. You will die of over-consumption for sure."

I decided to fit Father's joke into one of my Charlie McCarthy routines. But I wasn't sure anyone outside of my family would get it.

I got the idea to go to daily Mass when Sister Teresa said I should go for two weeks after I had the fight with David Plunkett. I figured that if I did at least twenty-six bad things a year, there was no getting away from going to seven o'clock Mass every day. After a while, waking up early got to be a habit, and I would lie in bed and think about all the times I didn't share, or didn't turn the other cheek, or disobeyed my mother, or dreamed of being a foot taller and punching out kids who were mean to me. There was nothing else to do but get up and go to Mass.

Once I got to church, I was always glad I went. There were mostly old ladies dressed in black, saying their rosaries and lighting candles. I still used my First Holy Communion missal that had the Latin on the left side and the English on the right. The priest said the Mass in Latin while I read the English part. The Mass only took a half-hour because there wasn't a lot of singing, and the priest didn't give a sermon except on Sundays and holy days.

One day as I left the church, Father Ambrose was standing on the front steps. It was a chilly day in late October. His hair was messed up and his black cassock was slapping in the wind like the sail of a boat. I started down the steps. As I passed, he put his hand on my shoulder. I stopped and looked up. He reminded me of a giant tree with a bird's nest on top.

"You ever think about being a priest, Peter?" Father asked. He sat on the step just above me. Our heads were on the same level, even though he was sitting and I was standing.

"The nuns at St. Antonitus were always asking me the same thing. I don't know. I'm not a good singer. My sisters say I sing off-key."

He chuckled. "Most priests can't sing very well. We mostly fake it."

"It's between that and playing centerfield for the Yankees."

He laughed. "Tough choice."

It seemed as though Father Ambrose liked being a priest. He was always laughing and joking. My sisters said he was so handsome. When Chickey said "so handsome," it sounded like it was spelled "soo-oh handsome."

When you think of it, being a priest is a pretty good job. You don't have to worry about the Depression or being out of work, because somebody has to say Mass, hear confessions, and do all the stuff they have to do when someone dies.

"When is the church bazaar?" I asked.

"Sometime in March. You still interested in selling raffle tickets?"

Besides Pasta

I nodded. I remembered what he said about getting me a mitt if I helped.

"Anyone selling at least ten books of raffle tickets will get a prize. Yours will be a lefty fielder's mitt---unless you want something else?"

"I can't think of a better prize than a mitt. What's the big prize for winning the raffle?"

"Two tickets to the World's Fair. All expenses paid. Food, hotel, travel...everything."

With a prize like that I was sure I could sell ten books of tickets. Everybody was talking about the World's Fair, even though it wasn't until next year. There were posters everywhere. In the Pathe news they told about all the things they were going to have, like showing pictures over the radio. They called it television. They said pretty soon people could buy television sets. Tony said they would cost a lot of money. That we would have to save up a long time to buy one.

I was already thinking of all the neighborhood stores I could get to buy tickets. Geraldine could take a book to work. Marky could help me sell tickets in his neighborhood or ask his father to put a sign in the delicatessen saying what the prize was and how they could buy a chance to win the grand prize. But it was only November and March was a long way off. There was plenty of time to think about it.

Somehow Mama got hold of an old Smith Corona typewriter for my sister Geraldine. I loved to watch Geraldine practice her typing. Her hands were a blur as they flew over the keys. I liked the crisp sound the metal made as it hit the paper. Like tiny firecrackers shooting off across the page.

A bell sounded as the carriage reached the end of the line and in a flash, she would snap the carriage back to start a new line of typing. It looked like magic the way the roller moved up one space so she wouldn't be typing over the line she already finished. But shorthand was even more like magic.

To practice her shorthand, she would listen to the radio and take down what they were saying by drawing funny squiggly lines that made no sense to me. But afterwards she would read back exactly what the person on the radio had said. I wasn't surprised when Mueller Brass hired her as a secretary at $12.00 a week.

We didn't make a big fuss over birthdays in my family. My mother would bake a cake or make zeppoles, and we would all sing "Happy Birthday." But if I didn't remind someone it was my birthday, some of the time it would be forgotten until a few days later.

A week after my tenth birthday, as we sat around the dinner table Phyllis looked up from a book she had propped on her lap." Mama, we forgot Peter's birthday." My mother looked at me with a sad smile. She explained that when she was growing up in Italy, they only celebrated the Saint's birthdays. I heard that excuse before. I thought that she didn't remember birthdays on purpose. There were too many kids to buy presents for and what was she supposed to do for money?

The teacher at school knew when I had a birthday because she kept a calendar on the wall. We had to write our name on the day we were born. I hated it when my teacher would tell the class to wish me a happy birthday. One reason was that I was a year older than the rest of the kids, and the other was that I had to lie when they asked me what I got for a present.

Besides Pasta

"Well, Mama, Peter goes to Mass every day. Besides, he says maybe he wants to be a priest. We all know he's not a saint, but daily Mass should count for something."

Everybody laughed including me, and my ears grew warm and red as they did when I had everyone's attention. I said with a serious expression, "I think I smell zeppoles, Mama."

Frances clapped her hands and shook her head in agreement. She gave me a big-eyed wink.

My mother laughed, came over and kissed me on the cheek and then got a large black frying pan from under the sink. She placed it on our gas stove. As she poured oil into the pan, I got flour, sugar, and a sifter from the pantry. I loved to watch my mother mix the sugar and baking powder and flour together. She never used a measuring cup for anything, but somehow everything she made turned out really good.

She dropped globs of the dough in the hot oil, and soon they puffed into odd shapes. They turned from white to gold. When she decided they were fried long enough, she lifted them with a slotted spoon, and placed them on a platter. I dusted them with powdered sugar. Soon the plate was piled high with zeppoles. The pile shrank fast as my brother and sisters crowded around for a taste, which came to three or four zeppoles each.

My sister Geraldine put her arm around my shoulder and said, "I'm sorry we forgot your birthday, Peter."

Everyone said my sisters were pretty, but that Geraldine was the prettiest. Her skin was clear and light like my mother's, her nose straight, and her eyes and hair the color of the chestnuts I liked to gather as I walked to school. She looked more like my mother than any of the children. That made her special, too.

Peter Rizzolo

"Christmas is just four weeks from now, and I want to get you something nice."

I knew exactly what I wanted but was afraid to ask because I knew it cost a lot.

"I want to be a ventriloquist, like Edgar Bergen," I said. "I need a Charlie McCarthy to practice my routines."

"I'm going shopping at Bamberger's this Saturday. Do you want to come with me?" Geraldine asked.

We took the number twenty-nine bus on South Orange Avenue. We got off on Market Street right in front of Bamberger's. Once in the store, we took an escalator to the fifth floor. I discovered that if I twisted the rubber handrail that moved along with the steps, I could get the handrail to stop, but not the steps. I did it when Geraldine was looking at a Christmas list she had taken from her purse.

A fat lady ahead of us screamed and fell backwards into a man just in front of us. We were lucky she was only halfway to the top, because it took two people to lift her. It they hadn't, her dress would have gotten sucked into the escalator when she reached the top. I guess nobody noticed that I had caused the handrail to stop for a couple of seconds. Geraldine gave me a funny look when I told her it was my fault the lady fell over. I don't think she believed me. It's funny, when someone doesn't like you, they can't believe you can do anything right. But when someone does like you, they can't believe you can do anything wrong.

The store was crowded with shoppers. The vacuum tubes they used to send messages from one department to another made a loud sound. It was like saying the word "soup" while at the same time you sucked

215

in your breath. When it reached its destination, a bell dinged at the counter where the salespeople waited on customers.

The store was filled with the smell of pine trees, perfume, and new things. We walked to a counter in the toy department. Geraldine asked a salesman if they had any Charlie McCarthy dummies. He took us to a glass counter where there were four or five dummies, different sizes, and each dressed in different clothes.

He pulled out a medium sized Charlie, one wearing a white felt cap, a blue blazer jacket with tiny gold buttons, and a red silk handkerchief in the left breast pocket. He wore a white shirt with glass buttons that Geraldine called *mother of pearl*. He wore a red bow tie and a white flannel cap. His sharply creased flannel pants rested on black patent leather shoes. His face looked exactly like the real Charlie McCarthy; with eyes made of glass that were almost scary they looked so real. The fixed wide-eyed expression was somewhere between a smile and a kind of smart-alecky look.

"This is our most exquisite model, and of course our most expensive." He looked at me and then raised his eyebrows like stuck-up people do sometimes. "We also have a nice Charlie in our basement toy department."

Geraldine looked at me and winked. She asked the man if I could try moving the dummy's mouth. He acted as though he didn't want to, but then reached into the glass case and removed Charlie. He handed it to me. I looked behind the head. There was a lever that controlled the eyes and a string with a ring on it to control the mouth. The salesman said you're supposed to rest the middle finger against the lever and place the index finger in the ring. I wasn't sure what he meant and Geraldine showed me how.

I rested the dummy on my arm and placed my other hand on the controls. Mustering my best Charlie imitation, I said, "Here's looking at you, babe." I rolled Charlie's eyes in a full circle. Geraldine laughed and I noticed even the stuffy salesperson smiled.

He took Charlie from me and placed him carefully back in the case. He handed Geraldine a small card with his name printed on it. "If you decide to buy one, please ask for me."

We went on to look at other things, and my sister never again mentioned Charlie McCarthy. My original excitement over Charlie began to fade because I figured he was too expensive, and I wasn't the only one Geraldine had to buy presents for. As we wandered through the toy department, I saw a million other things I wished I had. The ball bearing roller skates, whose wheels seemed like they would never stop spinning once I gave them a snap. Not like the learner skates my friends would let me borrow.

The smell and feel of real leather baseball mitts was almost too much to bear. And the rows of wooden baseball bats stamped with black lettering that said "Louisville Slugger," reminded me of the time I went to see the Newark Bears play at Ruppert Stadium with Phyllis and saw all the players' bats lined up in front of the dugouts.

When we got home, I had a real bad headache. I told my mother because I knew what she would do. She asked me where it hurt, and then she lifted me onto her lap. She rubbed the spot with her thumb as she quietly said prayers in Italian. I didn't understand what she was saying, but I knew that after a few minutes I would fall asleep and the headache would be gone when I woke up.

Besides Pasta

Geraldine didn't realize it, but I did notice the price of Charlie. It cost $8.99, almost a whole week's salary. She kept two dollars a week out of her check and gave my mother the rest. Out of that, she paid the bus fare to work and bought other stuff. It would take her a long time to save that much money. She did say she wanted to get me something special, but I knew I shouldn't count on getting Charlie.

My three oldest sisters, Helen, Geraldine, and Phyllis, shared a bedroom. It was only one week before Christmas and I couldn't stand it anymore. One afternoon, when none of them were at home, I sneaked in their room. I looked in the top three dresser drawers but didn't see a box big enough to hold Charlie. I pulled open the bottom drawer. Some clothes were spread over a cardboard box that was just about the right size. My heart was beating so loudly I doubt if I would have heard anyone come in the room. I removed the lid and there was something wrapped in tissue paper. Just then my sister Helen shouted at me, "Peter, what are you doing?"

Helen said it was the worst thing to do, to spoil someone's Christmas surprise, and she would tell Geraldine, so she could bring back whatever it was she got for me.

"Don't tell her, please! I swear...I didn't see anything."

My please didn't do a bit of good. That night, practically as soon as Geraldine got in the door, Helen told her. "I caught Peter snooping in the bottom dresser drawer this afternoon. He says he didn't see anything...but he had that box open when I caught him."

"I know I shouldn't have looked, but she came in before I saw what was in the box. Honest to God, I don't know what's in the box."

Without saying a word Geraldine took off her coat and hung it in the hall closet. "I wish you had seen what was in the box, because I don't want you to get your hopes up. There's no way I could afford to get you that Charlie."

I was sitting at the kitchen table doing a geography assignment. I couldn't make myself look up at Geraldine. Tears dripped onto my homework. She came over and kissed my cheek and said that when she was little, she probably would have done the same thing. She lifted my chin so I had to look into her face. She smiled. "It's okay."

She gave me a hug and then began to talk about work. I liked to hear all about what happened at work because by now I knew a lot about her boss and the other workers. She said that last year everybody got a $5.00 bonus for Christmas and that this year they might get even more because they got a big government contract to make brass fittings for the Navy.

Geraldine always wanted to start a family business. Her latest idea was to buy a used bus and hire it out to take people to Florida. The way she figured it, we could charge a lot less than Greyhound, and still make enough money to pay off the bus. Then pretty soon we could buy a second bus.

"I think it would be better to have a store like the Stillmans'," I said. "It wouldn't be a Jewish delicatessen because Mama doesn't know how to make *gefilte* fish or pickled herring and other stuff the Stillmans sell."

"Yeah," Tony said, "Mama can make ravioli, zeppoles, lasagna, and a million other kinds of macaroni. We could have balls of provolone and pepperoni hanging from the ceiling. The store would smell of Romano cheese, Italian spices, and fresh ground coffee."

219

Besides Pasta

"It takes a lot of money to rent and stock a store," Geraldine said. "The bus idea is more doable. Then after we save enough money, we could also have a grocery store."

"How about a bookstore?" Phyllis said. "I could see myself working in a bookstore."

My mother just shook her head. "Such big dreams."

But Mama had that look in her eyes that said she was proud of us. That she believed we could do it.

Every Christmas my mother would threaten not to buy a Christmas tree because they were too expensive. And every year, late Christmas Eve, she would go out with Helen and Geraldine to find a place where they had left-over trees. She would offer them ten cents for the tree. They would laugh and say the cheapest tree costs $1.50 and that they would sell all their trees before midnight. Usually by nine or ten Mama would come home with a nice tree. As we put the tree up and decorated it, we heard all about how Mama had haggled the price down to five cents. Helen would reenact the scene in Italian, with English on the side for us younger kids. My mother would start out very dignified but as the evening wore-on, and the price would not come down, she told the man selling the trees that her other five children were sitting at home in a cold flat with last year's tinsel in their hands, ready to put on the tree that would never come. She could see the man was becoming impatient. He finally gave up and told my mother to pick out one and to give him whatever she thought it was worth.

By the time Mama got home with the tree we had already cleared a place in the living room. Tony had spread a white cloth and had set a big metal scrub basin in the middle. They lifted the tree into the basin, then Tony filled it with coals he had brought from the cellar.

Frances and I started to put on paper ornaments we had made at school. Mama sent Frances, and Chickey and me to bed. I gave my school ornaments to Geraldine. She promised to put them up front where everybody could see them.

But before going to bed, I carried the presents I got for everybody and put them under the tree. They were mostly things I had made at school. By this time, I was really tired and didn't put up much of a fuss about going to bed. Usually I would fall asleep right away after getting in bed. But that night I must have counted a million sheep before my brain was knocked out enough to let me sleep.

It was still dark when my eyes popped open. My room was next to the kitchen. I shared it with my brother Tony. He was sound asleep. I thought nobody was up, but then I heard my mother's and Helen's voices in the kitchen. They were talking quietly in Italian, and for an instant I thought it was a Sunday morning because those were the sounds I heard every Sunday morning. Suddenly I realized it was Christmas morning. I shot out of bed and ran into the living room. Helen must have seen me. "Peter", she shouted, "don't open anything until everybody is up."

Propped up under the tree was a box wrapped in red paper. It was the same size as the box I had seen in the drawer. It had my name on it. The tag said from Helen, Geraldine, Phyllis Tony, Chickey, and Frances. I was sure they had filled it with old newspaper just to fool me.

Every year somebody would get a big box with a bunch of smaller boxes inside. And the smallest box would have something like a candy kiss in it.

Besides Pasta

I shouted to Helen, "Can't we wake up everybody now? Pretty soon we'll have to get ready to go to church."

She came into the living room and whispered, "They were up really late wrapping presents. I'll wake them around seven."

Just then Frances came into the room, still half asleep. She sat next to me in front of the tree. We started playing a game of trying to guess what was in the boxes by the size and shape. When Helen left the room, we held the wrapped presents to feel how heavy the thing was and shook them to see the kind of noises they made. Clothes in a box never made any noise when you shook it. We weren't interested in quiet boxes.

Waiting for seven to come was probably the longest hour I ever lived. Slowly, other family members gathered around the tree. Tony took charge. He found a present for each person and insisted we open only one at a time, so everyone could enjoy the surprise. I kept looking at the red box. I wished I could see right through it to the inside. I wondered why it had everybody's name on it. I was the only one there who didn't know what was in it.

When I finally opened the package, I couldn't believe there was the very same Charlie McCarthy I had seen at Bamberger's. I looked at Geraldine. "But you said you couldn't afford it." She smiled and said, "That was the truth. I really couldn't afford it all by myself. Everyone chipped in and we gave them five dollars down and I'm going to give the store fifty cents a week until it's paid off."

Over the next few weeks Charlie and I were inseparable. I probably drove everybody crazy with the little routines I made-up. I couldn't wait until Marky came over to put on a show for him. I knew he would rather play catch because he always brought his mitt. Sometimes he looked bored. But mostly, he would laugh at my jokes. He even gave me ideas for other routines.

"Why not have Charlie tell about going to Davega's to buy two baseball caps? One for himself and one for you."

"That's a great idea. We could tell how he didn't have enough money…"

"Yeah," Marky said, "and tell how the man asked, 'who the hell are the Stillmans?'"

"You want to try working Charlie's controls?" I asked Marky.

He tried, but he wasn't good at combining the eye motion, head turning, and mouth moving with what he was saying.

"It's not your fault," I told him. "They're left-handed controls."

Mama never really understood why I played with Charlie. I guess she was worried that her son was playing with a doll. But I didn't see Charlie as a doll, or even a toy. He was a friend. He had a personality, a sense of humor, he wasn't shy, and he would say things I was too shy to say. Through Charlie I could be more me than I could as myself. I once brought him to school and did a routine for my class.

"Well, Charlie, here we are at Public School 156."

Charlie looked about the room and rolled his eyes. "What a motley looking bunch of kids…."

"Now, now, Charlie. They're my classmates…."

"Well, I must say, you fit right in," Charlie said.

He looks at my teacher. "Hi, good-looking!"

"Charlie! That's my teacher. Show a little respect for goodness' sakes."

"Okay, Pizza Rizz, whatever you say…"

Besides Pasta

"My name is Peter. I don't care for pizza."

"First person I ever met who doesn't like pizza...."

"I like it to eat. Not for a name."

"Would you settle for Pete?" Charlie asked with an eye roll.

"Pete's okay."

Charlie scans the room. "I don't know about that. You guys think he's okay?"

There were a few giggles. Rosie said, "Yeah!"

When it was over, everybody clapped and shouted. Even the teacher joined in.

Rosie came up to me after class. "I could hardly see your lips moving," she said. "And it sounded exactly like your voice was coming from Charlie's mouth."

Other kids came up and wanted to try the controls and make Charlie talk. It made me nervous because they were a little rough the way they handled him.

I still didn't like the public school, but at least after that, the kids didn't tease me so much. Some of them even asked me when I was going to bring in Charlie again.

Peter Rizzolo

Chapter Twenty-One

Almost Spring and Summer 1939

I wouldn't mind if we had a big snow in March, but all we had was wind, rain, sleet, and freezing cold. In the front room of our house, there was a kerosene heater that we used when my mother didn't want to run the furnace. We had just finished dinner and my older sisters and brother were in the kitchen, sitting around the table talking about Hitler and how Roosevelt should stop him from taking over Europe. I went to find Frances. She was sitting on the floor playing cards by herself. She was close to the kerosene heater, where it was warm. Ginger was stretched out on the floor next to her.

"You want to play 'Go Fish?'" she asked me.

"Sure," I said. I sat next to her.

Just then, Chickey came into the room. She was reading a magazine as she walked toward us.

"Hey, watch out!" I yelled.

But it was too late. She walked right into the kerosene heater. It tipped over and crashed onto the floor next to where Frances and I were sitting. Chickey screamed. Frances grabbed Ginger. We both jumped back just before a wall of fire shot across the floor. Everyone came running in from the kitchen. My mother grabbed me and Frances and pushed us toward the stairs. The room was filling up with thick smoke. Mama ran into the kitchen. I stood frozen at the top of the stairs.

"Get blankets," Tony shouted as he ran to our bedroom. Phyllis ran after him. Tony came back with a blanket from our bed. He threw it over the burning stove. Phyllis rushed back in and threw a blanket over the line of fire.

"Oh God," Helen shouted, "Mama, the whole house is going to burn down!"

Chickey just stood there screaming and crying. Geraldine grabbed Chickey's arm and dragged her to the top of the stairs, where me and Frances were huddled together with our hands over our mouths because it was hard to breathe. Then both Phyllis and Geraldine started pulling Tony away from the fire. He was trying to stamp it out with his feet. Now the blankets were catching fire.

Mama came running in with a pot of water. "Go, go, *figli di Mama*," she screamed, as she splashed the water onto the flames. But it only got worse, with little puddles of fire popping up everywhere. When the curtains caught fire, the smoke was so thick it drove us all down the stairs and out of the house.

The family living on the first floor must have heard all the shouting and maybe even smelled the smoke, because they were already standing on the sidewalk looking at the second-floor window that was all lit up with flames. We were all shaking, partly from being cold and partly from being scared. All seven of us were packed in close to Mama.

"Oh my God," Helen said. "Mr. Bellini!"

There was no fire escape. He would be trapped in the attic.

"I'm going back in to get him," Tony said.

Phyllis grabbed his arm. Tony's face was black and his eyes red from standing over the fire. "No, no, Tony. I saw him leave the house. I'm sure he's not up there," Phyllis said.

"I saw him leave," Frances said.

My mother was crying. She held onto Tony, too. "Phyllis, you were in the kitchen. How could you be sure he didn't come back in?" Mama asked.

"I'm sure he didn't come back," Frances said. "I would have seen him."

None of us had coats. We scrunched together to keep warm. It seemed like forever before the fire engine came. I don't even know who called them. The street was filling with people.

When the firemen got there, they ran a big hose up the stairs. The fireman pushed people back away from the house. Then the front windows exploded and a shower of glass shot from the front of the house. I could see a fireman in the window. He was holding a hatchet. Black smoke came pouring out. After a few minutes we couldn't see any more flames, but still plenty of smoke. One of the firemen came down and talked to my mother.

"Must not have had much kerosene in that heater. The fuel was pretty much burned up by the time we got to it."

Besides Pasta

"We were almost out of kerosene," my mother said.

"Good thing you were. If the burner had been filled to capacity the whole house would have gone."

"My God," Helen said. "Everything's ruined."

Chickey was crying. She knew it was her fault for knocking over the burner. Mama put her arm around her.

"When can we go back in?" Mama asked the fireman.

"As soon as we get our equipment and hoses out of there. Be careful, there's glass all over the floor."

By the time Mr. Bellini got to the house, we were still cleaning up the front room. He said the most important thing was that no one was hurt. He ran upstairs and got a piece of canvas. He tacked it over the broken window.

By the time we got to bed it was really late. I was tired but couldn't sleep. Neither could Tony. He said we were lucky the kerosene didn't splash on me or Frances or Chickey. He said the fireman told him that it's best to keep a tippy burner like that in a corner of the room.

"He said it was a good thing we used blankets to smother the fire and not water."

"How come?"

"The water just spreads the kerosene."

Then I remembered what happened when Mama threw water on the fire. "But they used hoses," I said.

"The kerosene had burned out by then. That's why he said we were lucky the tank wasn't filled."

After we got back in bed, we talked about the World's Fair and the parish bazaar and Father Ambrose's raffle idea. Tony stopped talking. After a few minutes he started to snore. He probably saved the whole house from burning by thinking to grab that blankets. He smelled like smoke. I still couldn't sleep. I kept seeing the flames shoot across the floor and the curtains catch fire. Even the warm bed and the covers couldn't stop me from shaking. I snuggled against Tony. For once I didn't mind his snoring. The sound made me feel safe.

The following morning, I went into the living room to see what it looked like in the daylight. The linoleum was ruined. It was charred and bubbled up in places. The windows frames were black and partly burned away. The walls and ceiling were sooty. It was like being inside a giant chimney.

I went into the kitchen. Mama was at the sink filling a pail with water. She added Biancoline to the water. She carried the pail and a mop to the living room. Everyone else was still asleep because we had gotten to bed so late.

"Peter," Mama said, "Get the scrub brush and some rags from the back porch and wake up your brother and sisters. We need to clean up this mess before the landlady gets here."

Another bad thing that happened in 1939 was that the "Iron Man of Baseball," Lou Gehrig, had to quit when he was still the best player on the Yankees. He had a bad disease that was eating his muscles and making him fall a lot and not be able to run the bases. They had "Lou Gehrig Day" at Yankee Stadium so the fans could say goodbye to him. The place was so full, not a single extra person could get in. When he came to the microphone the people stood and clapped until their hands must have hurt. He stood in front of the microphones all by himself waiting for them to stop. Then he said with a shaky voice that people shouldn't feel sorry for him. He said, "Today, I'm the luckiest man on

229

earth." I saw it on the newsreel two times, and both times I cried. The sad thing was that even though he must have had the best doctors in the world, they still couldn't do anything to keep Lou Gehrig from dying.

One afternoon, a week after the fire, a delivery truck brought a bunch of boxes to the priest's house. Father had told me that the raffle tickets would be arriving any day. After the truck left, I went over and knocked on Father's door.

"Hi, Peter," Father Ambrose said. "I know what you're looking for."

I smiled. He led me into the rectory. He had already broken open one of the boxes. It was sitting on the hall table. He reached in and counted out twenty books and handed them to me.

"Make sure they fill out both the ticket and the stub."

"When are you going to hand out the rest of the books?"

"The Knights of Columbus meet tonight. I'll give them theirs then. The rest I'll hand out after Sunday Mass."

It was only Thursday. That gave me a three-day head start on everybody else but the Knights. I brought the books home, grabbed a pencil, and put two books in my shirt pocket. I told my mother I was going out to sell tickets. I would miss my radio shows, but I couldn't pass up having a head start.

I found that it wasn't that hard selling bazaar raffle tickets, because everybody wanted to go to the World's Fair. For ten cents, the cost of one ticket, you could win a chance to go to the Fair for three days and stay in a New York hotel for two nights! If I had two dollars, I would buy a whole book myself. I went to every house and store in the neighborhood. Most of the people were nice, but not everybody. I learned that there were some people who didn't care about seeing the World's Fair. They didn't say that, but it was a pretty good guess when they slammed the door, with me standing there with my mouth still open.

If the person was nice, and gave me a chance, I would say, "This next ticket could be the winning ticket. If you don't buy it, the people next-door will."

The first week I sold four books. That's eighty tickets. Some of the store people bought three or four tickets. But after the first week it got harder and harder because so many kids were selling tickets; even the stores themselves were selling tickets. But the best thing was getting Mr. Stillman to put up a sign on the counter in his store. Marky's sister made the sign for us. Mr. Stillman sold two books of tickets. Geraldine took a book to work and sold all twenty tickets. Phyllis took a book to work, but only sold half of the tickets. That came to seven and a half books. Two and a half more books of tickets, and I could get a prize.

The time for the raffle was only a week off. I had an idea. I went to the Stillmans' delicatessen to pick up the book stubs and money. Marky and I went to sit at the table in the back of the store. Mrs. Stillman was at the counter making a tuna salad. The smell was making me hungry.

"Whatever your mother is making really smells good," I said loud enough to be sure she heard me.

"Would you like some on a cracker, Peter?" Mrs. Stillman asked. "And maybe a glass of milk?"

"Yes, thank you."

Besides Pasta

She brought me a dish of crackers, piled high with tuna salad. Then she poured me a glass of milk.

Marky and I started checking to make sure all the stubs were filled out. Otherwise we wouldn't know who won the prize. I told Marky my idea.

"The people who go in the candy store are used to gambling because they play the numbers, right?"

"You want to stand in front of the candy store and sell tickets?" Marky asked.

"No. I tried standing in front of stores. Maybe one in million people buy a ticket, unless you're the Salvation Army with bells and a trumpet and a big pot."

Marky didn't say anything. It wasn't like him. He usually had lots of good ideas. He looked tired. I noticed his breath smelled bad. Like the last time I had tonsillitis. But I knew he didn't have tonsils anymore, so it couldn't be that.

"Buying a raffle ticket is like gambling." I said.

"I see what you mean. His customers should be interested."

"That's what I figure." I only had one tuna-cracker left, but I didn't want to finish it; otherwise she might bring me some more. I liked it, but she put too much horseradish in the salad. It was making my nose drip.

"Maybe he wouldn't want you taking business away from him," Marky said.

"There isn't much time left. I have to do something. I want to ask him to put the sign about the raffle in his store, like your father did."

"It's a business," Mrs. Stillman said. "He's not going to do it without being paid."

I didn't think she was listening to us. She was making potato salad. I wondered if she put horseradish in that, too.

"Okay. I'll tell him if he sells three books, I'll have my mother crochet him something nice for his store."

"Your mother crochets beautiful things. He would like that."

I took the sign and went next door to ask the numbers man if he would help me sell tickets. His wife, Frances, was in the store. She seemed glad to see me. I told her my idea.

"Okay, but just this once, Peter. And your mother doesn't have to make anything unless she wants to."

In the last three days of the raffle, the numbers store sold three books of tickets. Father Ambrose said that I sold more tickets than anyone in the parish, not counting the Knights of Columbus and the Virgin's Sodality. Marky laughed when I told him. He said, "Who can compete with an army of knights and virgins?"

"What's a virgin?" I asked Marky. The only one I ever heard of was Jesus' mother.

"It's a lady who wasn't ever married."

"That's not true. The Blessed Virgin was married to Joseph." I was surprised Marky didn't know that.

"I remember you telling me about mysteries," Marky said. "I guess that's one of them."

And as he had promised, Father and I went to Davega's and picked out a lefty fielder's mitt. Stamped right on the heel of the glove it said, "Genuine Cowhide." It was autographed by Nolan Richardson, the shortstop for the Newark Bears.

Besides Pasta

The pocket was deep and soft and I knew that once a ball sunk in there it wouldn't pop out like it did when I wore Paul's right-handed mitt on the wrong hand. Any ball coming my way would stick in there like it was glued. Grounders, line drives, fly balls, diving catches…bang! That was it. The batters won't have a chance.

I couldn't wait for baseball season to start so I could go to ladies' night with Phyllis. Maybe this time Marky could come, and with the two of us trying to catching foul balls, we were bound to get at least one. And this time I would have my own glove.

That summer, Father Ambrose began to organize the parish baseball team. I was surprised how many kids showed up for the first practice. Some of the eighth graders looked like they could almost play for the Newark Bears. It turned out that a lot of them played for the public school in the regular year.

Some of the seventh graders were pretty good, too. There were three sixth graders, but I was the only one going into fifth grade. The sixth graders and I played catch off to the side and helped shag fly balls. I wasn't good at judging the really high fly balls. They almost always sailed way over my head.

Because there weren't enough seventh and eighth graders to make up two teams, everyone took turns fielding and batting. Father had me back up the catcher because there was no backstop or fence to stop the ball from going into the street when it was a wild pitch or the catcher missed. I didn't need a catcher's mask or shin guards because by the time the ball reached me it was an easy grounder.

I knew I was nowhere good enough to play on the parish team, but I loved being around the team. I learned a lot about being a ballplayer. About how to slide so you didn't get tagged, how to crouch when you were batting to make the strike zone smaller, how to field grounders so you didn't get smacked in the balls by a bad bounce, how to judge and snag fly balls. But the best part was learning how to act like a big leaguer. How to knock mud from your spikes even though you weren't wearing spikes and there was no mud. How to always be chewing gum and spitting, especially when you got a bad call. How to dive for first base when the pitcher was trying to pick you off, even though there was plenty of time to walk back.

Father sometimes let me and the sixth graders take a few swings at the plate. I mostly struck out or hit pathetic grounders. But once I bunted and beat out the throw to first because nobody was expecting it. The only way I ever got on base, excepting that one surprise bunt, was from being walked. I got walked a lot. Father Ambrose said that when I crouched at the plate, the strike zone was about as big as the catcher's mitt.

Just two weeks into my baseball career with the Saint Rocco Rockets, I got a high fever and the worst sore throat I ever had. I couldn't hardly swallow, and spit kept coming out of the corner of my mouth. The doctor said my tonsils were infected and swollen. That there was nothing to do but take them out. He sent me to the clinic at the city hospital where they took one look at my throat and put me in the hospital. I wasn't scared at first because Marky had the same thing done. He said it wasn't so bad. But I guess it's not the same for everybody.

The worst part was getting knocked out. They rolled me into the operating room and had me scoot onto a table under a bunch of bright lights. There were three or four people in gowns and masks and rubber gloves standing around talking. A nurse tied down my legs and arms and wrapped a belt around my chest. Then she put this cup over my nose and mouth. It was like a tea strainer with cloth over the outside. She had a can of ether. She told me that's what it was. She started to drip it onto the cup. She told me to take deep breaths. At first the smell wasn't so bad, but then I started choking on it and felt like I couldn't breathe. I wanted to be brave, but it felt like they were trying to kill me. I started kicking my heels and tried to free my arms and shake my head. But someone must have been holding my head. My heels were making a loud noise banging against the table. I felt dizzy, as though I was falling from an airplane. My body felt like it was swelling and getting ready to bust.

The next thing I remember was waking up choking on a tube they had stuck in my nose and down my throat. My mother was standing there. She ran to get the nurse.

"Oh good, he's awake," the nurse said.

I guess she figured that out because my eyes were wide open and I was choking on the dumb tube that was sticking down my throat.

She slipped the tube from my nose and untied my hands.

I couldn't speak; my throat was too sore and my tongue felt swollen.

"Would you like to suck on a piece of ice?" the nurse said.

I nodded. She fished one out of a pitcher of ice water and slipped it into my mouth. She cranked my bed part-way up. The ice felt good in my mouth, but when I swallowed, it felt like splinters of glass going down my throat.

Peter Rizzolo

My mother held my hand. In her other hand she had rosary beads, and I could tell from her lips moving that she was saying prayers. I was glad she was there.

I looked around the room. There must have been ten beds, all filled up with kids who were knocked out or maybe just sleeping. There was a kid in the bed next to me sitting up and smiling.

"I thought you were going to puke your brains out," he said. "Who knows? Maybe you did."

I closed my eyes. When I woke up it was dark. My mother was gone. Next to me was a tray of cold soup and melted sherbet. I was hungry, but all I could think to put in my mouth was ice. I could hear a radio in the next room. I heard this deep familiar voice…

"Who knows what evil lurks in the heart of men? The Shadow knows!"

I didn't remember his real name, but it sounded like the same guy who scared everybody last year, when he said on the radio that a ship from Mars had landed in New Jersey. Nobody in our house heard the show and by the next day when we found out about it, everybody already knew it was just a made-up story. But I guess a lot of people got their pants scared off.

I guess I was still groggy from the ether. Even though I liked listening to the Shadow, I couldn't keep my eyes open. When I woke up it was daylight. I was hoping it was all just a bad dream. But this wasn't home. When I tried to swallow, I knew it really happened. I wondered how long I had to stay in the hospital. The kid in the bed next to me said everybody stays about a week. "It's to make sure you don't start bleeding to death. A kid the other day began spitting out gallons of blood. He had to go back to the operating room."

I wished my mother had left her rosary beads. I started saying the prayers using my fingers to count. Dear God, don't let me start bleeding and have to go back to the operating room. Sometimes I would see a tiny spec of blood in my spit and would real quick say another rosary. For the next two days, Hail Marys and Glory Be's were flying like crazy out of the window on the tonsil ward of Newark City Hospital.

It seems like there's always something to spoil a person's summer. Last year it was a broken wrist. This year my dumb tonsils. That time Marky asked me if I ever thought about dying. I told him no. But I did when I was in the hospital after the tonsil operation. It was after the intern and an older doctor came around one day and listened to my heart. They started arguing about what they heard. The intern said he thought I had a murmur from rheumatic fever. The older doctor listened again for a pretty long time.

"My sister had rheumatic fever but I never did," I said.

"I'm almost certain it's a benign murmur," the older doctor said.

"What's a B9 murmur?" I asked.

"It means it's not serious," he said.

"Is it worse than a B1 or a B2?"

The old doctor laughed.

"It's spelled b-e-n-i-g-n," the young doctor said.

I knew how to spell benign, because it was a word we had in a spelling bee at school. I was joking. I decided to put my joke in one of my Charlie McCarthy routines. It was a habit I had of making a joke when people around me were arguing. It's hard to be mad when you're laughing.

But I was worried. What if it's not benign and the intern's right? Maybe the old doctor couldn't hear as good as the young one. "Can a person have rheumatic fever without knowing it?" I asked.

"Yes. It can be like a mild flu. You know, aches, pains, and fever," the intern said.

"Do you get tired when you play with your friends or take gym at school?" The old doctor asked.

"I never get tired from playing."

"Good. Good. It's probably nothing to worry about," He said to the intern. "Tell his mother about the murmur. She should know about it."

I didn't want my mother to know because then she wouldn't let me do stuff. "You don't have to. I'll tell her," I said. "My mother doesn't understand English very well."

"You speak Italian?" the old doctor asked.

"A little." It wasn't really a lie. I did know a few words.

The intern shook his head and gave me a funny look. "I'll tell her."

After they, left I put my hand on my chest and felt my heart. It was thumping pretty hard, I guess because I was scared. I forgot to ask the doctor what a murmur is. The doctors had felt my neck with their hands. They both thought they could feel the murmur. I tried but couldn't feel anything but my heart beating. If a murmur is something you can hear, how can you feel it? I wish I had asked. I could ask Marky. Maybe he would know. Tony and my older sisters would know, but I didn't want to tell them.

Besides Pasta

I missed a whole month of summer from the operation. I only spent a week in the hospital, but the intern told my mother about my heart murmur. After that she didn't let me out of the house for three weeks. The doctor said to her that if I caught something from one of the other kids before my throat healed up, it could affect my heart. There was nothing to do but read, and play with Charlie McCarthy, and make up a bunch of routines, and listen to my radio shows.

Father Ambrose came around once and told me about the team. They played two games already but lost both. He brought me a baseball for a present. He said he ordered shirts with the team's name on the back.

"Maybe next year we'll have a sixth-grade team and you can try out for it." He looked at my mother as though he was asking her if that was okay.

We were sitting at the kitchen table. My mother was at the stove stirring something in a pot. She looked at Father with a serious face. She didn't say yes or no, but I know she was thinking about that stupid heart murmur.

"Can you stay for dinner, Father?"

"I'd love to, Antoinette, but I have to get to the hospital."

I was holding the baseball Father had given me. I felt like throwing it against the wall as hard as I could. Or maybe drop onto the floor, scream, kick my feet and pound my fists like a four-year-old. It wouldn't do any good, I knew I'd catch it good from my mother after Father left.

Mama said she was taking me to see Dr. DiGiacomo. before school started back up, to see ask him to excuse me from gym. I reminded her that I was transferring to St. Antonitus and that they didn't have gym class.

"They have recess. You play games. They have to know about your heart condition."

It was hard to fool mama. I hated to hear her say I had a "heart condition," because that's what she always said about Helen. Because whoever she was telling would shake their head and look sad.

I said a prayer to Saint Peter, Saint Rocco, and the Blessed Virgin to ask God that Dr. DiGiacomo wouldn't hear a murmur, or if he did, that he would say it was benign.

Chapter Twenty-Two

Goodbye Hunterdon; Hello, Eighth Street

It was my favorite type of meal. We weren't eating anything green. Even though it was my favorite color, the only green things I liked were pickles and green peppers.

A vegetable peddler had come on a truck that day selling corn on the cob. Mama bought a dozen ears. I knew how to make corn so she let me do the whole thing.

"I was just a year older than you," Mama said, "when my mother died. I was only twelve, but because I was the oldest girl, I had to cook for the whole family and even the people who worked on Papa's farm."

I wouldn't want to cook for a whole army like that, but it was fun to help Mama. I shucked the ears, washed off the blond hairs under the faucet, and then threw the corn in our biggest spaghetti pot. I filled the pot with water and added a teaspoonful of salt. Once it came to a boil, I turned off the burner and let it sit for five minutes before pouring off the water. The corn always turned out perfect.

At dinner time the whole family sat around the kitchen table. Mama took a pan of roasted potatoes, red peppers, and chicken from the oven. She set the hot pan on the table. She took a loaf of Italian bread from the oven, where she had warmed it. Tony began slicing the bread. The corn I had made was heaped up on a platter that Helen took from the stove-top. It wasn't anyone's birthday or a holiday, and we didn't have company, so I wondered why we were having such a special meal.

Everything smelled delicious and after crossing ourselves and saying grace, we started passing our plates to Phyllis, who was serving up the chicken, potatoes, and peppers.

I was buttering a piece of bread extra slow. I was thinking Mama always had a reason for everything she did. So why was she feeding us like we were prisoners about to go to the electric chair?

"*Mangia, figlio di Mama*," she said to me. "Why do you eat so little?"

"He eats enough," Tony said. "He's just chews everything so small he could probably drink it by the time he's done."

No one laughed because everyone was talking to the person next to them and didn't hear what he said. Our dinner table was like listening to five different radio stations all at the same time. You could tune in one, but it was hard to tune out the others.

Mama said something to Helen in Italian. I didn't get what she said. Helen banged on a glass. "May I have your attention please?" She banged the glass again.

I looked at Frances. Her eyes were wide. I could tell she was thinking the same as me. Here it comes.

"Mama has an important announcement," Helen said.

Besides Pasta

Sometimes Helen talked like a school teacher. One day she painted the stairs and railing going to the second floor. As each person came in the house, she told them, "Be careful not to touch the freshly painted surfaces!"

Everyone stopped eating and stared at Mama. She said, "You tell them, Helen." Mama got up and went to the sink and started cleaning pots.

"The landlady got a letter from the fire chief," Helen said. "It said that nobody can live in the attic unless the owner builds a fire escape. They told her the present tenant had to move out immediately."

"Mr. Bellini is going to have to move?" I asked. When I watched him draw, he would tell me opera stories. He would sing some of the parts in Italian. I loved watching him paint and listen to him sing. I had to try really hard not to cry.

"I already gave him notice," Mama said, without turning around.

"The worst part," Helen said, "is that the landlady was mad that now she has to build a fire escape and blames us because of the fire."

"God! Don't tell me we have to move?" Tony asked.

"Mama already found a nice place on South Eighth Street, just around the corner from St. Antonitus church."

"It's all my fault!" Chickey said. She must have felt bad because she had started the fire. She started crying and ran from the kitchen. She was mad because she was best friends with the girl who lived downstairs. We heard the front door slam shut.

Frances' big eyes were already swimmy with tears because she and Regina Biaocchi got to be good friends. Making new friends wasn't that easy for Frances, ever since we left South Orange Avenue and broke up the Blessed Trinity.

Just the other day I was telling Geraldine that I was beginning to like living on Hunterdon Street. There were a few kids in the neighborhood I was making friends with. And Father Ambrose said I could play on the sixth-grade baseball team next summer. And pretty soon the Saint Rocco's festival was coming. Besides, I was getting used to public school.

Geraldine said that she liked living on Hunterdon Street because the Biaocchis were such good friends and it was close to where she worked. Now Geraldine was looking at me to see if I was going to cry, too. I couldn't hold back the tears anymore but I didn't make any noise. I knew the whole family was sad about moving, and I also knew Mama couldn't do anything about it even if she wanted to.

Tony stopped eating. He got up from the table before he even finished his second helping of potatoes. "Damnit," he said. "I'm sick of all this moving. We might as well be in the circus!" As he left the kitchen he said, "I'm going to talk to Chickey."

I never heard Tony swear in front of Mama. She was the only one in the family who had permission to swear. And even then, only in Italian.

Mama came from the sink and sat at the table. She had tears in her eyes. Nobody knew what to say. I knew that pretty soon everyone was going to be complaining to her. It wasn't her fault we didn't have our own house; that we always had to move even when we didn't want to.

"It won't be so bad," I said. "We'll be closer to the Stillmans and just a block from school. I'll be able to come home for lunch every day. Maybe bring my friend Tommy."

"I'm sure Mama would love that," Phyllis said.

Helen, Phyllis, Geraldine and even Mama started laughing. I didn't see what was so funny. In my family we sometimes laughed when it seemed like we should be crying.

When it was time to move, my Uncle Pete came with a truck. Helen was in charge of packing all our stuff. Tony and my uncle carried out the heavy furniture. It took three truckloads to get us moved.

Mr. Bellini stood on the sidewalk watching us load the truck. He hugged all of us kids and then reached out to shake Mama's hand. She pushed his hand away, smiled, and gave him a big hug. Mama and Helen got in the truck with Uncle Pete. Frances and I got in the back of the truck. Tony, Phyllis, and Geraldine were still talking to the Biocchis.

Helen leaned out the truck window. "You want Uncle Pete to come back for you?"

"No," Tony said, "we can walk there."

I was wrong about one thing. I wouldn't be closer to Marky. Soon after we moved to South Eighth Street, Mr. Stillman sold his business. They moved to a faraway neighborhood. From South Eighth Street it took almost an hour to walk there. The first time I went, Marky took me through their second-floor apartment. Marky showed me his room that he shared with Paul. There were model airplanes hanging from the ceiling, a Captain Midnight poster hanging on the wall, piles of books, and a table with a half-finished model plane.

"Since Paul got a job, he's been buying expensive plane kits. This one here is going to have a tiny gasoline engine," Marky said. "He'll be able to steer it by remote control."

Peter Rizzolo

"Must have cost a lot," I said. The engine was on the table next to the plane. I picked it up and couldn't believe how light it was. I told Marky about me going back to Saint Antonitus for fifth grade.

"I have to change schools, too," he said. We went and sat at the kitchen table. I know it must have been my imagination, but the kitchen smelled exactly like their old delicatessen. Then I realized why. On the table was a loaf of Jewish rye, a bowl of pickled herring, a platter of lox, and an open package of Philadelphia cream cheese. The food must have been left over from their lunch.

Mrs. Stillman poured me a glass of milk and told me not to be shy, to help myself to whatever I wanted. She told me that Marky, because he had missed so much school last year, had to take a test in the new school to see if he could go into the sixth grade. He did so good in the test they said he belongs in the seventh grade. Marky's ears got red.

Seventh grade! Now he was two grades ahead of me.

"You want to go see my new school?" he asked.

I was eating a thick slice of rye bread piled high with cream cheese. My mouth was full. I nodded.

I noticed when we were walking that I had to walk fast to keep up with his long legs. He must have grown a lot that summer, because his pants were way above his ankles. His face looked different. After we had walked a couple of blocks, he started slowing down. He was breathing like he had run up and down a flight of stairs a few times. He stopped. He pointed to a dark, red brick building across the street.

"There's my school. There's a playground in back. But the doctor said I can't take gym or go out for sports."

"Your stupid kidneys?"

247

Besides Pasta

"Yeah."

When the light changed, we walked across the street and climbed the wide cement steps that led up to the school entrance. We sat on the top step. By this time Marky couldn't talk from being out of breath. We sat, watching the traffic go by, and didn't say anything for a pretty long time. I thought if I told him about my heart murmur it would take his mind off his kidneys.

"When I had my tonsils out, the doctor said I have a heart condition. He said it was probably from having rheumatic fever."

"I didn't know you had rheumatic fever."

I explained how you could have it and not ever know it. And how it could still damage your heart. I asked him if he knew exactly what a heart murmur was.

"A doctor came to our classroom. He explained all about the heart. When the valves get damaged from a disease, they don't close as they should. When the doctor listens with his stethoscope he can hear extra noises."

"That's what they call a murmur---right?" I asked.

Marky nodded. "The doctor said in some kids, even if their heart valves are normal, they can have a murmur."

"Yeah," I said. "That's what they call a benign murmur."

"You're right. That's the word he used. Benign. Yours has got to be benign. You can play and run all day and never get tired."

I told him my joke about B9. He always got my jokes and laughed twice as hard as anyone else. It wasn't from just trying to be nice, either. You can tell the difference.

In the playground I stood on one of the swings, and at first just went back and forth a short distance. Marky was sitting on the swing next to me. I told him to try it. He shook his head. I hooked my feet under the metal part where the chain was attached to the seat of the swing. I started to swing higher. At school you got yelled at if you stand on the swings. But there was nobody around. Standing was scarier and a lot more fun than sitting. I went higher and higher until I was practically facing the sky at the top of my swing.

When I saw that he wasn't going to swing, I slowed down and then sat on the swing seat. We talked about the Yankees and wondered if they would win the pennant again. We talked about Lou Gehrig having to quit baseball because he was dying from a weird brain disease. Marky wasn't a big Yankee fan like me, but he did like Lou Gehrig.

"At least he got to be one of the greatest ballplayers ever," Marky said. He was kicking the dirt under the swing where it was already dug out from people's feet.

I always talked with Marky about being a baseball player someday, but I knew I probably wouldn't ever be good enough, even to play for our school team. And Marky was even worse than me, so he must have known he could never play professional sports.

I remembered me and Marky once talking about his mother wanting him to be a doctor. He said he didn't know if he'd like being around sick people all the time. Especially sick kids.

"You ever try to picture yourself grown up?" Marky asked.

"I can't," I said. "As slow as I'm growing, I'll be a hundred before I'm grown up."

He looked at me then looked at the ground again. "You know, it's hard to have a serious conversation with you." With his kicking he had uncovered a stone half buried in the dirt. He pried it loose. It was the kind with all the sparkly pieces in it. He slipped it into his pocket.

"Sister Magdalene said you should always look at the good side of things."

"Shit. You're such a damn Pollyanna."

He stood and started walking. I just sat there. I felt as though he had hit me on head with a lead pipe. I jumped up and ran after him. He had never once called me a name. I didn't know exactly what it meant, but the way he said it, I knew it was probably a mean thing to say about a person.

"What the heck are you so mad about?" I asked him.

He didn't answer me. We walked a long way without either of us saying anything. He started breathing hard. I could tell he was out of breath, but he didn't slow down. When we got back to his apartment, we stood there just looking around, but not saying anything. His breathing started to slow down.

"I heard they're making a movie about Lou Gehrig's life," I said.

"Good for him," Marky said so softly I could barely hear him.

"I guess I better get started home," I said. "My mother said I had to be home before dark."

Marky said that if I had a dime, I could stay a little longer and take a bus to South Orange Avenue and then take another bus or the trolley the rest of the way.

I could tell he was sorry for calling me a name. "I don't have any money," I said. "I don't mind walking."

We sat on his stoop and talked a little longer.

"Hey, where'd you get the neat Captain Midnight poster?"

"I sent in labels from Ovaltine jars." He reached into his pocket. "Look."

He was holding a piece of metal that looked like a badge. "What's that?"

"It's a Captain Midnight Code-o-graph badge."

"A what?" I never listened to Captain Midnight because it was on the same time as another show I liked.

"They give you secret messages during the show." He picked up the badge and showed how he could rotate a knob in the center. They read off letters that don't make sense unless you have a decoder badge."

"Wow. Did you have to send in money besides?"

"Not for the badge. But I did for the poster."

"I'm going to ask my mother to buy Ovaltine."

"If you get one of these, we can send each other secret messages."

"Pigeons can carry messages," I said. "Maybe we can catch one and train it."

"That would be neat, but I bet it's pretty hard to train a pigeon. Let's just let the mailman be our pigeon."

"I like the idea of pigeons," I said, "but at least with the mailman you don't have to worry about him shitting on your front stoop."

We both laughed until we were practically crying. I could see he wasn't mad anymore. I told him about how I got my mitt by selling twenty books of raffle tickets. "Be sure to bring your mitt when you come," I told him. "We can play catch in the St. Antonitus school playground." We used to play catch in Valesburgh Park. There was grass there, not just cement like the playground. But I knew that Valesburgh Park was too far for him to walk.

On my way home, I looked at all the grown-ups and even old people walking all over the place and never even thinking what a great thing it was to be able to walk. And here Marky was just a kid, and he got so short of breath from walking that he couldn't even talk. It wasn't fair.

Marky was hardly ever wrong about anything, so maybe I am a Pollyanna. But the way he said it, you could tell it wasn't a compliment. I couldn't wait to look it up. I wasn't going to ask my brother or sisters what a Pollyanna was. They might agree with Marky.

The best thing about living on Eighth Street was that Joe Russo, who was the same age as my brother Tony, lived next-door. He taught my brother how to play chess. I liked to watch them play, and after a while I figured out all the moves, except for the knight. Tony had to explain that to me. I would sometimes play chess with my brother. He always beat me, so I tried to teach Chickey and Frances how to play. They didn't like chess. They thought it was too hard to learn all the different moves, and it took too long to play a game.

The other thing about Joe Russo is that he liked to argue about everything. The war, Hitler, Roosevelt, Russia, the Pope, the Catholic school, and just about anything you could think to talk about. Phyllis said Joe was narrow-minded and thought too highly of his own opinion. Tony said he was perverse, but he liked having him as a friend because he made you think about all the things a person takes for granted. I didn't bother asking Tony what perverse meant because I knew he would tell me to go look it up. I think it means stubborn or cranky. That's what I would call him.

Two weeks after we moved into the new flat, I started fifth grade at St. Antonitus. My teacher was Sister Magdalene. She was tall and thin. She wore glasses, had brown eyes, and the whitest teeth I ever saw. She taught all our subjects except music. For music we went to a different room and had a lady teacher, Mrs. Wagner. She had snow white hair and looked like a grandmother in a storybook.

I was always jealous when kids talked about their grandparents. All of mine were still in Italy. I never once saw any of them. I guess they were too old to make the long trip across the ocean. Helen said it would cost too much money for them to come just for a visit.

One day I was standing in the dining room looking at a large oil painting of my mother's father. He was wearing an old-fashioned suit and tie. He had dark hair and a fat mustache that covered the corners of his mouth.

"He looks like he might be a pretty stubborn, grouchy person," I said to Tony, who was sitting at the kitchen table doing a chess puzzle from the newspaper.

"Perverse, he looks perverse to me," Tony said.

I guess Mama felt as though she had to stick up for her father. "Papa was a good man," Mama said from the kitchen, where she was peeling potatoes at the sink. "He was nervous having to sit so long in his best clothes. He was worried, thinking how much the artist would charge."

"An oil painting is expensive," Tony said.

"They should use olive oil. You can buy a whole quart for fifty cents," I said.

Besides Pasta

"Yeah," Tony said, "and if you don't like the way it turned out you can always eat it. Good idea. Come here Peter. I figured out how to checkmate this guy in four moves. Let me show you."

It was good to be back in class with some of my old friends, especially Tommy Walker. He lived on Tenth Street, just two blocks up and a couple over from me. I went to his house to play after school because I didn't know any kids on South Eighth Street. In fact, I never even saw any kids my age.

Tommy could draw cartoons just about as good as the artists who draw the funnies and comic books. But he wasn't good at making up stories. I started writing stories and he drew the pictures. We filled up a whole scrapbook with comics we made up. It was fun at first, but it started getting harder and harder to think up stories. I knew I couldn't write a story every day like the cartoonists do. Our career as a comic strip team only lasted a few weeks, but it was fun for the time we did it.

One day Mrs. Wagner asked me and Tommy and a couple of other kids if we wanted to join the school choir. There were twelve boys in the choir, mostly fifth and sixth graders. We wore long red cassocks, fancy long-sleeved white shirts, buster brown collars, and silky red ties.

The choir practiced after school and sang for Holy-hour devotions on Thursday nights and at the nine o'clock Mass on Sundays. We got to sit in the sanctuary off to the side of the altar. I enjoyed learning the songs. I didn't have a very good singing voice, so I didn't sing loud enough to ruin the sound of the choir. When they hit the high notes, I just moved my lips. That always made Tommy laugh. Or sometimes we would start laughing for no reason. Holy-hour seemed like Holy-week when I had to bite my lip to keep from laughing out loud.

My favorite song was "Holy God We Praise Thy Name." I liked it for two reasons. First, it didn't have any high notes, and second, it was always the last song we sang after Holy-hour devotion, as we walked down the center isle of the church. I know that sounds as though I couldn't wait to get out of there, but to tell the truth, an hour is a long time to be holy.

There weren't any girls in the choir because they weren't allowed to be in the sanctuary. There was no reason that I could find out from asking Mrs. Wagner or Sister Magdalene. They said it's an old rule that got to be a tradition and no one thought to change it.

Between choir practice, piles of homework, and listening to my radio shows I never had any time to spare. I felt guilty not going to visit Marky. I never did get a Code-o-graph badge. It took too many Ovaltine labels and then I lost the ones I had. I did join the Captain Midnight Club because that didn't cost you anything. They sent me an official membership card with my name and a picture of Captain Midnight on it.

I wished we had a telephone so I could call Marky. Mama said it cost too much to have a phone. But with Geraldine and Phyllis working and Tony getting an after-school job at Bamberger's, it seemed we should be able to have a phone. Mama said she was saving up for a down payment on a house, and that a phone was a waste of money. Helen said a postcard only cost a penny to send. She said, "You and Marky can communicate via the postal service." That became another one of our family jokes, like the time she said, "Be careful not to touch the freshly painted surfaces." All of our family jokes weren't just about Helen's way of talking. Once, Chickey, after answering the door, came to Mama and said, "There's a very extinguished gentleman at the door, Mother."

The next day, I walked to the stationary store and bought two postcards. I wrote one to Marky when I got home. It was the first letter I ever wrote, except for Valentine's Day cards at school. Those didn't count because there was no writing. Just my name. This was my first communication via the postal service. I had to print small to get it all in.

February 1940

Hi, Marky,
    Can you come to my house this coming Sunday? We eat at three o'clock. Mama said for you to come for dinner. Bring your mitt if it's not snowing or freezing cold.
            Your friend, Pete

Every day, the week after I sent Marky the postcard, I checked the mailbox as soon as I got home from school. It wasn't like him to not to answer my letter. Maybe he never got it. Maybe a pigeon would have worked better.

I could have written the wrong address by mistake. But I checked it at least a couple of times. The post office could have lost it. Sure, that's what happened. The stupid post office lost my postcard.

Chapter Twenty-Three

Geraldine's Mysterious Sores

It was already Friday and I still hadn't heard from Marky. I checked the mailbox when I got home from school but as usual, it was empty. I ran into the kitchen. Geraldine had the ironing board out. She spit on the iron to see if it was hot. In a basket beside her was a pile of clothes. I wondered why she wasn't at work.

"I'm sorry, Peter, all we got in the mail today was our electric bill," Geraldine said. "When Mama sees it, she going to have a fit."

I didn't care about the stupid electric bill. I didn't know why Marky didn't answer my letter. How was I supposed to know if he was coming on Sunday or not? I went to the icebox and got out a bottle of milk and the butter dish. I took a crust of bread from the breadbox.

"I don't know if I like Marky anymore," I said as I buttered my bread.

Besides Pasta

"Why do you say that?" She set the iron down and put one of my shirts on the ironing board.

"He never wants to do anything. All we ever do is play cards…and talk. He doesn't even look the same as he used to."

"I did notice the last time he was here how puffy his face was. I guess it has to do with his kidneys."

"I don't care about his stupid kidneys. I'm sick of hearing about him being sick." Ginger came to the table and rubbed against my leg. I picked him up and put him on my lap.

"A person can't help being sick."

I felt bad because I knew what she meant. She was always going to doctors because of sores on her legs. She had to keep them bandaged because yellow stuff oozed out. Practically all the money she made at work went to pay for medicine and doctor bills. She never talked anymore about buying a bus and starting our own business.

"Between Helen's leaky heart, my stupid murmur, your sores and Marky's kidneys…I don't know; it seems like God's mad at us." I scratched Ginger behind his ears.

"Compared to what's going on in the war between Germany and England, our problems don't seem too bad."

Everybody was talking about the air raids over England. In the news I saw pictures of blown-up buildings and fires from the German planes dropping bombs. American ships were being sunk by German submarines. Mama was afraid Tony was going to have to go in the Army if America got in the war.

"Did you lose your job?" I asked.

"No. I had a doctor's appointment this afternoon. He's sending me to a surgeon for a second opinion."

"You need an operation? It's not your tonsils, is it?"

"He found a swollen lymph node under my arm."

"A what?"

"He explained it's a kind of gland that traps infection in a person's body. He thinks it might have something to do with the sores on my legs."

"Under your arm is pretty far away from your legs."

She laughed. "An infection can travel in the blood. It can end up anyplace in your body. The surgeon said that if he cuts out the lymph node maybe we can find out what's causing me to have the sores."

"Why don't they do that with Marky's kidneys?"

"You can't just cut out a person's kidneys." She stopped ironing and came over and sat in a chair next to me. She pulled her chair close to mine. "I want to talk to you about Marky."

I was getting scared because she looked so serious. When grown-ups get close to you and talk in a quiet voice, it's mostly never good news.

"Mrs. Stillman came by a couple of days ago. It was after Marky got your card. She wanted Mama to know what Marky could and couldn't eat and that he shouldn't get overtired."

I was chewing the last bite of my buttered bread. "She came all the way here just to tell her that? Marky knows what he's not supposed to eat." Ginger jumped off of my lap. He snapped his tail back and forth like he always did when he had enough petting. He walked off with his chin high in the air. Marky was too sick to even answer my postcard and my own stuck-up cat didn't care to be around me. I wished I was five-years-old again and could throw myself on the floor and have a tantrum.

"Mrs. Stillman said she wanted us to know how serious his illness is."

"What do you mean?" I asked. Geraldine's eyes looked like she might cry. She put her arms around me and hugged me. I could feel her tears on my cheeks. I felt guilty because I was feeling sorry for myself and not thinking how Marky must feel being so sick he couldn't do hardly anything. I started to cry too.
"The hardest thing in the world is to lose your best friend."

She held me tight for a long time. My ear was pressed to her chest. She was so skinny I could feel her ribs pressed against my face. I pulled away. "I don't know why I have to lose him. Why?"

But I didn't wait for Geraldine to answer me. I ran from the kitchen through the dining room and out the front door. I just kept running without thinking where I was going. It was cold and all I had on was a sweater. I found myself running toward the South Orange Avenue house even though the Stillmans didn't live there anymore. There was a stupid vegetable store there now. By the time I got there I was breathing hard. The cold air burned my lungs.

The metal icebox Marky and I used to sit on was painted green and covered with boxes of grapes. There were a few people shopping, picking through the fruits and vegetables. A big man with a mustache and wild hair stood with his hands on his hips. He looked at me like he thought I was going to steal something. He didn't know I used to live upstairs over his store. I turned away and walked to the church next to the vegetable store. I went through the gate into the churchyard and walked to the cemetery behind the church. I hopped over the iron fence. I walked around not knowing why I was there, when the minister's black cat came up to me and brushed between my legs. He remembered me. I picked him up and held him against my cold face. He was warm and purry. I wasn't mad at him anymore for skwooshing my model plane. He was the only person left in the neighborhood who knew me

I sat on some dead person's stone without looking to see whose name was written on it, or how old the person was when he or she died.

I knew Marky was going to die without ever growing up. I just knew it. He knew it, too. I could hear him talking in my head. Saying things about not being anything when he grew up, about babies who died, why it was that children had to die when some people lived to be a hundred. I sat a long time, thinking, crying. I couldn't get rid of the idea that Marky's kidneys would quit working, and his body would swell up like a giant balloon from not being able to pee. I wondered if it would hurt. And why couldn't the doctors make a hole someplace and let the piss out? I started thinking about our baseball caps and "who the hell are the Stillmans?" and me peeing in my pants from laughing. It was cold and dark. I put the cat down.

"Goodbye, Captain Midnight." I said. He started to walk away. He stopped and turned his head toward me. Then he ran off. I think he must miss the old neighborhood, too. Like I said, I wasn't mad at him anymore for ruining my Spitfire. I was lucky to have had it to build and then to see it fly. I still had the memory of it swooping low, then rising and curving to the right and sailing over the fence into the churchyard. And Marky saying, "Wow, that was beautiful." I could hear his voice as though he just said it.

Even though it was just once, I would always have the picture in my head. Your memory is like a giant store filled with all the things that ever happened to you. And there's no other store in the whole world that has the exact same stuff in it. When a person you love dies you can't make any new memories to store away, to think about. That's the worst thing. But the ones you already have are yours forever. I wiped away tears with the sleeves of my sweater and headed home.

Chapter Twenty-Four

.

Pearl Harbor and Mama's Nightmare

On Sunday, December 7th 1941, I was buying a newspaper, when I heard people in the store talking about the Japanese bombing American ships at Pearl Harbor. They said it meant we would declare war on Japan. I ran home and told my brother and sisters and mother. The whole family went to the living room to listen to the news on the radio. Mama sat in a side chair. Her eyes were shiny with tears. The rest of us sat on the floor, close to the radio. My insides were shaking, because I thought Japanese planes were coming to bomb us any minute. I saw in the Pathe News how they bombed the Chinese people. Planes dropped bombs, then swooped down and machine-gunned people who were running in the streets. They weren't even soldiers; mostly women and small kids. At school when we talked about it and looked on the globe, I couldn't believe how small Japan was, and how big China was, and yet the Japanese were beating up on them. And now they were starting a fight with us. Up until then the war always seemed so far away. I was scared for my family. Afraid my brother would have to go away to fight in the war.

Frances looked scared, too. Those big brown eyes were looking around, trying to figure out what was happening.

The voice on the radio said that in the early morning hours, hundreds of Japanese planes attacked unsuspecting American ships. They destroyed practically our entire Pacific fleet. The announcer said that hundreds of American sailors were killed.

"Are you going to have to go fight in the war?" I asked Tony. I didn't want him to go and get killed or gassed like my Uncle Jerry did in the other war.

"I registered for the draft last year. If this means war, they'll probably call me up pretty soon."

"With the way German submarines are sinking American ships," Phyllis said, "and now this, we're going to have to fight both Germany and Japan."

She was right. The next day Roosevelt announced that we were declaring war on Germany and Japan. I was thirteen, so I wouldn't have to go into the army for a long time yet. But Tony and some of my cousins would.

After a while I stopped being afraid of the war because we weren't being bombed, and the Japanese didn't invade California like everyone said they would. By the spring of 1942 the American Marines won their first big battle. The island was called Midway. In the newsreel they showed American planes bombing the island and Marines landing on the beaches. They even made a movie about it. Everybody said it was the turning point of the war. In Africa the

American Eighth Army and British soldiers were beating the Germans. A German field marshal named Rommel was running as fast as he could from our soldiers. My cousin Frank Araneo was one of the soldiers chasing him. He was in a jeep when it hit a land mine. The soldiers in the jeep with him were killed. Frankie lost part of his leg and was in the hospital a long time before they sent him home. Another one of my cousins, my Uncle Pete's oldest son, was a pilot in the air force. He was reported missing in action somewhere over China. We all prayed that they would find him. But they never found him or his plane.

To help win the war, me and my friends saved tin cans. We cut out the bottoms, then squashed them and stacked them in cardboard boxes. We asked people who smoked to save the wrappers. We removed the aluminum foil from the paper the cigarettes came wrapped in. I made a ball of aluminum foil the size of a softball. We probably saved enough tin and aluminum to build a whole airplane. There was meat and food rationing but Mama always managed to feed us okay. I guess she was already used to rationing from never having enough money.

Even though the Marines and our soldiers were starting to win battles, Geraldine wasn't winning the war against her sores. She started running fevers. Where the lump under her arm was, the skin broke open, like the sores on her legs. The surgeon removed the lump to have it tested. The report showed that she had tuberculosis; that it was spreading through her body.

My mother's worst nightmare had come true. In Italy Mama had seen entire families die from tuberculosis. Her two stepsisters both died at a young age of tuberculosis. Mama thought that by coming to

America she was getting away from it. I guess people weren't all her ship brought to this country.

Our whole family had to go to the health department and have skin tests for TB. I was scared when my arm got red and swollen where they gave me the skin test. Frances' arm looked the same as mine. The doctor said it meant our test was positive. But our chest x-rays turned out normal, so I couldn't understand what was going on. The doctor explained that the positive skin tests meant that Frances and I had the TB bugs in our lungs, but that our body had it under control for the time being. He said we had to have a chest x-ray every six months, until they were sure we weren't going to get tuberculosis.

It was scary to think those stupid TB bugs were inside of us and we couldn't do anything about it. At the time there was no treatment for tuberculosis, except staying in bed, and keeping the window open, even in the winter. Getting better had something to do with breathing plenty of fresh air. Sometimes they did an operation to collapse the infected part of the lung. But it didn't really cure anything. It just slowed the TB down a little. Geraldine never wasted time complaining or feeling sorry for herself. She never gave up believing that something could be done to cure her.

When TB was first diagnosed, she was put into the hospital until her phlegm didn't test positive. But she couldn't cough up enough phlegm for them to test, so they put a tube down her stomach, the first thing every morning. It made me want to throw up just thinking about someone putting a tube down my throat. I usually gagged when the doctor poked that little stick in my mouth.

Geraldine told me she never really got used to it. Sometimes she would gag so much they gave up trying for that day. But the next day, they would come with their bowl of ice water, with the tube curled up in it, just waiting to be swallowed. The only good thing was that if the test was negative three days in a row, she could come home. She went in and out of the hospital a lot, but mostly she stayed at home.

The TB hospital was in Verona, New Jersey. It was just for people with tuberculosis. You couldn't get there except by car. Mama never took us to see her, because she was afraid we would catch TB from some of the sicker patients who coughed all the time. We were always glad to see Geraldine when she came home from the hospital.

At home, Geraldine had a bedroom all to herself. It was usually cold in Geraldine's room because Mama turned off the radiator and insisted Geraldine keep the window open. Geraldine told me that once the doctor let her look through the microscope at a slide he made from her phlegm. She said the TB bugs stood out because they stained red. I could picture in my head when she coughed, millions of those mean red dots shooting in the air, looking for someone else to make sick. It made me afraid to breathe too deeply whenever I went in her room. Then I would feel guilty, because I didn't want her to think I was afraid to be with her.

She always ate dinner with the whole family. Mama kept her plates and stuff separate. She washed them in steaming hot, soapy water.

On good days Geraldine's old smile and spirit came back. But her eyes weren't sparkly like they were before. She couldn't hide that, even with powder and rouge. Phyllis told me that Mama felt guilty about Geraldine having TB. One of the doctors had told Mama that she probably gave TB to Geraldine. That Mama probably got it from her two stepsisters. But that was stupid, because Mama didn't even have a positive skin test. But she still blamed herself.

Some days Geraldine wouldn't even bother to get dressed. But if we were having company she would put on makeup and nice clothes. One day Phyllis took a picture of me, Tony, and my four other sisters. It was the only picture we had of all of us together.

I don't know where Phyllis got the camera. It was a Kodak Brownie. You looked in the top and could see the picture you were taking. It was sort of like an upside-down periscope. Geraldine looked sad in the picture and fatter than she did in person. People would see the picture and say she didn't look that sick. That's because she was wearing makeup and got dressed up. She didn't want people to feel sorry for her. It was my favorite picture, but I always wished Mama and Phyllis could have been in it.

For some reason Mama didn't like to have her picture taken. She never said why, but I think maybe she liked to remember how she looked when she was young and everyone said how pretty she was. It makes me mad to think nobody ever took a picture of her. If they had, I could see what she looked like back then. I wondered if there maybe was another reason for her not wanting her picture taken. Maybe she threw away all of her old pictures.

I wished we had pictures of my grandparents and relatives in Italy, and pictures of my mother's family when she was growing up in San Andrea. Marky was lucky. They had piles of old photographs.

One day he and I were sitting on the bed in the bedroom he shared with Paul. One of his family albums was open. I guess we were around seven or eight at the time. It was our favorite thing to do on rainy days. The bed was alongside the window that looked out onto our backyard.

But I couldn't see anything because it was such a dark day and the rain was coming down so heavy. I liked the sound it made when it hit the glass. It was a perfect day to think about old times.

The album was practically falling apart. The edges of the black pages were crumbly. You had to be careful turning the pages so you wouldn't crack the paper.

My favorite pictures were of his great-grandparents. Marky said they were taken in Russia in the late eighteen hundreds. I didn't even know they had cameras back then. Taking pictures back then must have been serious business because nobody was smiling, not even the kids. My favorite was one of this old man sitting on a horse. He had a droopy white mustache. He wore a fur cap and fur coat. A rifle lay across his lap, and what looked like a deer was draped across the back of his horse. In other pictures, people were posing in dress-up clothes.

Marky said the man on the horse was his great-grandfather's brother. Most of the pictures had names and dates written along the edges. Some of them were written in Russian, so we couldn't read them.

There was a newer album that had pictures of Marky's parents when they were little, school pictures, and wedding pictures. You could tell they weren't taken in Russia. He said his parents were born in New York. There was one of Marky, all sudsy and naked, standing in a bathtub with a washcloth draped over his head. Mrs. Stillman is sitting on the edge of the tub, laughing. I felt sad not to have old pictures of my family, especially of my mother and father.

One night at the dinner table, Geraldine said, "In the sanitarium the doctors are talking about new drugs being tested for treating TB." I think she was trying to cheer up Mama. "They told us that there's a doctor in Princeton who's working on it. It's a sulfa drug."

"That's what they make matches from," I said. Frances pushed her half-finished dish toward me. I forked a meatball and dropped it onto my plate. Mama sometimes put fennel seeds in her meatballs. Frances didn't like things with seeds.

"I guess it's chemically related," Geraldine said.

"Do you know the doctor's name?" Helen asked. "Maybe we can call him to see if you can get some."

"They've only used in lab animals. It'll be years before they will try it on humans."

"I'll call him," Tony said. "Find out his name."

Mama was at the stove. I saw her slip a pill under her tongue. She didn't say anything.

With Geraldine being sick, Mama decided we needed to have a phone in case we had to call a doctor for an emergency. She told us that the phone company charged extra for each call you made, so she was pretty strict about letting us use it. Soon after we got the phone, Tony found out the name of the doctor in Princeton who was using the new sulfa drug. He had a hard time getting hold of the doctor. He finally did, but it didn't do any good, because the doctor said he couldn't give her the drug. That they had to be very strict who to use the drug on, because it was experimental.

After school, before going out to play, I would stop in Geraldine's room to talk to her. She always wanted to know about school. I would get a glass of milk and a piece of bread and sit at the foot of her bed while I ate my snack. She was usually reading or typing or writing letters. I knew she typed to keep in practice. It was like saying, "I'm going to get better. I better be ready for when I go back to work."

"Who are you always writing to?" I asked.

"Someone I met in the sanitarium."

"A doctor?" I asked. It would be good if she married a doctor. Then he could take care of her.

"No. He was a patient. His TB just got started. It showed up on a skin test. He wasn't even sick."

"Does he have a job? Is he Catholic? Is he Italian?"

"You sound like Mama."

We both laughed. Those were the exact same questions Mama always asked when my sisters talked about a boy they met.

"His name is Bill Krebs," Geraldine said. "I believe his grandparents were from Germany. He's a really good piano player. He also teaches piano."

"Are you going to marry him?"

"We're just friends. We've only known each other a short time."

She put down the letter she was writing. "Hand me my bathrobe, Peter."

It was hanging over a chair by the window. It was white with tiny flowers on it. It was heavy, because it was two layers of cloth with cotton between the layers. In some places the cloth was worn and pieces of cotton were poking through.

I noticed it was starting to rain. I knew I wouldn't be playing outside. I handed Geraldine her bathrobe, then sat on the edge of her bed. "Mama got married right off the boat. She didn't even know our father."

"Yes, and we know how that turned out."

She stood and slipped on her robe. She went to the window and sat. From there she could see our neighbor's fenced in backyard. There was a bunch of junk back there. An old bathtub with weeds growing out of it; a pile of tires; a rusted lawn mower. The yard was full of crab grass. A clothesline stretched to a pole at the back fence. A row of sad looking clothes was getting wet instead of dry. It wasn't a pretty view for her to be looking at.

"How soon will you be able to get some of that sulfa drug?"

"It could be a year or two."

"How come so long?"

"They have to be sure it's safe before starting to treat thousands of people."

"Maybe you should volunteer to be a guinea pig."

"My doctor said I wouldn't qualify to take the drug as an experimental subject, because my disease is too far advanced."

"I don't understand that. It seems like that's a good reason you should be getting the medicine."

"Tell me how your baseball team is coming along."

Geraldine knew that because I had a stupid heart murmur, the school doctor wouldn't let me take gym or go out for the school baseball team. But even if they did, I would probably only be a bench warmer. I decided to organize one of my own. A lot of the neighborhoods had teams that played each other. The trick was getting nine kids who were good enough, and then be able to get them to show up for practices and games. I named the team the Ninth Street Bears.

"I lined up a few kids already. Junior Remendelli. He's going to be our pitcher. He walks a lot of batters, but if he gets it over the plate most kids can't hit the ball. He's our best hitter too. And Patsie Balsamo and his kid brother, Freddie. Patsie plays the infield. Either third or short stop. He's not afraid of grounders and has a pretty good arm. Tony Domico plays first base."

"Isn't he in high school?"

"Not until next year. We already had a couple of practices."

"You're half way there. You're a regular Joe McCarthy."

He was the manager of the New York Yankees. I was surprised Geraldine knew that.

"There's a Polish family that moved in, down the street. I noticed a blond kid about my age. And he's got a kid brother who's about my size. I'm going to ask him."

"What about you? Aren't you going to play?"

I was pulling on loose cotton threads in her bedspread. I didn't know if I should tell her. Besides, I felt guilty talking about my team with her being sick and not being able to do things she wanted to do. "I'm going to maybe pinch hit," I said. "In our practices I catch for both sides because we don't have enough players."

She smiled. "Don't worry, I won't tell Mama. You do use a mask and chest guard, don't you?"

"Sure," I lied. It wasn't as though our pitchers could throw the ball a hundred miles an hour. I wasn't afraid of the pitches, as much as the foul tips that could give you a pretty good smack in the head or even in worse places.

I could hear Mama and Helen in the kitchen putting away groceries. I whispered, "I'll probably be catcher for regular games when we don't have enough kids show up."

273

Besides Pasta

"Too bad Marky doesn't live closer. Is he good enough to be on your team?"

"If he wasn't sick, he could be our catcher. He's not a bad hitter either. Sometimes when he and I played catch at Valesburgh Park we would get in pickup games. Marky struck out a lot, but when he connected, he could smack the ball pretty far. One time he hit a triple, and then tried to score when the throw went over the third-baseman's head."

"That must have been exciting."

"I can still picture him running for home with everybody shouting and his long skinny legs wobbly from trying so hard to beat the throw."

"Did he make it," Geraldine asked.

"No, he never made it to the plate. He fell before he got there. Kids on the other team were laughing at him. He told me after the game that when he rounded second, he couldn't get his breath and on the way to the plate he lost control of his legs."

I'm sure he was disappointed. But he did hit a triple. That's something. I still wish he would have made it.

Chapter Twenty-Five

Eighth Grade

Helen couldn't work because of her heart problem, and with Geraldine being sick, and Mama's angina, our family depended on Phyllis and Tony. Chickey, Frances and I were still in school. Tony had a job working for Brewster Aircraft in Newark. He made good money because he worked a lot of overtime. But all that he and Phyllis earned went to support the family, and to cover the cost of medical supplies and doctor bills. We were no better off than when we were on Relief. Mama still couldn't save money to buy a car or to buy a house of our own. And with Geraldine having to have her own bedroom, we really did need a bigger place. We moved to a bigger flat on South Ninth Street. It was our shortest move ever, just one block!

Our three-bedroom flat on Ninth Street was on the first floor. We were surprised to find an old black upright piano in the living room. The people who moved must have left it. Tony told me that it cost a lot of money to move a piano, especially if the people were moving to a place on the second or third floor. I couldn't see why they couldn't take it apart and move the pieces.

A couple of keys were busted and the rest were as yellow as an old dog's teeth. One of the pedals didn't work either. But it still had a nice sound to it. Nobody in the family ever took music lessons so I was surprised when Helen sat down and started playing songs. Frances, Chickey and Geraldine and I crowded around the piano. Mama was standing on a chair putting up a curtain.

"Where'd she learn how to play?" I asked.

"We had a piano on Garside Street," Geraldine said. "You were a baby."

"We did? Don't they cost a lot?"

"It was there when we moved in," Geraldine said. "Helen taught herself how to play by ear."

"Wouldn't it be easier to use her hands?" I asked.

Everyone laughed. Even Mama.

"I bet you can fix those broken keys," Geraldine said.

"Maybe," I said. "I saw a man tune the piano at school. The top part comes off. And the part around the keys too. It looks like a harp inside. There are a million little hammers that strike the strings. It looked pretty complicated."

"If you get it fixed," Mama said, "I can sell it. We could probably get enough to pay for new linoleum."

"Please don't sell it," Chickey said. "I want to learn how to play."

"Tony Domico has a piano," I said. "I heard him play *Rhapsody in Blue*. I couldn't believe he knew the whole song by heart."

Peter Rizzolo

"That's one of my favorites," Chickey said. "Please, Mama. I really want to learn to play."

I wondered if Mama remembered who Tony Domico was.

"You know the Domicos Mama. They live in the one-family house just a few houses from us."

Mama nodded but didn't say anything. She kept putting up the curtain. Helen stopped playing. No one knew what to say. I was pretty sure no one but Mama cared about the stupid linoleum. Except maybe Helen, who always fussed over the house. The linoleum was old and had worn out places where you could see the wood floor.

"We can cover the holes with furniture, or you could crochet doilies to put over them," I said to Mama.

Everyone was looking at her and waiting to see what she would say. She stepped down from the chair and went to the piano and sat on the bench next to Helen. Helen had tears in her eyes. Mama put her arm around her. "*Al diavolo di pavimento! Continuare a giocare, figlia di Mama!*"

Helen laughed and hugged Mama then started playing again.

I nudged Geraldine. "What did she say?"

"She said, 'to hell with the linoleum. Play on, my child'."

The broken pedal was easy to fix. A nut was missing from the rod that was supposed to connect to the peddle. I took the rod to the hardware store and got a new nut. But I couldn't fix the keys because the felt pads were missing and I didn't know where to get thick pieces of felt. But the piano still sounded pretty good to me.

Whenever anybody came over it was the first thing we showed them. Helen had scrubbed, waxed and polished it. She cleaned the keys with Biancoline. They got almost as white as Ginger's underbelly. I was glad we weren't still on Relief, because there was no way Mama could hide a piano from the social worker.

Mama slept on the living room couch and Helen, Phyllis, Chickey, and Frances shared a room that had two beds in it. Tony and I shared the third bedroom. We slept in the same bed. Geraldine had a room all to herself. The house was almost directly across from the Saint Antonitus Catholic School. Some of the priests got to be good friends of the family. The reason we got to know so many priests was that all of us kids, except Frances, went to the Catholic school, and also from Helen and me going to daily Mass. There weren't usually that many people in church. After Mass the priest would sometimes stand in front of the church and talk with us.

Not long after we moved into the flat on Ninth Street, Mama awoke one night with strong pain in her chest. She started vomiting. Tony ran to the doctor's house, which was ten blocks from where we lived. He got the doctor out of bed. They drove back to our house in the doctor's car. When the doctor saw how sick Mama was, he called the ambulance. I didn't find out about it until the next morning because I slept through all the commotion.

They said she was having a gallbladder attack. They operated on her that same night. But after coming home from the hospital two weeks later, she started getting chest pains again. It was the exact same pains she had before her gallbladder operation. The doctor gave her tiny pills to put under her tongue whenever she got the pain. The medicine was called nitroglycerine. The same as the stuff they use to blow up things. It made the pain go away but gave her a bad headache.

The doctor called it angina. He said she probably had a heart attack at the time of her gallbladder operation.

Sometimes she would forget where she put the pills. We would all run around the house looking for her nitroglycerine. We were sure she was going to die if we didn't get it to her in time. Mama was the only one who stayed calm. It would scare me even more when she would take out her rosary and start praying. It reminded me of the time I went to my dead aunt's wake. She was holding rosary beads in her hands as she lay in her coffin.

We all tried to keep Mama from working so hard, but she kept doing things anyway. She started keeping her pills in her apron pocket and would turn her back when she slipped one under her tongue. But you could tell, because she got pale when the angina came. She learned that if she took a pill before she washed clothes or scrubbed the floors, the pain wouldn't come.

We were careful not to get Mama excited, because the doctor said that too much worry and aggravation put a strain on her heart. That it could bring on another heart attack. But it wasn't easy trying to keep Mama calm. She worried about Tony having to go in the army. She worried about all her nephews who were already in the army; she worried about Geraldine, about Helen's leaky heart, and even my stupid heart murmur.

One-night Father Morris came to our flat. He blessed our flat with holy water. He had a big appetite for Mama's cooking and liked to sing and tell jokes. In church he was always serious and pious. But when he was in our house, he was just like one of the family. He could play the piano even better than Helen. He would play and sing songs

I never heard before. His favorite was "Give Me that Old Time Religion." We all learned the words and sang along with him.

One night when Father came for dinner, Mama made his favorite, her usual spaghetti and tomato sauce but instead of meatballs she made something special. It was flank steak sliced thin, covered with pine nuts, spices and rolled up like a blanket. She tied it with string, browned it, and then cooked it in the tomato sauce. After dinner Father Morris, Geraldine, Phyllis, Tony, Chickey, Frances and I were sitting around the table as Mama and Helen cleared away the dishes. Mama set a platter of homemade zeppoles on the table. Father Morris told my mother that I should go to Saint Benedict's Prep after I graduated from St. Antonitus. I heard about the school because they always had good baseball and basketball teams. But I didn't know where the school was.

"It's an all boys' school run by Benedictine monks," Tony said. "It's on High Street in downtown Newark, just a couple of blocks down from Central High."

"That's right," Father Morris said, as he bit into a zeppole. I had to laugh because he had a ring of powdered sugar around his mouth.

"Do you have to pay to go there?" Mama asked. She poured Father a cup of coffee.

"Yes," he said. "The tuition is one hundred and fifty dollars a year."

Mama just shook her head but didn't say anything.

"He may be able to get a full scholarship," Father said.

"Who pays for the scholarship?" Tony asked.

"Saint Benedict's gives each Parish in Newark one scholarship a year. And from what I hear, Peter's one of the top students in the eighth grade."

My ears got hot and red. I wondered how he knew about my grades. I figured he must have talked to my teacher. "Two kids in my class say they're going to Saint Benedict's when they graduate from Saint Antonitus. Mike Patterson and Tommy Walker."

"Why only boys?" Chickey asked.

"Because girls aren't allowed," I said. "They have to let boys go, or the monks wouldn't have anyone to teach."

"That's stupid," Chickey said. "Why is everything always for boys?"

"Our Lady of the Valley is a high school for girls," Father said. "It's just that when boys and girls get to high school age, many people believe they do better when they're not mixed together."

I knew what he was talking about. The guys in my class were always talking about girls…who they liked, and who was the prettiest. I never said who I liked, because if I did, somebody would tell the girl and she would expect me to talk to her or something. To tell the truth, there was this one girl, I couldn't help looking at all the time. I had to be careful not to stare; otherwise someone would notice. I do think she noticed, because once she caught my eye and smiled. I turned around, thinking maybe she was looking at someone behind me. During recess she was always talking with this one guy from the other eighth grade class. He was tall, had blond hair and fewer and less fierce-looking pimples than most of the rest of us. He was on the school basketball team.

"They have boys and girls together at Saint Rose of Lima's Business High," I said. "Phyllis, Geraldine and Tony went there. I could go there. And it doesn't cost anything."

"Theirs is a two-year program. If you want to go to college or the seminary, you'll need to go to a regular high school," Father Morris said.

I looked around. Nobody said anything. I wasn't sure I wanted to go to an all boys' school. No one in my family got to go to college. It didn't seem fair, and besides, I didn't see how I could. Unless I went to the seminary. I knew that was free.

Geraldine was the first to speak. "Give it a try, Peter. If you can get a scholarship for high school, who knows, maybe you could get one for college."

I knew that Geraldine wanted me to be a doctor. Once, she told me that our family could use a good doctor who wouldn't charge us anything. She said it like she was joking, but I could tell by the way she looked at me that she wanted to see what I thought about that. I told her sure, and that maybe I could someday find a cure for TB and Helen's leaky heart valve. But I knew it was like talking about how someday we would have a family business, a house in the country, horses, and grow tomatoes as big as grapefruits like Mama did in Italy.

"Will he have to take a competitive exam?" Phyllis asked.

"Acceptance is based on the academic record and need," Father said. "They're not going to give a free ride to a kid whose family can afford the tuition."

I wished Marky was in our parish. I felt pretty sure his parents could afford to send him to Saint Benedict's. Then if I got to go, we would be in the same school. "Do you have to be Catholic to go there?" I asked.

"Most of the students are, but it's not a requirement," Father said.

"If I weren't sick," Geraldine said, "he could go there without a scholarship." Her voice was shaky like she might start crying.

"Now, now, Geraldine," Father said. "You have nothing to feel guilty about. Besides I've asked all of the parish priests to remember you in their prayers. You're going to get better and back to work before you know it."

"Is there some kind of application form we would need to get from Saint Benedict's?" Tony asked.

"Not that I know of. Take your brother to see the pastor. Ask Father Moran to put Peter on the list of candidates. He knows who Peter is. He sees him at Mass."

If Father Morris asked all the priests in the parish to pray for Geraldine, that was a lot of prayers. There were about a dozen priests living in the rectory. Only four were regular parish priests and the rest were missionary priests who lived there when they weren't away giving retreats in other parishes. They belonged to the Dominican order and wore white robes, not black ones like our regular parish priests.

Another priest who came to our house was Father Bunjak. He was at least six feet tall, and whenever he came over it was like a cyclone came through the door. He would hug and kiss everybody. Me and Tony he just hugged. He said Mama was his adopted mother. His mother was in Czechoslovakia and I guess he missed her a lot. He had pizzazz; that's for sure. He would tell jokes and sing. He almost always brought something when he came; a cake, or a bottle of wine, or candy. You never knew when he would come through the door because he was a missionary priest who went all over the country giving retreats. He would only get to stay in our parish a few days before he had to go off on another retreat.

Geraldine said that the retreats were to fire up the Catholics in parishes where people were mostly falling asleep in church. Once, he gave a retreat in our parish. He was the best preacher I had ever heard. He could make you laugh, and cry, but mostly make you want to be thankful to God for loving us and to enjoy every second of being alive. At the end of his sermon he would always ask the people to pray for his dear mother.

When he came to see us, we didn't often see his serious side, except when he talked about the war and his mother being in Czechoslovakia and him not knowing if she was alive or dead.

Phyllis told me once that priests had to go wherever the Bishop sends them, and that on purpose he would always send them far away from their own family. And because they couldn't get married, they got pretty lonely living with other priests.

"I wouldn't like that part of being a priest," I told her. "A family is a lot to give up. And why can't priests get married and have their own family?"

"It's been that way for hundreds of years." she said.

"The nuns all say that if you're meant for a religious life, you'll hear God's voice calling you."

When I went to Mass I would always be listening, but all I heard was the priest saying the Mass prayers in Latin. If God is going to call me, I hope he speaks in English. Even Italian would be okay; I could understand a little.

Marky was in tenth grade, but because he was in and out of the hospital so much, he had to have a tutor come to his house. I was lucky if I got to see him once a month. Mostly I went to see him, because it was too hard for him to come to see me. And I think his mother was afraid for him to spend much time in our house because of Geraldine being sick.

When I would go to his apartment we talked about baseball, and about the team I was organizing. We played chess or checkers or cards. He liked word games. I stumped him once with a four-letter word beginning with *t* and ending in *i*. His brain must have been tired from playing chess. I bet you figured it out already. And it can't be a person's name either.

He liked to talk about what he was studying in school. I liked school, but it wasn't anything I talked about with my neighborhood friends. Between going to classes and doing homework, school already took up practically my whole life.

But Marky was always excited about stuff he learned from school, or from reading science books, or the newspaper. He made me think even harder than my teachers did. He was sometimes surprised how much I knew, even though I was two grades behind him. That was because I was a good listener. I learned a lot from my older sisters, and Tony and Joe Russo arguing all the time.

Rosemary O'Malley, that's the name of the girl in my class that I was always looking at and thinking about. She had long hair that was the color of a new penny and so light that it was always in motion when she moved her head. She had blue eyes and freckles, but not too many freckles. She was smart, excepting in math. That's how come I got to talk to her. One day as we were leaving class, she was right in front of me. She stopped, turned, and smiled at me. When I stopped someone behind me ran into me, and I bumped into Rosemary. Her eyes up close had little specks of gold in them.

"I'm sorry."

"It's okay," she said. "I've been meaning to ask if you would help me with my math. I just don't get fractions."

I stood up really straight, trying to make myself an inch taller. "Yeah. Okay. Sure, I can do that."

"I'm going to watch basketball practice after school. Can you meet me in the auditorium?"

"Okay."

"Maybe you'll help me get an A on the math test we're having tomorrow."

The auditorium had folding chairs. After school they had to be cleared away so the basketball team could practice. I went to the boys' bathroom before going there. My hair was messed up, as usual. In the morning it was neat, because I wet it and slicked it back before leaving the house. But by the afternoon it was dry and springy with curls. I didn't want to wet it because she would be able to tell, so I used my fingers as a comb and tried to make it look less messy. I sniffed under my arms. They were sweaty but didn't smell.

She was sitting with her legs crossed when I got there. She smiled and waved me over. I sat next to her in a folding chair. We didn't talk for a while. We both watched the players.

"The guy who just sunk the basket…that's Sandy. He's my friend. He's in the other eighth grade class."

"I know."

"Do you play sports?"

Peter Rizzolo

"I manage the Ninth Street Bears. Sometimes I catch and pinch hit."

"That sounds like fun. I like baseball."

"So does my sister Phyllis."

"I wish they had a girls' team."

She removed her math book from her book-bag. "Okay, fractions." She flipped through the book. She showed me the place in her book. "This problem here... how do you do it?"

She pointed with her finger. She was wearing nail polish the color of watermelon. It was a word problem. It said a family sold their house for $2,500 which was 125% of what they had paid for it. How much had it cost them and how much profit did they make?

I was glad it was such an easy problem.

"What you know is that the house cost 100% and the profit is 25%"

"So far I'm with you."

"Then 2500 is four quarters plus one quarter or five quarters." I wrote it down on the pad I brought. She leaned over close to see what I was writing. I could feel the heat from her face. She smelled like roses. I guess it was from the soap she used.

"Hmm...$2,500 is five quarters. I get it."

"Right. The original cost of the house is 100% or four quarters. If you divide $2,500 by five you get $500. That's one quarter of the original cost."

"Okay."

"And four quarters is four times $500, or $2000. That's what they paid for it when the seller bought the house. They made $500 profit!"

Besides Pasta

"You make it seem so easy." She was shaking her head and smiling. Her boyfriend walked over to where we were sitting.

"Hey, Rose what's going on?" he asked.

"Peter's helping me with my math."

He looked at me as though he smelled something he didn't like. "Get lost. I want to talk with my girlfriend."

"Sandy!" she said.

"It's okay. I guess we were finished."

"It's not okay. What's the matter with you, Sandy?"

The basketball coach blew his whistle. Sandy just turned and left without answering her.

"I hate that. He acts like he owns me. I'm sorry, Peter."

I didn't want to leave, but I noticed Sandy kept glancing over. The eighth-grade dance was coming up in two weeks. I didn't have the nerve to just walk up to a girl and ask her. For one thing, I never knew what to say to girls. But with Rosemary, we could talk about fractions and baseball.

"You want to go the dance with me?"

She smiled. "I bet you're a good dancer."

"Chickey showed me how to do the fox trot."

"A chicken taught you how to dance?"

We both laughed. I knew she was joking because in a class report I told about my family.

"I'd love to go to the dance with you, but Sandy already asked me. You don't have to have a date to come. I'll save you a dance."

I told her yeah; maybe Tommy Walker can be my date. But I didn't go to the dance. I was only joking about Tommy. He was just as shy as I was around girls.

Peter Rizzolo

After that day, I made up stories in my head about how I rescue Rosemary. Sandy would be pushing her and yelling at her. She looks scared. I come up to them and tell him to leave her alone. He puts up his fists and wants to fight. I tell him it wouldn't be fair, because I'm a jujitsu expert and I didn't want to hurt him. He comes at me like a bull, and I calmly flip him onto his back. After a few hard flips, he runs away.

Rosemary hugs me and kisses me on the cheek. I'm not shy or nervous, because I pretend I'm Rick in Casablanca. I give her my best Bogy half-smile, then kiss her on the mouth. Then we hold hands and walk to the ice cream parlor on South Orange Avenue. We share a banana split. I ask her if I could be her boyfriend. She smiles, and says I already am.

Mama's Braciole Recipe

Ingredients:

Flank steak (beef)

Pine nuts

Breadcrumbs

Salt, pepper

Garlic

Parsley

Parmesan cheese

Mama placed the flank steak on a board and pounded it with the side of a butcher's knife until it was as thin as cardboard.

She then mixed together bread crumbs, pine nuts, garlic, Parmesan cheese, parsley, salt, pepper and olive oil. She spread this mixture evenly on the steak before rolling up the steak and tying it with string.

She browned the rolled-up steak in olive oil before placing it in tomato sauce.

Chapter Twenty-Six

Miles to Go Before I Sleep

I did get a scholarship to Saint Benedict's. The school was located just a few blocks from the Newark court house, a public high school, and several movie theaters, including the former Newark Opera House where there was now a burlesque show. One time when Marky and I went to a downtown movie to see *Pride of the Yankees*, the life story of Lou Gehrig, we stopped in front of the burlesque theater. There were giant pictures outside of women with hardly anything on.

"You want to go here instead of to see the *Pride of the Yankees?*" Marky asked.

"I don't know," I said. But it was so close to Saint Benedict's. What if one of the monks was to see us walking out of there? And just looking at the pictures made the hairs on the back of my neck stand up. Even with five sisters, I never once saw one of them without any clothes on. Sometimes in the morning, one of them would be ironing

a dress, and only be wearing their slip. Mama would say "*indescento*!"
Then they would go put on a bathrobe.

"I wasn't serious," Marky said. "They don't let kids in. You have to
be at least eighteen."

I wanted to tell him about Rosemary, but there wasn't that much to
tell. All the things I did with her were just inside my head. I was
surprised he made a joke about the burlesque, because he never talked
about girls. We continued walking toward the Paramount Movie
Theatre.

"We're not kids anymore," I said. "Besides, grownups already
know all about naked women."

"So do the kids at my school," Marky said. "You should see the
pictures they pass around."

"It's the same at our school. The nuns almost have a heart attack if
they catch a boy with dirty pictures."

Marky laughed. "I've seen my mother and father naked. And even
my sisters sometimes. It's not such a big thing."

"You mean your father's" He looked at me funny, then we both
busted-out laughing.

He changed the subject. "How do you like St. Benedict's?"

"I like it a lot."

"What's it like?

"All the buildings are dark red brick. There's ivy growing up the
sides."

"Sounds like a college."

"There's fenced in courtyard in the front, and a field across the
street where the teams practice. The building the Benedictine monks
live in is between the school and a small church."

"What's it like inside?"

"There's lots of dark wood and it smells like shoe polish. I guess because all the kids have to shine their shoes every day. The gym, though, smells like old sneakers."

We were almost to the Paramount Theater. We were standing on a corner waiting for the traffic light to change.

"Most gyms do," Marky said.

"The wooden floor's so smooth and shiny it looks as though you could ice skate on it. And there's a balcony that's used for a running track. For basketball games, they set up folding chairs on the track."

At the theater we bought our tickets, but had to wait in a long line to get in. While we waited, he asked me more questions about St. Benedict's.

"I have to take a bus to get to school. All my teachers are Benedictine monks. They aren't anything like the nuns at Saint Antonitus. Sometimes they even say hell and damn when some of the guys get them mad. Religion class is like listening to my brother Tony and Joe Russo arguing religion." Marky started looking bored so I didn't say anything more about St. Benedict's. I couldn't wait to see the movie. When we finally got, in most of the good seats were already taken. We had to sit in the balcony.

My favorite courses in high school were English and math. I liked math because there was always a right answer, and once you learned the rules you didn't have to memorize anything. In English class our book was Prose and Poetry of America and my favorites were Mark Twain's short stories and The House of the Seven Gables by Nathaniel Hawthorne. My favorite poem was by Robert Frost. It was called

Besides Pasta

"Stopping by the Woods on a Snowy Evening." As an assignment we had to write down what we thought the last stanza meant.

The woods are lovely, dark and deep,

But I have promises to keep,

And miles to go before I sleep,

And miles to go before I sleep.

One day, after getting home from school, I went into Geraldine's room with my English book. I read the poem to her. I asked her what she thought the last stanza meant.

"What do you think?" she asked. She was propped up in bed reading a magazine. She kept flipping the pages, but I could tell she was listening to me. When she looked at me, she had tears in her eyes. I thought that maybe it was from reading.

Geraldine should have been a teacher, because they never tell you the right answer, except when they correct your test paper. Then it seems to narrow down to just one right answer.

"It's cold," I said, "it's snowing, it's late at night and even though he wants to just sit on his little horse and enjoy the scenery, he knows he'd better get going."

"That's the literal meaning. You know what a metaphor is?"

"It's when you say one thing, but you're really talking about something else."

"Can you give me an example?"

I had to think. "How's this: sometimes in school my head is a balloon that's so filled up it's ready to bust."

"That's pretty good. What about the woods being lovely, dark and deep? Suppose that's a metaphor like your balloon."

I read the last stanza to myself. "I can't think of anything that's lovely, dark and deep. Except maybe a wishing well."

She put down her magazine and drew up her knees. "That's an interesting idea. Write about that. And let me know what some of the other kids think."

It turned out this brainy kid in class said Frost was talking about life. How it can be beautiful, and at the same time mysterious and sad. And how a person is meant to do something with his life and better get started because no one knows how long they're going to live.

I never did tell Geraldine what the right answer was, because I knew now why she had tears in her eyes. She already knew.

I took German because the guidance counselor said the best scientists in the world were German. He said American scientists had to be able to read German. For some reason, he decided I should be a scientist. Maybe because I was good at math. I don't know exactly.

I had Father Archibald for German. He had escaped from Germany just before the war. He had a crew cut, and a head like a bulldog. When he got mad, which was pretty often, he would pound the desk and call us *"dummkopfs!"* If anyone from Hollywood ever saw Father Archibald, they'd hire him on the spot. Maybe he really was a German actor making believe he was a priest so he could escape from Hitler. Even if it wasn't true, it would make a pretty good story.

I liked learning a new language, but it was hard, because Germans say things backwards and you have to memorize whether a particular noun is masculine or feminine. It made me afraid to say a word, because Father Archibald would get mad if I gave the word the wrong gender.

Besides Pasta

The only thing I didn't like about Saint Benedict's was not being able to take gym or go out for sports because of my stupid heart murmur. Two other things I didn't like was having to always wear a jacket and tie and having to wear a freshman beanie.

Saint Benedict's had a tall metal fence that separated the courtyard from the sidewalk on High Street. During recess some of the boys would line up along the fence and watch the girls who were going to Central High, as they walked to school. The boys would whistle and say things to the girls. The girls would sometimes wave and smile. Some of them had their skirts pulled way above their knees. They swung their hips like Betty Boop.

The priest who was the monitor of the recess would come over and chase the boys away from the fence. But it seemed he always waited awhile before he chased them. If you were wearing a freshman beanie you got chased by the upper classmen before the priest chased everyone else away. The upperclassmen said we were too young for that kind of stuff. I sometimes wished Rosemary was one of the girls walking by, but I wouldn't want them all whistling at her. Besides, I knew she couldn't be. She was going to Our Lady of the Valley High, which was nowhere near St. Benedict's.

Because I couldn't take gym, I had a free period three days a week. Mostly I would start in on my homework in the school library. But sometimes I played chess with this kid who was a foot taller and probably weighed about the same as me. He had long arms, a big head and had a funny walk. He was the smartest kid in the whole school. For some reason he didn't take gym either. He looked goofy, but was a nice friendly kid. I think he let me win at chess, just so I'd keep playing with him. In a way he reminded me of Marky, who didn't have a goofy walk, but was brainy and didn't have any friends besides me and his cousin, who really didn't count because Marky didn't like his cousin that much.

Of all the times Marky was in the hospital, I only got to see him once. He never stayed longer than a few days and by the time I found out about it, he was already home. But this one time his mother phoned my mother to tell her that Marky was very sick and had asked for me to come see him. I wanted to but was afraid to go. Between my broken wrist and two operations, going to a hospital was right alongside of rushing into a burning building to get the bottle of cod-liver oil my mother kept in the icebox. But I had to go. I wanted to see him.

"Mrs. Stillman never before called me when he was in the hospital. He must be really bad this time."

Mama was at the counter next to the kitchen sink snapping string beans and putting them into a pot. I liked the sharp popping sound it made when she broke off the ends of the beans. I was at the table drinking a glass of milk. She dried her hands on her apron and came over and sat beside me. "She said he is very sick," Mama said.

"What else did Mrs. Stillman say?" I could tell Mama wasn't telling me everything. "Is he dying, Mama?"

Mama's eyes were filled with tears. "The doctors say there is no more they can do for him. She said you better come see him right away."

My head filled up with so many thoughts and feelings. I felt like throwing my glass of milk across the room. Why didn't I go see him more times? I couldn't stand the thought of him being gone forever. Why didn't God listen to our prayers? We were all praying for him;

me: Mrs. Stillman, Sister Patricia. I knew now that I made a big mistake not telling more people to pray for him. Marky was the best person I ever knew. My best friend. Why would God take him from me?

"The doctors don't know everything," I said. "They could be wrong." I put my head in Mama's lap. I cried for a long time.

To get to Beth Israel Hospital, I had to take two long bus rides. I had no trouble finding the hospital, because the driver of the second bus gave me directions. Mrs. Stillman met me in the lobby. She looked worried.

"Did you have any trouble getting here, Peter?"

"No. It just took a long time."

She took my hand and we walked toward an elevator. "Marky has been asking for you and his brother."

I liked Marky's mother. She was my idea of a perfect grandmother. Not that she was that old. It was her old-fashioned glasses and her gray hair that she was always brushing from her face. I never once heard her raise her voice or lose her temper. But after all, she's not Italian and didn't grow up near a volcano. Mama could be calm one minute and blowing her top the next. But it didn't mean she didn't love us. It was just the way she was. I was thinking these things on the way to Marky's room.

I knew Marky's brother was overseas. "Is Paul coming?" I asked her.

"The Red Cross is trying." She had tears in her eyes. We were at the door to Marky's room. "Visit as long as you want. I'll be at the nurses' station."

I knocked. There was no answer. I knocked again.

"Come in."

When I saw him, it took my breath away. It was his voice, but it didn't look anything like him. His face was so puffy that his eyes were practically closed. The skin on his forehead was dry and looked like someone had sprinkled it with salt. I wouldn't have known it was him except for his nose. He had a sheet over him. You could tell his belly was enormous.

His right hand was on top of the sheet. He lifted it part way, as though he wanted to shake my hand. Then he dropped it. I laid my hand on top of his. I was shocked at how cold it was. I stood there with my throat knotted up. I couldn't talk. Even if I could, I wouldn't know what to say. You're my best friend. I never once told him that. I guess we both knew that anyway. I wanted to tell him that he was going to get better like he always did. But from seeing the way he was, I knew he wouldn't.

"Can I have a sip of water?" he asked. His voice was hoarse.

There was a glass and a straw on a table beside the bed. I put the straw in the glass. I held it to his lips. I could see that his tongue was dark, and dry as leather. He took a tiny sip. He couldn't open his mouth all the way because the corners of his lips were stuck shut.

"I'm glad you came."

"Yeah. Me too."

"My mother says Paul's on the way. Last we heard he was in Italy." He looked out the window. "I don't think he's going to get here in time."

I followed where he was looking. You could see the tops of buildings. There were flowers and trees growing on some of the roofs.

"Remember how we used to sneak up on the roof at South Orange Avenue and spy on the neighborhood?"

"Yeah," I said. "Mama would have killed me if she knew."

He turned from the window and looked at me. "I guess I was born a little too soon," he said.

I knew what he meant. About a year ago we were sitting in his room talking. It was February and we were both sick of winter. I had gotten a black wooden bat for Christmas. I brought it to show him. He was sitting on the floor, cross-legged, pounding a baseball into his oiled fielder's mitt.

"I read about doctors in England experimenting with taking a kidney out of a healthy person and putting it in someone who was going to die if he didn't get a new kidney," Marky said. "It's called a transplant operation."

"Could I give you one of my kidneys?"

"The person you get the kidney from has to be a twin brother," he said.

"Just a regular brother wouldn't work?"

"It wouldn't last very long," he said. "Your body kills off cells that are different from its own. They're working on drugs to prevent that."

"It's weird, isn't it? Like we have little armies inside of us."

I stood at Marky's bedside, thinking about that conversation. Maybe by now they learned more about how to do a transplant that would last. "Can't your brother Paul give you one of his kidneys? Even if it doesn't last very long, maybe by then scientists will figure out how to do it, so that it does last."

He just shook his head. Neither of us said anything for a while.

"Remember us talking about being mad scientists?" he said. He tried to laugh. It wasn't much of a laugh, but I could see his belly shake under the sheet.

"Yeah."

"So, are you going to be a mad scientist, or a priest?"

"I don't know yet." It didn't seem right talking about what I was going to be.

"Be whatever you want to be. Not what the nuns or anybody else want."

I wanted to ask him if he was scared of dying. But I couldn't make myself say it. Neither of us said anything for a long time. He closed his eyes and went to sleep. I could see that he was still breathing. My hand was cold from holding his. The nurse came in. She said I had better go. That he needed to rest. She said Mrs. Stillman was waiting for me.

Two days later, when I got home from school my mother was sitting at the kitchen table, crying. I asked her what was the matter.

"Mrs. Stillman called about Marky."

I threw my coat and books down. I ran out of the house. I started walking up South Orange Avenue toward Valesburgh Park. I can't remember crossing streets or seeing anybody. It was a cold day and felt like it might snow. I was cold, because I left without my jacket or gloves. I jammed my hands in my pants pockets. After walking a few blocks, I passed the giant Hoffman soda bottle. I was halfway to Valesburgh Park.

When I finally got to the park, I went to the ball field. I ran around the field, I don't know how many times, before dropping onto a bench by the batter's cage. I pictured all the times Marky and I played ball there. How pathetic we were at first, and how after a while we got to be pretty good. And how we always went and bought ice cream cones when we had the money. And how we argued which team was better, the Yankees or the Dodgers.

A bunch of kids came to the field with balls, bats and mitts. I was surprised to see them because it was so cold. They started duking-up sides. They were looking at me because I was crying and kicking the dirt under the bench.

"Hey, Rizz, you want a game?" one of them shouted. I recognized them from the times me and Marky would be there and they would ask us to play when they didn't have enough guys.

"I can't. I have to go."

"Where's your friend, Marky?" one of the guys asked.

"He's dead," I said.

"Geez," the guy said.

They all were staring at me. I couldn't believe I said it. "He's dead," I said again. I turned from them and started the long walk home. My feet were getting numb from the cold. I thought of the last time I saw Marky in the hospital. I shivered as I remembered how cold his hand was. I was glad he had asked me to go see him, but I wished I didn't have that picture of him in the hospital bed. I guess that's why I went to the park. To picture him chasing fly balls, running bases, fielding grounders, and sometimes sharing an ice cream cone. Other memories flashed into my head. The Saint Rocco's street fair. Marky chasing after the little girl with the two balloons; us sitting on the icebox in front of Stillman's spying on the Greek numbers man; going to see the movie about Lou Gehrig's life and us sitting in the balcony of the

Peter Rizzolo

Paramount Theater when it was over, embarrassed when the lights came on, because we were both crying; all the cold rainy winter days we sat in his room in the back of the store, oiling our mitts and longing for the warm weather. Even though there were tears freezing on my cheeks, I couldn't help laughing out loud thinking about how Marky looked when he tried on my baseball cap, and the salesman at Davega's asking us who the hell are the Stillmans?

I started walking faster because I was beginning to shiver. I didn't want it to be dark by the time I got home. Mama would be worried with me running out of the house with practically nothing on. She'll say, "*Figli di Mama*, you'll get pneumonia!" I know that Marky's soul is in a better place than this crazy world, where people are always having wars and killing each other. But I still wish he were here.

When I got home, Mama threw a blanket around me because my lips were blue and I couldn't stop shivering. She lit three gas jets; a pot of tomato sauce was simmering on the fourth. She sat me front of the stove. The whole family excepting Mama crowded around me. She was at the sink pouring spaghetti into a colander. I could see the steam rise up from the sink. I was beginning to feel warmer already. Helen said Marky was the smartest kid she ever knew. Tony said that Paul had told him that Marky beat his father at chess when he was only eight years old. Geraldine said I was lucky to have such a good friend. Helen got up and began setting dishes on the table.

Chickey and Frances had tears in their eyes but didn't say anything. No one said anything about the funeral. I didn't want to talk about it either. I told them about the time Marky and I went to Davega's and the salesman wouldn't let us pay on credit. I told him the Stillman's

303

Besides Pasta

always did. He said, "Who the hell are the Stillmans?" I told them how we kept saying "Who the hell are the Stillmans?" all the way home and how I wet my pants from laughing. Pettty soon everyone was laughing and telling funny stories. Mama said the pasta was getting cold. But nobody seemed to care.

Made in the USA
Columbia, SC
26 March 2019